Judy

It was great to
see Jan — the
Hunter Valley

LEN EVANS'
COOKBOOK

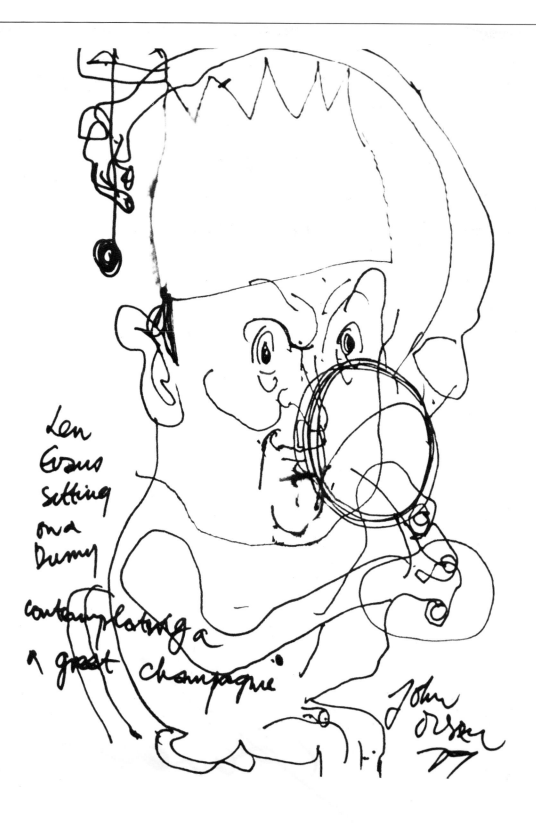

Len Evans sitting on a Dummy contemplating a great champagne

LEN EVANS'
COOKBOOK

GOLDEN PRESS

This book is dedicated to Trish,
whose insistence that I settle down to a steady job
(and stop playing about with writing)
got it all going.

ACKNOWLEDGEMENTS
I would like to thank those people who have made a particular con-
tribution to this book: Sally Cleaver and Carolyn Divjak for helping
with the food photographs, Annie Kaden for doing all the work
without a murmur, the two beautiful ladies of M & B, Barbara
Beckett and Bryony Cosgrove, and all the enthusiasts with whom
I've enjoyed some of the great food and wine of the world.
LEN EVANS

GOLDEN PRESS
Published in Australia by Golden Press Pty Ltd
Incorporated in New South Wales
5-01 Henry Lawson Business Centre
Birkenhead Point, Drummoyne, 2047, Australia,
and 717 Rosebank Road, Avondale,
Auckland, New Zealand

Created and produced by
Mead & Beckett Publishing
139 Macquarie Street, Sydney, Australia
First published 1985

Edited by Bryony Cosgrove
Designed by Barbara Beckett
Photographed by Ray Jarratt & David Young
Typeset by Asco Trade Typesetting Limited, Hong Kong
Colour by Bright Arts, Hong Kong
Printed by South China Printing, Hong Kong

National Library of Australia
cataloguing-in-publication data
Evans, Len, 1930–
The Len Evans cookbook.

ISBN 0 7302 0209 7.

1. Cookery.   I. Title.

641.5

Page one: One of my two
original Fred Williams. He
was a great bloke as well as a
magnificent artist.

Page two: A cartoon by my
great mate John Olsen.

Page four: My favourite cartoon, the original masthead of
the Indulgence column.

Introduction

The past 30 years, in Australia, have seen a dynamic change in food and drink habits; perhaps the most dynamic in the history of the world.

The migrant influence, increased affluence, cosmopolitanism brought about by travel, an increase in the various types of media, and many other factors, have brought about a huge growth in catering, in restaurants, hotels and clubs, a tremendous interest in cooking in the home, and the establishment of a table wine industry among the world's finest.

I have been part of this growth. I came to Australia the same 30 years ago, and have had the pleasure and privilege of working during this most volatile time in the food and beverage industry. This book chronicles some of my experiences.

I was asked to write my memoirs, but I didn't like the idea—for one reason I'm still living them, and for another my many conceits do not include a belief that my life has been particularly fascinating. However, you may be amused by some of the incidents that have taken place.

The recipes I've collected over this time, many of which appeared in my columns in the *Australian Women's Weekly*, the *Weekend Australian* and the *Sunday Mirror* among others, have been put into a less haphazard shape, and I've added others from colleagues and friends.

I'm very proud to be part of the industry I chose for my living. I haven't become rich, but I live richly—rich in experience, rich in friends. And we deal in joy, for good food and good wine should lead to feelings of well-being, good humour and fun.

Some years ago I told someone that I had met all sorts of people at my table, and how nice so many of them seemed to be. It was then I realised that I had met them in the best possible circumstances: when they were relaxed, eager to appreciate and having a good time. I sincerely hope that this book helps you do the same.

Anders Ousback chose this photograph to represent our relationship when he started his wine and food career with me at Bulletin Place.

Contents

CHAPTER ONE

Stocks and sauces: the Chevron Hilton

Working at the Chevron Hilton in Sydney, from 1960 to 1964, was the greatest learning experience of my life. I had entered the hotel trade in 1958 as a glass washer at the Ship Inn at Circular Quay, working from 6 am until 10 am and all day Saturdays. This gave me time during the week to write radio and television scripts, meet people in the business and attend rehearsals.

But soon the hotel business started to encroach. I became a barman, then a bar manager, then a stock taker and systems analyst. The last jobs involved analysing the gross percentages and potential profits of hotels. The manager of one of the hotels I used to visit at fortnightly intervals mentioned that he was leaving to become Beverage Manager of the Chevron, the great new hotel, and he suggested that my scrutineering talents could be used there.

Within a few weeks, my systems of stock control had been accepted by the Chevron management, but on the condition that I worked for them, rather than as an outsider. Finally, with some misgivings, I joined the management team, thinking I would learn from the others about my great love, wine. Instead, I found that my meagre knowledge was in demand, for nobody knew anything about anything, in wine terms.

Almost five very happy years followed. The initial General Manager was soon replaced by Frank Christie, the Coordinator General of the Chevron chain. The Hilton people came and went, creating friendships that have lasted to this day; we went into receivership, but still battled on; and I continued to learn.

The Chevron went into receivership because it was a hugely capitalised, strange type of hotel to run. It was intended to have over 1000 rooms, which shows the great foresight of the planners, for it would still be Sydney's dominant hotel today. (The huge hole-in-the-ground remains, like an earnest spinster, still waiting for a proposition.) The hotel finished up with only 220 rooms, but it had the 650-seat Silver Spade theatre restaurant, an 800-seat ballroom, the 600-seat Oasis Lounge, the 200-seat Grill, function rooms for another 200 and oodles of public and cocktail bars to boot. With double seating for some shows, we were capable of serving 3000 dinners in an evening. In spite of all the activity, however, and with

New Year's Eve 1983: Rudy Komon, myself, Andre Simon, Frank Christie, King Watson and Tony Bohdan.

all the accommodation full, we still couldn't match the impossible interest bill bequeathed us. Hence the receivership.

But things carried on. I became Beverage Manager with 85 staff, then Food and Beverage Manager with 350 staff, including 80 cooks and apprentices. As far as I know, this was and will be the last time in Australia that two full brigades of chefs operated: sauciers, grillardins, rôtisseurs, garde-mangers, pâtissiers, poissonniers and so on. Kitchen discipline was very strict, and I would be invited formally by the Executive Chef to join the sous-chefs for their simple meal prior to service, to chat about their careers, the great chefs, the great restaurants, the old times. Fascinating stuff for a green enthusiast.

When I was made Food and Beverage Manager I received a wonderful lesson from my associate Tony Bohdan. Frank Christie put me in charge of the two departments 'to bring them together as one kingdom, not to operate as separate fiefdoms'. Tony (now a successful consultant) was the Assistant Catering Manager and John Tully (now a catering school teacher) was Assistant Beverage Manager. They were each to be elevated in rank and pay, with me as their boss.

Since Tully had worked for me for two years, I knew there would be no problems with him. But Bohdan was something else—abrupt, brusque, determined. I called him into my office to give him the news, and then I stated, 'Bohdan, I realise you know a great deal about food, more than I will ever know, and that you can make me look a fool and undermine my position. If you do I will promise you one thing. I will take you down with me.' Bohdan nodded his understanding. 'Now,' I went on, 'my biggest problem is will the chefs accept me?' Bohdan smiled. 'Surely,' he said, 'after what you've just told me, the problem is the chefs. Will you accept them?'

'If you're put in charge, be in charge. If you have the responsibility you must ultimately answer for the success or failure of the operation, so it might as well be you who determines the action.'

I have never forgotten that. If you're put in charge, be in charge. If you have the responsibility you must ultimately answer for the success or failure of the operation, so it might as well be you who determines the action. Tony Bohdan and I formed a happy and active partnership, a great blend of his professionalism and my entrepreneurial bulldust.

We all worked hard at the Chevron—8 am until 7 pm at least, often into the night, often until 1 am the following day to return only hours later. At least one duty at weekends, and we would come in anyway if it was a big Saturday, as it almost always was.

The early 1960s saw the beginning of table wine popularity in Australia. The Chevron had lists of Private Bin wines where few had been seen before. We originated 'Cellarmaster's Suggestions', which is now almost mandatory on wine lists, and we took wines from behind the counter and put them within reach of the customer in open shelves, split barrels, stacked cartons. Perhaps it's difficult to appreciate that this was only about 20 years ago. However, very few establishments then presented wine as it is offered everywhere today.

During this time we built up the greatest cellar ever seen to date in

An early group at the Chevron Hilton, 1960. Charles Bell, third from left, went on to become an international executive for Hilton Hotels International.

Australia. In addition to all the top French wines, all the Premier Grands Crus, all the great vineyard Burgundies and endless Champagnes, we had an Australian cellar of extraordinary range. Don't forget that Murray Tyrrell didn't start bottling until 1962. The Chevron stocked his first wine, and a year later, when I ordered 60 dozen red, 20 each of three Vat numbers, Murray thought he was hearing things. 'Jesus Christ!' he shouted. 'That'll pay the wages for a month or two.'

I had particularly strong relations with Hardy's, Lindemans, McWilliam's and Yalumba in those days. Dick Heath, the chief wine maker of Hardy's, complained in 1960 about the buildup of old red wine stocks. We soon fixed that, offering 1945 reds at ten shillings a bottle. The marvellous Lindemans whites of the 1950s and early 1960s were my benchmarks for the Hunter semillon style. I bought O'Shea reds from McWilliam's at six and seven shillings a bottle (and kept some until the mid-1970s). When John Stanford came to work for the Wine Bureau, of which I was founding director, he would have the pick of my cellar. Invariably he would choose the 1952 Mount Pleasant Stephen Hermitage of O'Shea, 'Just have to get the taste right in my head.' No wonder there's none left. Sadly, this great cellar was dispersed when new owners arrived in the late 1960s. However, I was able to buy some of it, as were friends of mine, so I still occasionally get to taste one of the wines I laid down nearly 25 years ago.

From 1963 to 1964, my last couple of years at the Chevron, I had the number two position at the hotel as Frank Christie's assistant. I shall never cease to marvel at his forebearance and attitude regarding delegation of authority. I wonder often if I would have done the same thing in his position. He was always clearly in charge, and he was always there, but he allowed the staff an extraordinary amount of licence to implement new ideas, to create special functions, and to

Armati, the maitre d' of the Silver Spade, Chevron Hilton, and myself, together 20 years on.

attempt new promotional concepts. I shall never forget that chance. Frank and I are still great mates; he has run the Melbourne Hilton since its opening, in 1974, and I always stay there when in that city.

Frank wasn't always forebearing. On one occasion, Ken Kendrick, the Catering Manager, and I put on our own private dinner party at the opening of a new floor show in the Silver Spade. Ken had created a magnificent banquet from items in the day store and freezer which would eventually have been thrown out, because they were no longer on any menu. In the same way, I had found various wines which were no longer moving, 'odd' bins and samples. But the Food Controller of the day, a not very popular gentleman who wasn't invited to the party, put the wines through the billing process at full price. The party was a brilliant success. We arrived at work next morning with massive hangovers and received a curt 'In my office, immediately' from Frank. There I received one of the greatest dressing-downs of my life: responsibility to the General Manager, to the receiver of the company, to ourselves, etc. etc. etc. I managed to get in about four 'Yes sirs' in a rather one-sided conversation, and that was that. Never did it again, and temperance in all things has dominated my life ever since.

We had some marvellous fun, in spite of all the hard work. Friday lunch was set aside for the great Friday Club, quite the best thing of its kind I've ever attended. Eight of us would bring various masked bottles and sit down to some excellent food. However, when Tony Bohdan took charge of the food, strange things happened. Bulls' testicles, yearling thoroughbreds, cows' udders, and other even more unmentionable things made their appearance. Our job was to identify the type of food, the sauce, the various components. That was before the wine tasting started. The bottles would be passed in their paper bags, and soon we learned to put our fingers on the bottom of the bottle to see if it had a 'punt', denoting a French wine. So we put pieces of cardboard over the punt. Then pieces of cardboard over plain Australian bottle bottoms to make believe they were hiding something. Once I declared a Lindemans Bin 1333 1959 *must* be French, or I would eat my hat. I was wrong, and later a highly elaborate pastry hat arrived. After four courses and eight wines I didn't know quite what was required of me. Luckily, my day was saved by another guest, Joe Franks, who wanted the hat for his boy to wear to a fancy dress party that weekend. So we baked him pastry spats and he went as a meat pie.

It was at this luncheon that Gus Pfafflin went to sleep. A huge man, with a deep gravelly voice, he awoke with a start and said, 'You know those ones called morning glories when you wake up and feel good, well, I've given them up.' Since Gus was in his sixties we weren't really surprised, but we did have the decency to ask why. 'It's like this,' he said, 'you never know what may turn up during the day.'

On another occasion that savage wit Ron Tarrant listened with apparent awe to Frank Thorpe, then President of the Wine and Food Society of New Zealand, give a brilliant dissertation on a wine: 'This reminds me of a wine I tasted last year with Prince Metternich. There we were, on the slopes of the Rhine, drinking one such as this, when we got to talking about the war. There we were, in the brotherhood of wine and we found that we'd fought in the war—on different sides, of course, he in the Panzer Corps and me in the New Zealand Antitank Brigade. Sipping that wine, we found that we had fought in the same theatre of war, in North Africa. Not only in the same theatre, but the same battle. And not only in the same battle, but in the same action. Comparing notes, here we were, in the brotherhood of wine, and we found that we had fired and fought against each other 20 years before.' Tarrant had had enough. 'It's a good thing you were both flaming incompetent.'
The learning curve continued. Wine companies made a special fuss and invited me to all sorts of functions and tastings. I was lucky to be in the right spot at the right time, for it would be so much harder to be recognised today. I was asked to serve as an associate judge, and the next year, when someone became ill at the last moment, I was made a judge. In 1962, seeking more wine information, I suggested to Peter Hastings, the then editor of the *Bulletin*, that he start a wine column. 'Good idea,' he said. 'You write it.' Thus 'Cellarmaster of the Bulletin' was born, drinking deep until 1973, and then, after sporadic sorties from there until 1981, returning to the home cellar.

During this time the Chevron was host to the greats of the world,

'Once I declared a Lindemans Bin 1333 1959 must be French, or I would eat my hat. I was wrong, and later a highly elaborate pastry hat arrived.'

especially from show business and the arts. I met Vivien Leigh, Judy Garland, Ethel Merman, Louis Armstrong, Nelson Eddy, Nat King Cole, Rudy Nureyev, Dame Margot Fonteyn, Frank Sinatra, Igor Stravinsky. Stravinsky stayed at the Chevron while the Beatles were across the road at the Sheraton. Someone suggested that Stravinsky and the Beatles should get together. Both parties agreed, but the young Beatles demanded that Stravinsky cross the road to meet them. 'Alas,' the great composer sighed, 'my old legs will not carry me over there.'

The Beatles were to have stayed at the Chevron; I accepted their booking while Frank Christie was on holiday. He returned to cancel it. Too much trouble he said. So they went across the road, and we got all the crowds and all the police and all the rioting and none of the money. Evans 1, Christie 0, as he cheerfully conceded. Later, the score was evened when I refused an unknown act, Wayne Newton, a decision which Frank also countermanded. Wayne was a great success at the Silver Spade, and thereafter, whenever Carlos Gastell, his manager, came to town he would always ring me. 'Len,' he would sigh, 'Wayne sends his love.'

The Governor-General of the day, Viscount de Lisle VC, made an unofficial visit with his family to see Eartha Kitt perform. He wished to talk to her afterwards, and although she saw no reason to, good manners prevailed, and she agreed. They got on extremely well—a ten-minute interview lasting an hour—while the rest of his party waited downstairs. I remember one particular exchange. We were talking of the civil rights program. 'Not much has been achieved in 180 years,' declared Eartha. 'But my dear,' said His Excellency, looking down his nose, 'you've done wonders. After all, that's only seven or eight generations.'

Those were memorable days, and I will always be grateful for them. One of the amazing things about that particular team is that we've always kept in touch; in 1980 there was a staff reunion attended by nearly a hundred people.

In the Chevron kitchens there were three great 'steamers' anchored to the floor. Into them every day went the fish and seafood pieces, bones and skins, all the parings of meat plus bones, and the chicken and game carcasses. From these came the three basic stocks that ended up as soup, stock, glaze or essence. The sauciers would send the apprentices over with large pots to top off the basic fluid. During the day the quantities in the pots became smaller as they simmered on the stoves. These stocks were skimmed, ingredients were added, taken away, strained and further reduced, the whole process developing the great sauces that were then the backbone of the cuisine.

It was here that I learnt the value of such stocks. No one can do without them because they are the basis of so much that's good in cooking. One of my favourites of those days was Madeira Sauce, and now my own children love it and will undoubtedly teach it to theirs. It's very simple to make, but you must start with a good stock.

'In the Chevron kitchens there were three great steamers anchored to the floor. Into them every day went the fish and seafood pieces, bones and skins, all the parings of meat plus bones, and the chicken and game carcasses. From these came the three basic stocks that ended up as soup, stock, glaze or essence.'

Stocks

To be a good cook, it is essential to have a store of good stocks—for soups, sauces, glazes, casseroles and so on. These stocks take time to prepare, but with the amount of freezing space available today, it becomes necessary to make each stock only once or twice a year. The stock can then be put into small containers that are either labelled or, better still, colour coded: blue for fish stock, red for game, yellow for poultry and so on. Thence it becomes a simple matter of pulling out the appropriate container as required. The basic stocks are: vegetable, fish, meat, game, white veal, brown veal and poultry.

When clarifying stock, apart from skimming, letting cool to remove fat, and racking (pouring off sediment from one vessel to another), final clarification may be obtained by two easy processes—ice and egg fining.

Let stock cool to moderately hot, add shaved ice and bring to the boil, stirring all the time. Strain. This will remove much coagulated solid matter. Then, let stock cool to moderately hot, add a couple of lightly beaten egg whites and again bring to the boil, stirring all the time. Strain through a very fine sieve or muslin.

If the stocks are fairly well reduced (i.e. beyond soup stage), they should become aspic when chilled. As such, they can be used in all sorts of interesting entrées: duck pieces in game aspic, prawns or fish pieces in aspic and so on.

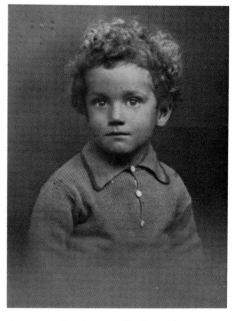

Apparently, I was a little sod.

Vegetable stock

It is not necessary to make and store this, since it is so simply and quickly done. However, it is useful to have a store for soups or vegetarian sauces.

100g onions	*3 litres water*
100g carrots	*bay leaf*
100g celery	*pinch thyme*
100g leeks	*2 cloves*
100g cabbage	*salt*
100g tomatoes	*black pepper*
100g butter	Makes 2 litres

Dice all vegetables except cabbage and tomatoes. Melt the butter in a stockpot and simmer diced vegetables for 10–15 minutes. Add diced cabbage and tomatoes, water and rest of ingredients. Simmer for half an hour. Strain.

Fish stock

4kg of fish pieces, bones, trimmings
250g onions
250g celery
250g leeks
250g tomatoes
100g mushroom trimmings

50g butter
bottle white wine
6 litres water
salt
pepper
Makes 4 litres

Dice vegetables and gently sauté in butter in a big stockpot. Add all other ingredients and bring to the boil. Simmer for 20 minutes only, gently skimming. Strain through diminishing sieves, let cool, and take off the fat. Reheat to boiling. Reduce to 4 litres for stock. Reduce further for soup. Reduce further for fish glaze.

Geraldine Pascall took over my *Indulgence* column.

Meat stock

2kg veal bones and pieces
2kg beef bones and pieces
8 litres water
500g pork skin or bacon rind
500g chopped onions
500g chopped carrots
500g chopped celery

½ cup chopped parsley
pinch thyme
bay leaf
salt
pepper
Makes 4 litres

Roast veal and beef pieces until brown. Place in cold water, bring to the boil, and skim the scum. Sauté the vegetables and add to the water with other ingredients. Bring to the boil, simmer for 2–3 hours, skimming off fat and scum occasionally. Strain through diminishing sieves. Let cool, then remove the final fat. This broth may be enjoyed as such. Reduce further for soup. Reduce further to make rich stock. Reduce further (just prior to burning on the bottom of the pan) to make a glaze.

Brown stock

250g gravy beef (cheap lean beef)
6 beef bones
1 medium carrot

2 medium onions
1 bouquet garni
water to cover

Cut carrot and onions into chunks. Chop gravy beef into 2.5 cm cubes. Place meat, vegetables and bones in a hot oven (220°C/425°F). Roast until bones and vegetables are golden brown. Transfer to a saucepan, add bouquet garni and water to cover. Simmer for 6 hours. Strain through muslin.

Early Chevron days: Frank Christie, Eartha Kitt, Jeffrey Penfold-Hyland, Eartha's secretary and myself.

Brown sauce

1 carrot
1 onion
2 rashers bacon
125g butter

1 cup flour
5 cups brown stock
¼ cup tomato purée

Chop the carrot, onion and bacon into 1 cm cubes. Melt the butter, add flour and cook until it is a good dark brown. Add stock gradually and bring to the boil. Sauté the chopped vegetables and bacon in a little butter. Add to the sauce. Add the purée. Simmer the sauce gently until reduced by half. Strain through muslin.

Game stock

As for the meat stock, except that one uses whatever game pieces and bones are available. An ideal blend would be venison, hare and wild duck. Yet a superior game stock can come from wild duck only.

White veal stock

4kg veal bones and veal pieces,
    trimmed of fat
8 litres water
2 or 3 chicken carcasses (if available)
250g chopped onions
500g chopped carrots
250g chopped leeks

250g chopped celery
½ cup chopped parsley
pinch thyme
bay leaf
salt
pepper

Makes 4 litres

Break veal bones into small pieces, break up chicken carcasses, and with small veal pieces, add to the water and bring to the boil. Skim and add all other ingredients. Boil for 2–3 hours, occasionally skimming off the fat and scum. Let cool and strain through diminishing sieves. Reduce to 4 litres. Let cool and remove the final fat.

Brown veal stock

As for white veal stock, except that the veal bones and pieces are roasted until brown before being boiled. Tomatoes and mushroom pieces are added to the mixture, and meat broth (i.e. meat stock before reduction) is used for the boiling rather than water.

Poultry stock

As for either white or brown veal stocks, depending on the delicacy of sauce or lightness of soup required. To emphasise poultry flavours, simply add heaps of poultry bones or trimmings if these are available, or a couple of boiling fowls. Don't think this is extravagant, since you are making a decent quantity of stock.

Christmas 1949 in Germany, with my father and mother, and brother Martin in my arms.

Artichoke sauce

4 large artichokes
1 large onion, finely chopped
30g butter
¼ cup reduced chicken stock
½ cup cream
salt
pepper
sugar

Boil the artichokes, cool and cut out the heads, removing all traces of the 'beard'. Sauté the onion in butter until tender. Combine stock and cream and reduce by half. Put in the blender together with artichokes and onion, and season with salt, pepper and a little sugar. Blend to a light purée.

Béarnaise sauce

4 eggs
juice of 1 lemon
2 cups melted butter
salt and pepper
2 tablespoons capers
¼ cup chopped parsley
1 tablespoon tarragon vinegar

In the top half of a double boiler, beat the egg yolks and lemon juice. Cook slowly over very low heat, never allowing the water in the bottom pan to boil. Slowly add melted butter to the above mixture, stirring constantly with a wooden spoon. Add salt and pepper to taste, capers, parsley and vinegar. Stir to blend. This is an interesting variation, suitable for serving with fillet of beef.

Béchamel sauce

My variation of this sauce is quick and easy to do, and acts as a base for all kinds of white sauces. You can flavour it with whatever takes your imagination.

60g butter
½ cup flour
hot milk
pepper

thyme
salt
3 tablespoons white veal stock

Heat the butter and cook enough flour in it to make a stiff roux. Allow to cool. Add enough hot milk, a bit at a time, whisking constantly to make a smooth creamy sauce. Add a pinch of thyme, salt and pepper. Add white veal stock, simmer for a little while, occasionally stirring. Now add whatever flavouring you require—herbal, vegetable and so on.

Crayfish sauce

This is made from Australian saltwater crays, often wrongly called lobster, though much the same kind of sauce can be made from the freshwater variety (yabbies).

1 medium-sized crayfish
3 tablespoons olive oil
30g onions, finely chopped
30g mushrooms, finely chopped
30g carrots, finely chopped
60g tomatoes, blanched, skinned,
*   seeded and chopped*

20g chopped fresh dill
¼ cup brandy
½ cup white wine
2 cups reduced fish stock
⅔ cup cream (optional)
salt
cayenne

Mother, father and me in 1932; I don't *think* that was our house.

If the cray is alive, place it in very hot water for a couple of minutes. Cut the cray in half lengthwise, then chop it up across the halves of body and tail. Heat olive oil in a heavy bottomed large saucepan, add the cray pieces and work to cook all parts of the cray until the shells are red. Add the chopped onions, mushrooms and carrots, the tomatoes and the dill. Add the brandy and flame. Add the white wine and the fish stock. Bring to the boil and cook for five minutes.

Let cool, remove the cray pieces, take out the tail meat and put to one side. Pound the rest of the pieces in a large mortar to a paste. This is tedious and does require some elbow grease but it is worth it. Return the paste to the stock. Bring to the boil and simmer for 20 minutes. Strain through descending sieves (i.e. big one, followed by medium, followed by fine). Return to the heat and reduce the stock to a creamy consistency, being careful not to let it burn. Add cream if you wish. (I do, though many better cooks than I don't; I like the soft richness it gives.) Heat, correct seasoning and serve. A beautiful sauce with fish, or with the cray pieces, or with cray halves grilled with butter.

Cumberland sauce

There are many variations of this famous sauce. Greg, the original cook of the Tasting Room, used this version to serve with baked ham. It was one of his specialties. Alan Whicker, the television commentator, who is an old mate of mine, said this was the best lunch he ever had in Australia. Traditionally, the sauce was used to accompany cold venison and other game.

Mount Isa 1956. The pick and shovel kept me fit.

10g butter
1 tablespoon orange peel, pith removed, sliced in thin strips
1 tablespoon lemon peel, pith removed, sliced in thin strips
sugar
½ cup redcurrant jelly

1 cup tawny port
juice of 1 lemon
juice of 1 orange
1 teaspoon English mustard
pinch ginger
pinch cayenne

Melt the butter, add the strips of orange and lemon peel, cook for a little while, sprinkle with a little sugar, work together for a while longer. Add the redcurrant jelly and port and heat together. Add the lemon and orange juice, the mustard, ginger and cayenne. If the mixture is too thin, thicken with a little cornflour.

Cumberland sauce

Or you might like to try this one.

2 oranges
2 lemons
1 cup tawny port
1 cup redcurrant jelly
½ cup white wine vinegar

salt
cayenne
teaspoon of mustard
spoonful of honey (for a sweet sauce)

Peel the rind from the oranges and lemons. Make sure there's no white pith. Shred finely and boil in a little water for 10 minutes. The rinds can now be removed and thrown away, but I like to leave them in. Add the port, redcurrant jelly, white wine vinegar, salt, cayenne pepper, the juice from the oranges and lemons and a teaspoon of mustard. Boil for 5–10 minutes until reduced to a thin sauce. Sometimes a spoonful of honey helps to fill out the flavour if you like it a little sweeter. Others add chopped preserved cherries, but I prefer the sauce without them. Whatever, it's a delicious accompaniment.

Hollandaise sauce

1 tablespoon white vinegar
20g spring onions (white only)
black pepper
3–4 egg yolks

250g clarified butter
lemon juice
salt

Heat the vinegar and cook the finely chopped onions. Grind in some pepper. Add a little cold water and then the egg yolks, a little at a time, over a very low heat, stirring constantly. Work into a thick creamy consistency. Take off heat and work into the mix the clarified butter, which has been melted, a little at a time. Correct seasoning, add a squeeze of lemon juice. Strain the sauce through a fine sieve and serve. Should the sauce separate, add an ice cube until it binds together again. Different flavours may be obtained by using different vinegars, of which there is now an almost bewildering range.

Hunter sauce

30g butter
100g very finely chopped onions
2 teaspoons brandy
½ bottle good soft red wine
2 cloves garlic, crushed
1¼ cups brown veal glaze
60g finely sliced champignons

60g finely chopped white of spring onions
vinegar
½ cup cream
salt
pepper
Tabasco

Heat the butter to moderate temperature, add onions and sauté until soft. Add brandy and flame. Add red wine and garlic. Reduce by half. Add veal glaze, champignons and white spring onions and a little dash of vinegar. Reduce to a consistent thick texture. Correct seasoning. Add cream and a drop of Tabasco. Heat, add the green spring onion rings, serve. This is a robust, full flavoured sauce suitable for steaks and roast beef.

New Zealand, 1953. Gordon's Knob in the South Island is in the background. My Daniel Boone phase.

Mustard sauce

60g butter
½ cup flour
4 egg yolks
⅔ cup cream
salt

pepper
lemon juice
mustard of choice
Makes 2 cups

Melt the butter, mix with flour, and cook for a little while. Add some boiling water and whisk to a smooth, creamy consistency over moderate heat. Allow to cook for 2–3 minutes without boiling, stirring from time to time. Beat the egg yolks, cream, salt and pepper and a squeeze of lemon juice, and add slowly to the butter and flour mix, stirring constantly. Add a little more butter if necessary. Add whatever quantity of whatever mustard you prefer. A combination of French and English mustard achieves an interesting, almost nutty flavour. The sauce can be served with corned beef, baked ham or even pan-fried sardines.

Madeira sauce

15g butter	thyme
20g very finely chopped onions	½ bay leaf
½ cup Madeira, preferably Portuguese	1½ cups brown veal stock
	30g butter (optional)
salt	100ml cream (optional)
pepper	

Heat a little butter and sauté the onions until tender. Add Madeira, salt, pepper, thyme and pieces of bay leaf. Boil vigorously for a little while. Add the stock and reduce. Strain. Some people finish this sauce with the rest of the butter, but I quite like to add cream.

Oyster sauce

1½ cups reduced fish stock	cayenne
3 egg yolks	¾ cup cream
lemon juice	2 dozen oysters
salt	Makes 2½ cups

Heat the fish stock. Take off the heat and slowly add beaten egg yolks, returning to the stove to maintain heat from time to time, stirring constantly. When a good consistency has been attained, add a touch of lemon juice, salt and cayenne, then the cream, working in well. Heat, add oysters and serve. Good with poached fillets of fish.

Red wine sauce

½ bottle good red wine of the softer styles (shiraz, pinot, burgundy)	pinch thyme
	½ bay leaf
50g butter	¾ cup concentrated meat glaze
120g finely chopped onions	salt
1 clove garlic crushed	black pepper

Heat half the butter over moderate heat and sauté the onions. Do not brown. Add the red wine, garlic, thyme and bay leaf. Reduce by half. Add the meat glaze. Reduce until a smooth thick sauce is obtained. Strain through a fine sieve. Add the rest of the butter slowly over low heat. Correct seasoning and serve. This is a very strong-flavoured sauce. It can be reduced by using brown veal stock, or brown poultry stock.

Sauce soubise

500g minced onions	pepper
100g butter	sugar
1½ cups béchamel sauce	½ cup cream
salt	Makes 2 cups

Heat most of the butter gently, add the onions and simmer until tender. Do not brown. Add sauce, salt, pepper, a couple of pinches of sugar and simmer for 15 minutes. Rub the sauce through a sieve if you want a fine texture, or leave if you prefer onion pieces to remain. Add cream, correct seasoning and serve. Delicious with boiled beef and corned silverside.

Tomato and onion sauce

1kg ripe tomatoes
2 large onions, finely chopped
2 tablespoons olive oil
3 cloves garlic, crushed
salt

black pepper
pinch oregano
teaspoon chopped fresh basil
sugar
Tabasco

Heat olive oil in saucepan, add onions and sauté until tender. Blanch, skin and seed tomatoes and cut into small pieces. Add to the pan with crushed garlic, salt, freshly ground black pepper, oregano and basil. Sprinkle a pinch of sugar on the mix. Let simmer for half an hour. Work occasionally with a wooden spoon to prevent burning. Cook until tender and nearly all liquid has evaporated. Correct seasoning and add a dash of Tabasco. This sauce is ideal, as is, with pasta (more chopped basil can be added at the end), or as an accompaniment to steaks and fish.

Sauce vinaigrette

20g shallots or white of spring
  onions very finely chopped
1 clove garlic, crushed
10ml red wine vinegar
10ml olive oil

10ml walnut oil
teaspoon French mustard
dash lemon juice
salt
plenty of freshly ground pepper

Boil the shallots, garlic and vinegar together until half reduced. Work in the oils and mustard little by little. Season and add lemon juice to taste. Bottle. Always shake the bottle before use.

David McNicoll, Ron Saw and between them, the Cellarmaster of the *Bulletin*.

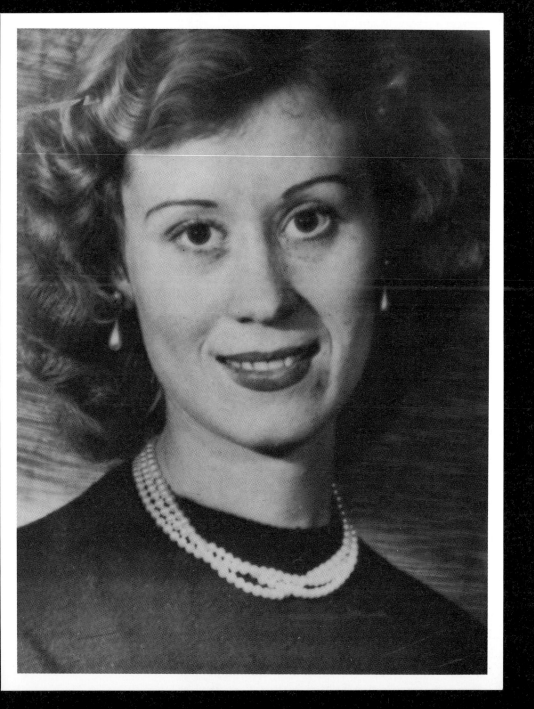

CHAPTER TWO

Soups: Paddington

WHILE WORKING IN THE OUTBACK, ring-barking, fencing and scrub clearing, I wrote occasionally for magazines. I wrote more during a stay in Mount Isa, where I worked as a labourer, a steel-hand, a foreman, and a stores manager while running a chicken and duck farm which was cleared out by a dingo in one night, giving golf lessons at the weekend, and writing and performing in revues for charity in the evenings. My life was as confused as that sentence—no one could ever say that I don't cram a lot into a day. I still do. As more and more articles were accepted for publication, I thought it would be a good idea to try my luck in the Big Smoke. I arrived in Sydney in early 1958.

Although the writing in Sydney looked quite promising, it was necessary to get a part-time job. I replied to an advertisement for a 'CASUAL YOUNG MAN wanted as a glass-washer, Ship Inn, Circular Quay'. Jack Moody was the manager and I still see him from time to time. I got the job, obviously because of my casual attitude, and started work at 6 am each day.

Bob Plastow, the owner of the hotel, was a very experienced publican who taught me a great deal. Life was not without its moments. After months of washing glasses, I learned how to pull a beer. Finally, the day arrived when I was taken off glasses to become a beerman. Every morning, as soon as the bar opened at six, hail or shine, a particular man used to come in and buy a schooner of beer. My first day and I would show them. As he came to the counter I presented him with his schooner. And he looked me straight in the eye and said, 'Brandy and soda, please.'

Mr Plastow nearly went berserk. 'Never pour a beer until it's ordered,' he shouted. 'You owe me one and nine.' I carefully put the beer in the fridge. 'What the devil are you doing?' he asked. 'If I've paid for it, I'm going to drink it,' I replied. The dreaded bullet wasn't far away, yet he smiled and nothing more was said.

One day a stocktaker arrived, a slightly mystical figure who reported on the bar percentages and therefore let the owner know just how well everyone was performing. I was told to call for him—to count the stock per item and give him the result. As I did this I specified the item first, Johnny Walker Red Label, Lindemans Mon-

My darling girl, Trish, in Mount Isa, 1956.

tillo Dry Sherry, and so on, and then counted the number of bottles. 'Why are you calling the names before the total?' the stocktaker asked. 'So you can find it on your sheet while I do the counting.' Incredibly, that was the reason why I was soon offered a stocktaking job, and, looking back, it was the pivot upon which the direction of my life turned.

Meanwhile, my writing career was making progress. 'Café Continental', an ABC show featuring Hal Wayne, which had gone on for years, needed a continuity writer. This led to work with Dawn Lake, Bobby Limb, John Bluthal, Fred Maxian and others. Indeed, on one night I had three major sketches on television, one each in Sydney, Melbourne and Adelaide. The total fee received was £19/7, including all interstate releases and reruns.

During this time, my greatest thrill was being employed as a humorist by *Observer* magazine. The editor was Donald Horne, the assistant editor Peter Coleman, and the financial editor Michael Baume. Another ad hoc contributor, an architectural student called Robert Hughes, did cartoons. The *Observer* was amalgamated with the *Bulletin*, and relationships were formed which last to this day.

However, there was a slight hitch. In Mount Isa I had met an English girl, the local beauty queen and daughter of a hardrock miner. After three years of courtship, my bride-to-be still did not approve of my bohemian career and demanded that, if we were to be married, a steady job was the requirement. So I took the stocktaking offer and became a hotel systems analyst. That job led to the Chevron, a meeting with Frank Christie, the big hotel boss of the day, and subsequently my joining the hotel. Now, after more than 25 years of marriage and three children, Trish sometimes asks, 'Why are you so busy? Surely you could make a comfortable living just writing.'

My dearest Trish overcame her reservations, and we were married at St Mathias in Oxford Street, Paddington, on 18 July 1959. Since we had been in Sydney only a year, there were no parents available so we did the whole thing ourselves. We had saved up £110, and that paid for everything. I remember that the red at the wedding break-

Our renovated lounge in Paddington. We did all the work ourselves, including knocking down the wall.

fast was Fiorelli, and the white Bianchini. The wedding was small, with perhaps 30 new friends present. Happily, six of them were able to come to our Silver Anniversary dinner. We had taken a very small flat in Paddington, with a bed/sitting room, a verandah/dining room/kitchen and a tiny bathroom. It cost £4/10 a week and we resolved to save £10 a week from then on so that we could buy a house. When our collective savings were withdrawn to pay for the wedding, I left some money in the account, for our future.

Our honeymoon was short, but it was a very nice day. Married on Saturday, on Sunday a honeymoon cruise to Hunters Hill and back on the ferry—we couldn't even afford the big one to Manly! And when we put our first deposit in the bank as a married couple, I found that the previous balance was not the 10 shillings I had believed, but 10 pence.

Trish and I started to decorate our tiny flat. I remember a table top that I painted with Dali-like surrealism, which, alas, has been lost to posterity; a collection of miniature bottles; my first pewter, a William Edom (or Edem), tulip-shaped tankard of about 1725 bought for seven guineas from Bill Bradshaw, the celebrated antique dealer of Ocean Street, Woollahra; and a large range of Australian liqueurs, which an enthusiastic maker had sent for my examination.

I left the liqueurs for Bob Oxenbould, a banker whom Ron Saw of the *Bulletin* renamed, with justification, 'The Dreaded'. Bob used to like a drink in those days, so one night he tasted the lot. Tasted! He drank, enjoyed, swilled in, guzzled, engulfed those liqueurs until not a drop was left. I don't know how or when the Oxenboulds left the flat, but we didn't hear from them for about 15 years, it seems. We wondered whether he had finished up as a tugboat captain on the Amazon, until he reappeared, still a banker, and the only fanatical fisherman I know who doesn't like fish.

The Oxenboulds were among the first we entertained. Rabbit fricassees, chicken stews and the eternal chump chops were all standbys of the day, but none so much as Trish's ham and pea soup. For a few months, Trish worked for Anderson's, the bacon and ham suppliers. There she was able to obtain great ham hocks and bacon bones which she turned into marvellous soup, making pots and pots of it so that at least there was something for people who popped in. It remains a staple to this day, and in winter time it's among my favourites. I suppose the love of soup was born in me, for in Wales there was always some bubbling on the stove.

At this time, many wine companies started to give me lots of different bottles as samples. We had no place to store these except under the bed. As the bulge from under the bed grew, it emphasised the gap between us, a sort of oenological prophylactic. So, we had to entertain more to use up the wine to bring ourselves together. Seemed a good system then and it still does. The greatest bottle can be opened only once. We drank old O'Sheas from the Hunter, Roger Warren's Thomas Hardy reds of the 1940s and early 1950s, and Colin Preece's marvellous Great Western reds, all with ham and pea soup.

'Bob Oxenbould used to like a drink in those days, so one night he tasted, drank, enjoyed, swilled in, guzzled, engulfed my collection of liqueurs until not a drop was left. I don't know how or when the Oxenboulds left the flat, but we didn't hear from them for about 15 years, it seems.'

Cream of artichoke soup with crushed hazelnuts

10 medium-large artichokes
2 cups chopped onion
2 bay leaves
1/4 cup butter
3 tablespoons sherry
8 cups chicken stock
1 teaspoon salt

1/8 teaspoon white pepper
3 cups ground, toasted, unblanched
   hazelnuts, divided
1/3 cup rice flour
1/3 cup dry white wine
2 cups cream
Serves 10

Remove leaves, stems and thistles from the artichokes; cut the remaining artichoke hearts into 5 mm slices. Cook the onion, bay leaves and artichokes in butter until the onion is soft. Add 1 tablespoon of the sherry, the chicken stock, salt, pepper and 2½ cups of the nuts. Bring to the boil; reduce heat and simmer for 25–30 minutes.

Make a paste of flour, white wine and 1 tablespoon of the sherry. Add to artichoke mixture; cook and stir until thickened. Add the cream; simmer for another 15–20 minutes.

Strain twice, once through a medium then through a fine sieve. Add the remaining tablespoon of sherry. If necessary, add more salt. (This will vary, depending on the saltiness of chicken stock.) Serve garnished with the reserved hazelnuts.

My great-great-great-grandfather's friend. His picture hangs in the Tasting Room.

Beef soup with liver dumplings

6 cups reduced meat stock
150g finely diced cooked beef
pinch mixed herbs
salt and pepper
teaspoon chopped parsley
for the dumplings:

150g veal or calves liver
1 egg
3 slices bread
1/3 cup milk
30g finely chopped onion
Serves 6

Bring stock to the boil, then simmer and add beef pieces. Season with herbs and salt and pepper. Make dumplings by roughly blending liver, egg, bread, milk and onion into a stiff paste. Scoop into small spoonfuls and simmer in the broth for 5 minutes. Place dumplings in plates, pour soup over, and sprinkle with chopped parsley.

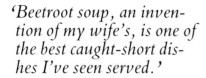

'Beetroot soup, an invention of my wife's, is one of the best caught-short dishes I've seen served.'

Beetroot soup

2 tins whole small beetroot
2 cups reduced chicken stock
1/2 cup cream

salt and pepper
Serves 6

Pour the beetroot liquid into a saucepan and add the chicken stock. While this is reducing over a fierce heat put the beetroot, together with a little liquid from the saucepan into the blender. Add this to the reduced liquid and blend it again. Put the liquid back in the saucepan and heat it again, then add the cream, salt and pepper.

This soup, an invention of my wife's, is one of the best caught-short dishes I've seen served. We had unexpected guests for a dinner and there was no first course. My wife took some chicken stock from the freezer and opened two tins of whole small beetroot. The soup was quickly made and well received.

Carrot vichyssoise

2 cups potatoes, peeled and diced
1¼ cups sliced carrots
1 leek, sliced (white part only)
3 cups chicken stock
salt
pepper
1 cup cream
carrot for garnish
Serves 4–6

Put all ingredients into a saucepan. Bring to the boil and simmer for 25 minutes or until vegetables are tender. In an electric blender, purée half the vegetables and liquid at a time for 30 seconds on high speed. Empty the purée into a mixing bowl. Stir in a pinch of white pepper, 1 teaspoon salt and the cream.

Serve in chilled bowls, ice cold, with a topping of shredded raw carrot.

My great-great-great-grandfather. His picture hangs in the Tasting Room.

Clam chowder

A richer version of this is my favourite. Instead of boiling the potatoes in water, I use a rich fish stock. This makes a dish that is a meal in itself. I always add a dash of vinegar before serving.

2kg pipis
2 rashers bacon, finely chopped
2 onions, chopped
1kg potatoes, peeled and sliced
½kg carrots, scraped and sliced
butter
thyme
salt and pepper
cream
Serves 8

Make sure the pipis are purged (see page 30). Place them in a large pot with some water in the bottom and steam until the shells open. Let cool, take the pipis out of their shells and retain liquid.

In a large pot heat a little butter, add the bacon and cook for a couple of minutes. Add the onions and cook until transparent, then add the potatoes, carrots and thyme. Season with salt and pepper. Cover with liquid, bring to the boil and cook until done.

Add the cream and the pipis, correct the seasoning and serve.

Manhattan clam chowder

Another seafood soup variant, one which uses the often available and reasonably priced local clam, the pipi. If you dig up pipis from the beach, keep them in fresh water with a dose of sugar or oatmeal. This will free them of sand.

*4 large, firm, ripe tomatoes, or 4
    cups chopped, drained, canned
    tomatoes
8 dozen pipis or cockles
3 tablespoons butter
1 cup finely chopped onion
¼ cup finely chopped carrot
¼ cup finely chopped celery*

*3 cups water
1 medium-sized bay leaf
½ teaspoon crumbled dried thyme
freshly ground black pepper
3 medium-sized potatoes, peeled and
    cut into 3 mm dice*

Serves 6

'If you dig up pipis from the beach, keep them in fresh water with a dose of sugar or oatmeal. This will free them of sand.'

If using fresh tomatoes, drop them into boiling water for 15 seconds, then peel off the skins with a small, sharp knife. Cut out the stems and cut the tomatoes in half crosswise. Squeeze the halves to remove the juice and seeds, then coarsely chop the pulp. Canned tomatoes need only be drained thoroughly and chopped. Steam the pipis, or cockles, until they open and save 3 cups of the stock; sieve to remove any shell residue.

In a heavy 3–4 litre saucepan, melt the butter over moderate heat. When the foam begins to subside, add the onions, carrots and celery and, stirring frequently, cook for about 5 minutes, until the vegetables are soft but not brown. Add the chopped tomatoes, pipi liquid, 3 cups of water, bay leaf, thyme and a few grindings of pepper, and bring to the boil over high heat. Reduce the heat to low, partially cover the pan and simmer for 45 minutes.

Stir in the potatoes and continue to simmer, partially covered, for another 12 minutes. Add the pipis and cook the chowder for another 2–3 minutes. Remove and discard the bay leaf.

Taste the chowder for seasoning and serve at once from a heated tureen or in individual soup plates.

Crab bisque

*24 live blue swimmer crabs
125g celery, finely diced
125g carrots, finely diced
125g onions, finely diced
olive oil
1 teaspoon tarragon, finely chopped
1 bay leaf
½ teaspoon thyme, finely chopped
½ teaspoon rosemary*

*10 cups fish stock
¾ cup dry sherry
1 tablespoon Cognac
10 tomatoes, skinned, seeded and
    finely chopped
½ cup cream
8 whole crab legs
salt and white pepper to taste*

Serves 8

Put the live crabs in cold water with a little salt and leave them to soak for one hour. Remove and drain the crabs. Heat the olive oil in a large sauté pan and sauté crabs until the shells turn red. Combine celery, carrots, onion, tarragon, bay leaf, thyme, and rosemary. Add to the crabs and stir. Add dry sherry and Cognac. Reduce liquid. Add the fish stock and simmer over low heat for approximately one hour. Strain through a conical strainer. Combine the chopped tomatoes with tomato paste and add to the stock in which the crabs were sautéed. Stir well and reduce over medium-high heat.

Pass this stock through a sieve and then a muslin cloth. Combine the stock with the purée of crab flesh and add the cream. Heat without boiling. Cut the whole crab legs in julienne strips and add to the bisque. Add salt and white pepper to taste.

Combination soup

This is my standby recipe for overcoming the effects of a glass or two too many. Well, it has happened from time to time. Some people use coffee, I use this soup, especially if it comes from the Peacock Gardens, my friend Matthew Chan's excellent establishment in Crow's Nest, Sydney. The soup is quite easy to make and is an excellent restorer of jaded tissues.

3 cloves garlic, chopped
10g ginger, chopped
30ml oil
150g prawns, chopped
250g barbecue pork, sliced
12 wontons
1 litre chicken stock
250ml prawn stock (if available)

100g Chinese mushrooms or canned champignons
100g Chinese cabbage or spinach stalks, sliced
100g bean sprouts
100g egg noodles
100g crab or crayfish meat
30g shallot tops, finely sliced crosswise

'Combination soup is my standby recipe for overcoming the effects of a glass or two too many. Well, it has happened from time to time.'

Fry the garlic and ginger in a little hot oil. Add the prawns, barbecue pork, wontons and the chicken and prawn stock and boil for 2–3 minutes. Add soaked Chinese mushrooms or canned champignons, Chinese cabbage or spinach stalks, bean sprouts, egg noodles, crab or crayfish meat and shallot tops. Simmer until hot, do not overcook.

Duck soup

The best soup I ever ate was at the Chevron Hilton in the early 1960s. A huge banquet was organised for 600 car dealers. Each was served roast duck as the main course. The catering manager noticed that the roasting pans each contained the remnants of the basting liquid, wine, duck blood and fat. He had all of this put into a huge pot, chilled it and removed the fat, re-heated the stock and strained it. The stock was then reduced to enough for eight people. The resultant liquid was highly concentrated in flavour, to say the least, but slightly salty. He then added some old Hunter wine, the saltiness disappeared, and he served eight people the reduced soup.

So, if you want the recipe, first take 600 ducks. . .

———————— ❦ ————————

Clear game soup with vegetables

A simple dish, yet one which constantly receives the highest accolades.

Trish's pea and ham soup
(recipe page 39).

8 cups clear game stock	*10g bean sprouts*
20g carrots	*10g champignons, thinly sliced*
20g onions, thinly sliced	*salt and pepper*
20g celery	Serves 6–8
20g leeks	

A good game stock is the basis for this soup. It must be seasoned and clarified. Into it place a julienne of the celery, carrots and leeks, plus the shaved onions, mushrooms and the whole bean sprouts. Heat and simmer until the vegetables are tender. Do not overcook. Serve.

ALTERNATIVES: If you wish to particularly impress, in the centre of each soup plate place a 'gesture'—cream, a liver quenelle, a slice of truffle, a dumpling, a soft-boiled shelled game egg (gull, quail, pigeon). I've even made individual puff pastry letters of my guest's names and floated them in the soup.

———————— ❦ ————————

W.A. fish soup

fish heads	*tomatoes*
skins	*onions*
bones	*salt and pepper*

This recipe evolved on a rough fishing trip with Peter Doyle and Michael Kailis, who owns the Perth fish markets. We were catching lots of snapper and each night I boiled all the skins, heads and bones with tomatoes and onions, straining off the liquid after about 20 minutes and discarding all solids. The next night I would skim the muck off the top, pour off the sediment and, using the same liquid, repeat the process. By the third night the soup was fantastic. It was so gelatinous, and there was so much of it, I discarded the top and bottom of the set jelly, retaining only the clear, quite solid aspic in the middle. Finally, I heated this for the last time, adding diced onions, potatoes, tomatoes, and a pinch of saffron, and when the vegetables were almost cooked, I added cubes of fresh snapper. It was absolutely delicious, a marvellously intense taste. While we were eating it, a local professional fisherman walked in. We gave him some of the soup. 'Who made this?' he asked. 'I'm looking for a cook for next season.' 'Oh,' I said, 'I'd cost $50 a day and keep.' 'Fifty bucks and keep!' he cried. 'For that you'd have to help with the nets.'

Gazpacho

1 loaf French bread (2 or 3 days old)	2 cloves garlic, sliced
½ teaspoon salt	3–4 medium-large tomatoes
4 tablespoons wine vinegar	1 cucumber, peeled
8 tablespoons olive oil	Serves 6–8
2 medium-large onions	

Cut the bread in small cubes, add just enough water to cover it, add salt. When the bread has absorbed the water, place it in a blender with the other ingredients and blend. Pour into a jug, add about 12 cubes of ice and serve. As a complement, on small individual plates serve cubes of cucumber, tomatoes, capsicum, bread and onions.

Warm fish salad with a sherry vinaigrette (recipe page 62).

Leek and potato soup

Some may consider this a version of Vichysoisse. All I can say is that we were making this in the Welsh hills when the Romans had a lot of gall.

300g leeks, finely sliced	2 cups meat stock
300g onions, finely sliced	300g potatoes, diced
50g butter	salt and pepper
½ bottle (375ml) white wine	¾ cup cream
1 cup brown poultry stock	Serves 6

Cook the leeks and the onions in butter in a large saucepan. Add the wine, poultry stock and meat stock and some water. Add the potatoes. Bring to the boil and simmer until tender. Blend. Put back in the saucepan, season to taste and add the cream to make a smooth, creamy soup.

Lentil soup

Traditionally, this soup was called *purée conti*. Now, one of the most famous vineyards in the world is Romanee-Conti in Burgundy. Did Prince Conti give his name to both?

500g lentils	bay leaf
60g lean bacon, diced	2 cups brown poultry stock
100g carrots, finely chopped	2 cups brown veal stock
100g onions, finely chopped	salt and pepper
thyme	Serves 8

Soak the lentils overnight. Put them into a large saucepan with the bacon, vegetables, herbs and stocks. Bring to the boil, then simmer gently for two hours, adding more stock if necessary. Remove from heat, allow to cool slightly, then put through a blender to make a purée. Re-heat, garnish with croûtons, and serve.

Thick meat soup

This is an easy to prepare caught short dish, which varies depending on the available ingredients The essentials are the potato and lettuce base, the rice and cheese and some form or forms of meat.

2 medium potatoes
2½ cups chicken stock
6 large, dark green outer lettuce
    leaves
150g lean minced meat
2 shallots, finely chopped
3 tablespoons red wine
teaspoon thyme, fresh or dried
teaspoon basil, fesh or dried

½ teaspoon nutmeg
2 x 190g cans champignons
1 tablespoon grated Parmesan cheese
⅓ cup cream
3 tablespoons cooked rice, noodles or
    cous-cous
salt and freshly ground pepper
Serves 4

Cook potatoes in stock until tender. Add lettuce leaves and cook for a further 10 minutes. Blend to a smooth purée. Stir-fry the meat, add shallots, wine, potato and lettuce purée and the herbs. Simmer for 15 minutes and then add remaining ingredients. Season with salt and pepper, and serve in large bowls accompanied by side salads and bread or biscuits.

The second best spitter in Australia.

Thick Mulligatawny soup

There are many variations and styles of this famous Indian soup. This one is easy to prepare and makes a good, thick winter soup.

4 cups strong beef stock flavoured
    with vegetables
8g cardamom seeds
6 whole peppercorns
8g coriander seeds
4g fenugreek seeds
1 bay leaf
pared rind of half a lemon

2 tablespoons desiccated coconut
1 cup boiling water
60g onions or shallots
30g butter or dripping
¼ cup flour
1 teaspoon curry powder
seasoning
Serves 4–6

Bruise all the spices lightly and put them into a muslin bag (like bouquet garni) with the bay leaf and lemon rind. Simmer for half an hour in the prepared stock, then remove the bag and put the stock aside. Pour the boiling water over the coconut and allow it to steep for half an hour. When required, strain it through muslin. Chop the onion finely and fry slowly in the heated fat, add the curry powder and continue frying for a few minutes. Remove from the heat to add the flour, then cook for a minute, and add the stock. Simmer for a quarter of an hour, strain through a sieve and add coconut milk. Return to the saucepan to heat, check the seasoning, and serve with bread or croûtons.

Soupe de coquilles St Jacques

½ medium-sized white onion	600g fresh scallops
2 carrots	3 tablespoons cream
30g butter	salt
1 cup dry white wine	freshly ground pepper
1 cup water or fish stock	Serves 6

Finely chop the onion and grate the carrots. In a large saucepan, gently sauté the chopped onion for about 2 minutes in 10g of the butter. Add the grated carrot and sauté for 5 minutes. Pour the wine and water (or fish stock) into the saucepan, bring to the boil and simmer for 5 minutes. Next add the scallops, allow to boil for 30 seconds and incorporate the rest of the butter. Add the cream, season to taste with salt and freshly ground pepper and serve immediately.

Quick mushroom soup

2 cans cream of mushroom soup	½ cup sherry
250g field mushrooms	⅔ cup cream
50g butter	Serves 8
freshly ground black pepper	

Make up cans of soup as directed. Slice the field mushrooms, and sauté them in butter. Add them to the soup with freshly ground black pepper and the sherry. Just before serving stir in the cream.

'Sometimes there's no point in starting from scratch if a can of soup will do half the work for you. The other ingredients give this quick soup a fresh and delicious character.'

Mussel soup

4 dozen mussels	100g chopped carrots
2 cups cider (dry, not carbonated)	50g butter
½ cup white wine	¼ cup flour
dash white wine vinegar	1¼ cups milk
200g chopped leeks	½ cup cream
100g chopped onions	salt and pepper
100g chopped celery	parsley

Into a large saucepan put the cider, white wine and vinegar. Bring to the boil and continue boiling as the mussels are dropped into the saucepan. Simmer for 20 minutes, then cool. Take out the mussels and remove them from their shells. Put the mussels to one side. In another saucepan melt the butter, add flour and cook for 2–3 minutes. Add milk, which has been heated, and stir constantly until thick. Strain the mussel stock, cook the vegetables in it, and add all to the white sauce. Mix thoroughly, then stir in the cream. Correct seasoning with salt and pepper, add parsley, add mussels and re-heat gently. Being a vinegar addict, I always add another dash of white wine vinegar.

Oyster soup

125g butter
125g celery
125g shallots
1 tablespoon plain flour
1 clove garlic

5 cups oyster liquid plus water
4 dozen oysters, shelled
2 bay leaves
salt and black peppercorns
Serves 6

Sift the flour. Finely chop the celery and shallots. Finely chop the garlic. Measure the oyster liquid and add water to obtain the required amount.

Melt butter in a saucepan, add celery and shallots and sauté until tender. Add the flour and cook slowly for 5 minutes, stirring constantly. Add the garlic, oyster liquid, bay leaves, 2 dozen oysters and season with salt and pepper. Simmer for 20 minutes. Remove the bay leaves, add the remaining oysters and serve.

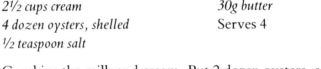

Oyster stew

This is a typical dish from New Orleans. The oysters there are larger and a little more rugged than Sydney rock oysters.

2½ cups milk
2½ cups cream
4 dozen oysters, shelled
½ teaspoon salt

⅛ teaspoon cayenne
30g butter
Serves 4

With the great Rudy Komon, MBE, at the Sydney Wine Show.

Combine the milk and cream. Put 2 dozen oysters, salt, cayenne and butter in a saucepan and heat until boiling. Reduce heat and simmer 5 minutes. Add the remaining oysters and serve.

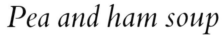

Pea and ham soup

This recipe is from Carolyn Divjak, chef of the Tasting Room.

1.5kg bacon bones
2 carrots
2 onions
2 stalks celery
parsley
bay leaf
few peppercorns
4 litres water

300g yellow split peas
½ packet frozen green peas
carrot, cut into fine julienne strips
turnip, cut into fine julienne strips
celery, sliced finely
watercress for garnish
Serves 12

To make the basic stock, cover bacon bones with water and add peeled carrots, onions and the celery, parsley, bay leaf and peppercorns. Bring to the boil, skim and then simmer for about 3 hours. Strain and skim fat off the stock. To the stock add the yellow split peas. Simmer for another hour or until the peas are softened. Add more water if necessary.

To finish the soup, about 4–10 minutes before serving add the frozen peas and simmer until tender. When ready to serve, blanch the julienne of carrot and turnip and the celery for a few seconds, and put a little in the bottom of each soup plate. Pour over the soup and garnish with watercress or mustard and cress.

Trish's pea and ham soup

This was one of the great standbys of our early married life. At one time we lived on this soup and chump chops because we couldn't afford anything else. I worked hard in those days, starting very early in the morning and getting back to our little flat 12 hours later, sometimes having eaten only a sandwich in the meantime. The ultimate pleasure was to find there was some hot pea and ham soup waiting.

1kg split peas	*3 stalks celery*
1kg ham hocks	*3 onions*
1kg bacon bones	*12 slices salami (optional)*
4 carrots	Serves 10

Soak the split peas overnight. Boil ham hocks, bacon bones, carrots, celery stalks and onions in water until all the goodness is out of everything. If there is substantial meat on the hock, take it off and chop it into chunks. Otherwise, strain the rest and press it through a sieve. Chill and then remove the fat. Add the peas to the stock. Cook fairly quickly for about half an hour.

ALTERNATIVES: cook chopped fresh onions, carrots and celery in the stock before the split peas are added. Another way is to add sliced salami with the peas. These slices 'sweat' and add a delicious flavour.

Pimiento bisque

This recipe is from the Tabasco people, who make their fiery sauce from the hottest peppers, fermented and then matured for three years. Use sparingly, but do use occasionally.

4 cups chicken stock	*1 egg yolk*
4 tablespoons uncooked rice	*½ cup cream*
4 pimientos (red capsicums)	*whipped cream to garnish*
¾ teaspoon of salt	*paprika*
¼ teaspoon Tabasco	Serves 4

Bring stock to the boil. Add rice; simmer for 15–20 minutes until the rice is tender. Put clean, seeded pimientos through a blender, then add to the stock with salt and Tabasco. Bring to the boil. Beat egg yolk slightly with cream. Gradually stir some stock into the egg mixture, then stir this into the stock in the saucepan. Heat, stirring until hot but not boiling. Garnish each portion with a dab of whipped cream; sprinkle with paprika.

'Hugh Birch, the famous Qantas flier, once remarked, "My wife and I have been married so long we're on our second bottle of Tabasco."'

Sydney Harbour prawn soup

I devised this dish with Graham Kerr, many years ago. It was our version of bouillabaisse. There are endless variations; sometimes I add pipis, different kinds of prawns, Balmain bugs, other fish, anything that's available. When Nora Gregory was cook in the Tasting Room, this was a celebrated standard dish that never failed to please.

60g onions	garlic
10 spring onions	60g butter
1 clove garlic	2 sprigs parsley
2 medium tomatoes	1 bay leaf
250g black bream fillets	1 teaspoon orange peel
300g John Dory fillets	8 mussels (in shells)
250g king prawns	salt, white peppercorns, to season
250g crayfish	4 cups fish stock
1 French loaf	¼ teaspoon saffron
butter	Serves 6

Slice the onions finely, cut top leaves from the spring onions, leaving about 12 cm of green. Peel the garlic clove. Skin, seed and dice the tomatoes. Make the fish stock. Cut fish fillets into 5 cm × 2.5 cm pieces. Peel the prawns and cut crayfish meat into chunks. To prepare the garlic bread, slice loaf thickly, not entirely severing the slices, butter each slice and spread with a little squeezed garlic. Wrap the loaf in aluminium foil and place in the oven at 190°C/375°F for 15–20 minutes.

Place butter in a deep saucepan and add to it the onion, spring onions, tomatoes, crushed garlic, sprigs of parsley, bayleaf and orange peel. Sauté for 2 minutes only. Add the prepared fish and mussels in their shells and season with salt and pepper. Cover with fish stock in which the saffron has been dissolved. Bring to the boil then reduce heat to a fast simmer and cook with the lid on for 4 minutes. Add the cooked prawns and crayfish (together with crayfish legs) and heat through.

Strain the liquid into a serving bowl and arrange the steaming hot fish in a decorative manner on a serving dish (remove bayleaf and parsley). Surround the dish with slices of garlic bread.

You can't win them all!

King prawn curry soup

This soup is a special of Berida Manor, part of their 1000 calorie-a-day regime. (I usually spill that much in wine.) As with all seafood dishes, this soup should not be overcooked.

25 green king prawns, peeled and deveined	2 carrots, finely chopped
	6 shallots, finely chopped
5 cups chicken stock	500g natural yoghurt
4 tablespoons curry powder	Serves 8

Using a little of the stock, mix curry powder into a fine paste. When smooth, add the remaining stock and the carrots, and bring to the boil. Allow to simmer for 3–4 minutes, add the prawns, diced into even pieces, and the shallots. Blend in the yoghurt, stirring gently for a few minutes; do not allow to boil. Preferably, add the yoghurt over a double boiler. Season to taste and serve with melba toast.

------------------- ❧ -------------------

Pumpkin soup

30g butter
2 onions, chopped
1 leek, chopped
3 shallots, chopped
1.5kg butternut pumkin
2 large ripe tomatoes

2½ cups chicken stock
salt and pepper
½ cup cream
parsley or chives
Serves 8

Sauté the onions in butter with the leek and shallots. Peel the butternut pumkin and cut into chunks. Skin and chop the tomatoes and add these vegetables to the onions. Cover with the chicken stock, season well and simmer until the vegetables are soft. Blend, check seasoning, and add the cream. Garnish with parsley or chives.

------------------- ❧ -------------------

Rabbit soup

2.5kg fresh rabbit
smoked ham hock
3 litres water
3 medium onions, thinly sliced
2 medium, firm tomatoes, skinned
  and finely chopped
2 teaspoons finely chopped garlic
1 teaspoon dried thyme

1 teaspoon salt
few grindings of pepper
3 tablespoons butter
6 tablespoons flour
½ cup dry white wine
1 cup cream
Serves 12

'Rabbit soup is an old bush recipe, and for the rabbit you can substitute anything that happens to be handy—fish, meat, vegetables, or if you're lucky, a ham hock.'

Put fresh rabbit, smoked ham hock and water into a large pot. Bring to the boil over a fierce heat. Skim off the foam and scum as it rises to the surface. Add the onions, tomatoes, garlic, thyme, salt and pepper. Reduce heat to very low, cover the pot tightly and slow simmer for about 2 hours. Transfer the meat to a plate and discard the ham hock. Extract the bones from the rabbit and cut meat into bite-sized pieces. Strain the stock through a fine sieve set over a deep bowl, pressing down hard on the vegetables with the back of a spoon. Discard the vegetables. Put butter into the cooking pot and melt. Stir in flour to make a roux. Add one cup of the strained stock, stirring constantly until the mixture thickens. Still stirring, pour in the remaining stock slowly. Add the meat and dry white wine and bring to the boil. Remove the soup from the heat and leave to cool for a moment before stirring in the cream. Check seasoning and serve in plates or pannikins with plenty of soppers to scoop up the liquid.

Home-made ravioli soup

8 cups meat stock
for the stuffing:
250g chicken livers
60g spring onions
60g butter
1 clove garlic, crushed
250g blanched spinach leaves, well-
    drained
¼ cup chopped fresh parsley

1 tablespoon chopped fresh basil
salt and pepper
2 eggs
for the pasta:
1¼ cups plain flour
3 beaten eggs
½ teaspoon olive oil
water
Serves 6–8

Slice the chicken livers and chop the onions. Heat the butter and sauté the livers. Add onions, garlic, chopped spinach, parsley, basil, salt and pepper. Simmer gently for a little while only. Remove and cool, then add beaten eggs and make into a paste.

To make the pasta, heap flour, make a well in the middle, add eggs and oil and gently fold in flour, making a very stiff paste. Add a little water if necessary, but the dough should be quite hard. Make two sheets of thin pastry from the pasta. Lie one down, and wet it with a finger or brush, painting a grid pattern on the pasta. The unwetted squares left should be just over 2 cm square. On each unwetted portion put a little mound of the filling. Lie the other sheet over the top, press around each mound of filling, and cut it with a sharp knife or crimp around it with a ravioli cutter. (There are also ravioli trays available.)

Heat the meat stock until it reduces slightly, correct seasoning, then poach the raviolis until the pasta is cooked, about 4–5 minutes.

Scotch broth

One of the best of all winter soups and so quick and easy to do. But you must start with a good lamb stock, which is made the same way as meat stock, using lamb bones and pieces instead of beef.

8 cups lamb stock
100g cooked lamb, diced
¼ cup pearl barley, soaked
30g onions
30g carrots
30g celery

30g leeks
dash vinegar
30g butter
½ cup chopped parsley
salt and pepper
Serves 6

Dice all the vegetables. Heat butter in saucepan. Add onions and cook until transparent. Add remaining vegetables, cooking for 2–3 minutes. Add the barley, which has been well soaked and drained. Add lamb stock and bring to the boil. Cook until everything is tender. Add the lamb pieces, a dash of vinegar and the parsley, and the salt and pepper to taste.

Tomato and basil soup

4 cups brown poultry stock
425g can tomatoes
1 medium onion, chopped
2 large ripe tomatoes, skinned,
   seeded and chopped

salt and pepper
½ cup chopped fresh basil
Serves 6

Mix stock, canned tomatoes and onion together and put through a blender. Heat in a saucepan, and add ripe tomatoes. Season with salt and pepper. Simmer until tender. Add chopped fresh basil and serve.

———————— ❧ ————————

Thin tomato and vegetable soup

4 cups meat stock
½ cup tomato paste
2 firm tomatoes, skinned and seeded
¼ red capsicum
¼ green capsicum

4 spring onions
salt and black pepper
1 tablespoon cooked rice
Serves 4

Make sure meat stock is quite clear. Add tomato paste and simmer until combined. Add tomatoes, and capsicum diced into 3mm squares. Cut whites of spring onion into 5mm pieces, then green leaves into rings. Add to the soup. Season with salt and pepper and simmer gently until tender. Add rice, then serve.

———————— ❧ ————————

Cold vegetable soup

This is really a purée version of the famous Spanish soup, gazpacho. There are many arguments about what exactly goes into gazpacho, so let me just recommend this soup as an ideal summer luncheon dish.

A cartoon by Ward O'Neill from the *Bulletin*.

1 large cucumber
250g ripe tomatoes, skinned, seeded
   and chopped
1 large onion, chopped
½ red capsicum, chopped
½ green capsicum, chopped
2 cloves garlic, finely chopped
dash malt vinegar

¼ cup olive oil
1 cup brown poultry stock
pinch oregano
pinch thyme
¼ cup parsley, chopped
¼ cup basil, chopped
salt and pepper

Peel cucumber, slice thinly and remove pips. Place slices on a flat dish and sprinkle with salt. Put a plate, weighted down, over cucumber. Let stand for half an hour, then rinse slices. Mix all ingredients in a large bowl and let stand overnight in the fridge. In the morning put the mixture through the blender, making a purée. Correct seasoning. Chop up part of the rest of the red and green capsicums into 3mm squares. Mix and scatter on top of each serve.

CHAPTER THREE

Fish: Doyle and the rest

P ETER DOYLE, OF THE FAMOUS SYDNEY fish family, was once a fishing inspector. On an inland posting, he found illegal traps on a section of a river under his jurisdiction. Determined to catch the culprit, he waited for two days and three nights by the traps. All that time he put up with the discomfort of flies and mosquitoes, packed cold food, no hot drinks. Finally, at dawn on the third morning, a furtive figure slunk to the riverside. Doyle's patience was vindicated.

The poacher began hauling in the traps. Doyle quietly crept up behind him and placed a large hand on his shoulder. In complete confusion, the man looked up and shouted, 'Who the hell are you?'

'I'm the local fisheries inspector,' Doyle replied. 'Thank God for that,' cried the poacher. 'I though you was the bloke that owned the traps.'

Fishing has been an important part of whatever leisure time I've had, and the two people that figure largely in my memories are Doyle and the eminent wine man, James Halliday.

I met Doyle through my great mentor, father figure and friend, Rudy Komon. Rudy had insisted on eating some fresh seafood one day, and said there was no place better for it than Doyles, Rose Bay. Marching straight into the kitchen he demanded of the rather hot character who was cooking the chips, 'Do you have any live crays?' 'Yes mate,' replied Pete Doyle, without looking up. 'They're all over the bloody floor.'

We looked down. Sure enough, the sack of live crayfish had come undone, and crays were walking all over the place, under the stoves, in the corners, marching out of the door. Completely unfazed by this, Rudy inspected them in turn until he pointed and declared, 'Good. I'll have that one.'

So began a friendship with Doyle which is now over 20 years old. We've had a couple of rows, a hundred or more fishing trips together, and thousands of laughs. Doyle is not a joke teller, but he's a great anecdotalist, with a compulsive love of the sea. The kind of fishing mania he possesses is typified by a story he tells of when he was young.

He was live fishing for kingies at night with one of his old uncles

Some of the Doyle family (and others) at their Pyrmont opening. Alice is under the wine glass and Jean and Peter are centre.

from Watson's Bay. The fish were biting, and since other boats were sniffing around, the Doyles kept their lights doused. They were kept busy hauling lines in, throwing the fish under one arm and holding them to the body to get the hooks out. It was a hot night and Doyle was only wearing shorts. Another big one bit, and Doyle hauled the line in, pulling the large fish into the boat and grabbing it under his left arm. In the dark he didn't realise there was a dreaded blue-bottle on the line, and suddenly his body was covered with huge weals. The pain was intense and he nearly blacked out.

The old uncle was a bit of a tippler and had a couple of bottles of sweet sherry on board. Doyle swears he drank about a bottle and a half before he finally passed out. At least the drunken sleep covered the pain.

A couple of hours later, he was wakened by the old salt. Thick-headed, cross-eyed, still hugely puffed out and still in pain, Doyle asked, 'What's up?'

'Pete,' his uncled whispered, 'they're on again.'

Fisherman have their own subculture. At the time when nude beaches had become popular, Doyle took me out in his boat one day. 'I want to show you something,' he said, heading for one of the beaches. Frankly, I was rather disappointed that Doyle should not only prove to be a voyeur, but also assume I was one. He passed the beach without a word. 'There,' he said finally, 'see that rock? That's where I caught the biggest bream I've seen in my life.'

Doyle, ever one to deflate the pompous and laugh at the ridiculous, claims he was present when there was a big ceremony of some kind at Constitution Dock in Hobart. The wife of the chief official at the function was asked by one of the fishermen present if she would like a cray. 'Yes,' she replied, 'as long as it's a fresh one.' The fisher-man dipped his hand into the box and brought out a huge cray, holding it by its back. The cray's tail swished and its head jerked repeatedly as it tried to escape.

'Oh,' cried the woman. 'It's huge. But is it fresh?'

'What the hell lady,' was the reply. 'Do you think I wind the flaming things up?'

Years ago, fishing with the celebrated American wine man Bob Mondavi, about 16 kilometres outside the Heads, we had all the big gear out, trolling. It was a hot, still day, and there were not many fish about. Happily, a large tuna hit with some vengeance and Bob had a great time reeling it in. Not long after, Doyle, saw something way off, from the flying bridge. It turned out to be an elaborate deck chair, obviously thrown off a passenger liner by some early morning drunks. With some difficulty we hauled the chair aboard. About 15 minutes later we spotted another. That, too, was hauled aboard. 'Reel in,' shouted Doyle. 'Get the poppers. Get those lines in.' Why? It was still a lovely day and there was plenty of time. 'We've got two chairs. What I want now is the table to make up the set.' Unfortunately for Doyle and his dreams of sybaritism, it wasn't to be.

Fresh fish are wonderful to eat, especially on the spot. There's

'Fresh fish are wonderful to eat, especially on the spot. There's nothing quite like a beach barbecue of jewfish, tailor or whiting, landed while the fire was burning down.'

nothing quite like a beach barbecue of jewfish, tailor or whiting, landed while the fire was burning down. One of the greatest taste sensations I've ever enjoyed was by the side of Lake Eucumbene, in the Snowy Mountains.

With father, fishing off Sydney Heads.

I was fishing with Bob Sanders, Bob Raymond and 'Stringy' Lowe, and we'd caught a one-and-a-half-kilogram fish in time for lunch. After landing it on shore, a twig fire was quickly established while the fish was gutted and cleaned. Dotted with a spot of butter and some freshly ground pepper, it was then wrapped in four sheets of newspaper, one at a time, each being soaked separately in water. One doesn't have to wait for the fire to die down, for, although the outside paper becomes charred quite quickly, the inner ones steam and cook the fish. After about 20 minutes, we lifted the fish from the fire and gently removed the paper. The skin came off with the paper, leaving the moist flesh intact. This was pulled off the bone, placed on Vogels slices liberally coated with fresh, unsalted butter, and sprinkled with pepper. It was marvellous. We enjoyed it with an old Hunter white and couldn't quite believe that the world was such an excellent place.

One hot summer's day, 'Stringy' Lowe and I were trolling (before I became a fly fanatic) in companionable silence. After several hours he said, 'Do you mind if I ask you a personal question? What was the greatest single instance of lovemaking you ever had?'

I thought for a moment. 'Do you mean emotional, physical, sensuous, spiritual, combinations of these?' I mused. Then I told him of an occasion when I was single, quite young and deeply in love with an older woman. It took a little time. No matter, we had plenty of it. After I had finished, he thought for a while, then said, 'The greatest time I ever had ...' and recounted, at great length, a story of an African princess.

Then he too finished, and again we were silent. The sun blazed, the breeze stirred the top of the water, the clouds shifted lazily. Stringy again broke the silence. 'Tell me,' he said. 'What was the second best one?'

I've cooked some great meals beside Lake Pedder, in Tasmania, though the trout, giants weighing up to seven kilograms, are better smoked. I suppose I could have cooked some of them by sonic wave, thanks to Doyle, his mate Alby George and another self-invited guest, who turned out to be the greatest snorers of all time. We were camped in a tiny caravan, and the racket they made drove me mad. So, although I suffer from claustrophobia, I finished up wedged in the back of the station wagon among all the gear and fish.

The Doyles have owned Watson's Bay for years, though for a time in the 1960s it was leased to Michel Ray. Once I was asked to entertain John Scott, an editor of *Time*, and I decided to take him to lunch at Doyles. I arrived to collect him two minutes late. Neatly dressed in bowtie and suit, he commented on my lateness. At Watson's Bay he watched the bikini-clad girls walk by, tasted some wine and took off his coat. More wine, then his tie. More wine, and he loosened his shirt. Seven hours later, after tasting Michel's new imports and the complete range of Cognacs and Armagnacs available, I deposited him at the harbourside home he was to visit. Mr Scott was as red as a letterbox, and looked ready to explode. He had lost his tie, trailed his coat, his trousers were at half-mast, and his hair stood out like a cartoon koala's. Regarding the steep house site, I asked if he would take the funicular. Mr Scott's shouted reply was lost in the wind, but I remember it was splendid alliteration.

Peter Doyle now manages the family business at Watson's Bay, with his parents, Jack and Alice, in attendance, and brothers and nephews and daughters abounding. The many times at sea I've shared with him and others mean a great deal to me. One day we were some distance out in his faithful *Grand Banks*, and after seeing whales and a couple of sharks, we found ourselves in a school of porpoises. There must have been over a thousand of them. Soon the bow waves were crowded, and more started playing behind the boat, then by the side, doing jumps in pairs, then counter pairs, with some showoffs leaping far out of the water and falling flat on their backs. 'Jeez mate,' shouted Doyle. 'You wouldn't be dead for quids. But when I do go,' he added, 'I hope it's pissing down with rain.'

James Halliday's humour is more cerebral, but infectious none the less. He taught me to cast a dry fly and introduced me to the wonders of stalking trout in gin-clear streams. A group of us used to go fishing for a week or so, and each of us was responsible for catering for one day. What meals, what wines! I can remember a tasting of Grange Hermitages from the 1950s, for lunch by the riverside, for example, and Bordeaux and Burgundies from the 1920s and 1930s, accompanied other wonderful meals.

The first trout I caught on a fly was a cause of great celebration, and Dr Don Francois and I took it back to the shearer's hut we shared

James Halliday and Andy Clayton show off their catch.

to cook it for lunch. Making a champagne sauce, I stood the cooked fish to one side on a rack over a pan, then added the juices from it to the sauce. Instant froth and a bubble flambé, for I had added not juice, but detergent. The trout was lost in a sea of foam, but finished whiter, brighter than ever before.

Some of the lads were experienced fishermen, some were not. One hapless gent never caught a single fish and only experienced the 'scream of the reel' when his fly, on a back cast, caught in the rump of my dog.

One day, a long way from anywhere in the heart of the highlands country, fishing the Maclaughlin River, I was accosted by a fellow who appeared out of the blue. 'I say,' he said, as people do, 'aren't you Evans?' I agreed that this was possibly so. 'Seen you on TV,' he said. 'That story about the Chinese.'

He was referring to an ABC show called 'Would You Believe', in which teams of three told stories about a picture, painting, photograph or object, only one of which was true. This particular story was about three Chinese brothers, and mine was false. 'These are the three Ling brothers,' I had said. 'One became a politician, and his name was Stee. One a doctor, and his name was Hee. The last became a celebrated gigolo and his name, apparently, was Fee. Fee Ling had a very promising career cut short when he succumbed to a Chinese version of a dreaded organic disease called the "Rots of Ruck".'

When I told this story in the studio no one laughed. No one laughs even now. But here was this chap, arriving from nowhere and recalling it. 'Yes,' he shouted. 'Rots of Ruck. Never laughed so much in my life.' And he disappeared. It's nice to have one fan, even though I've never seen him again.

James Halliday introduced me to Jason 'Snicky pooper' Garrett, a true eccentric who now owns London Lakes in the heart of Tasmania: a man-made lake covering over 300 hectares and stocked full of big trout. At present he is building a fishing lodge, and I hope he does as well out of it as he deserves. It would be difficult to find work for him, otherwise.

I've fished for mackerel off Noosa, watching them herd in pilchards and be herded themselves by sharks. I've fished off Exmouth in Canarvon in Western Australia, with Michael Kailis, for magnificent catches of trevally, mackerel, tuna, marlin, snapper and cod (up to 45 kilograms). I've fished off Kangaroo Island with Wolf Blass for whiting. At Lake Taupo I fished for trout and caught many on lures, before changing to a fly and then catching nothing, and having fun doing just that. I enjoy the company of my fishing mates, and I've enjoyed seeing the development of my son's interest, which is now much more fanatical than mine.

My preference is not just for freshly caught fish, but also fish stew. A pot of one of the endless variants, with new bread and cold wine, enjoyed while watching the water, must be one of the greatest pleasures in the world of gastronomy.

'Making a champagne sauce, I stood the cooked fish to one side on a rack over a pan, then added the juices from it to the sauce. Instant froth and a bubble flambé, for I had added not juice, but detergent. The trout was lost in a sea of foam, but finished whiter, brighter than ever before.'

Court-bouillon for poaching fish

1 bottle dry white wine
2/3 cup white wine vinegar
250g chopped carrots
150g chopped onions
150g chopped leeks
100g chopped celery

2 cloves garlic
small bunch parsley
bay leaf
pinch thyme
salt and pepper

Put all ingredients in a large pot, season with salt and pepper, and boil until all vegetables are tender.

Fish with anchovy sauce

Oyster tartlets (recipe page 88).

This dish is very good served with simple, boiled potatoes. If you ever obtain a fresh salmon (or a very large trout) it's an excellent sauce, though the cooking may take a little longer.

any firm fleshed fish suitable for cutlets (mackerel, kingfish jewfish)
500g butter
large glass of tawny port

dash of ketchup
freshly ground pepper
four fillets of canned anchovy

Melt the butter and mix all ingredients together. Cut the fish into cutlets. Place in an ovenproof dish, pour over the sauce and bake in a preheated hot oven until fish is cooked (20–35 minutes). Do not overcook.

Fillets of fish Antilles style

This recipe is from Millie Sherman, who runs cooking classes in Sydney's northern suburbs.

1kg fish fillets
1 large green capsicum
3 tomatoes
4 mushrooms
2 small onions
3 bananas
3 slices pineapple

100g butter
1 cup peanut oil
flour
salt and pepper
1 tablespoon finely chopped parsley
1 lemon
Serves 6

Slice capsicum into strips, peel tomatoes and quarter. Wash and slice mushrooms, peel and slice onions, peel bananas and slice. Dice pineapple. Melt butter in a frying pan and sauté onions gently without browning. Add capsicum, mushrooms and tomatoes. Simmer until the vegetables have softened and lost their juices. Add pineapple and bananas, heat gently for another five minutes. Taste and season. While sauce is cooking, dredge the fish fillets in flour and fry in peanut oil, using a second frying pan, two to three minutes on each

side, depending on the thickness of the fillet. Arrange fish on a serving plate, cover with sauce, sprinkle with chopped parsley and serve with lemon wedges. This dish is ideal as an entrée; with the addition of boiled rice it will make a delicious main course.

———————— ❧ ————————

Layered fish pâté

250g scallops
1 egg white
½ cup cream
1 carrot, grated
½ bulb fennel, chopped

250g fish fillets
200g cooked spinach
½ cup fish stock, concentrated
Serves 6

Blend scallop whites, egg white and cream into a mousseline consistency. Spread into a lined or greased pâté tin, adding as you go a thin layer of grated carrot, some chopped fennel, the coral of the scallops, and some pieces of fish fillet, so that the cut-across section will have variety and appeal. Cook gently until set, then allow to cool. Invert from the tin and coat with a blend of cooked spinach and concentrated fish stock. Allow to cool and set. Cut into slices and serve with a cold fish sauce of some kind (I would use a light nantua sauce whipped with cream).

———————— ❧ ————————

Barramundi Glen Norris

This recipe came from Glen Norris of Maryborough, Queensland, a reader of the old 'Indulgence' column of the *Weekend Australian*. Suprisingly, the sausage/fish mix does come off, in a hearty way.

barramundi fillets, in slab form
  (fresh or frozen)
cooking oil
steamed long-grained rice
Hungarian sausage
tomato

onion
capsicum
margarine
½ cup dry white wine
salt and pepper

Lightly lubricate a sheet of foil with cooking oil. Sprinkle a bed a steamed long-grained rice on the foil. Loosely cover the rice with thin slices of Hungarian sausage and sprinkle with oil. Place barramundi fillets on the sausage and rice. Add thin slices of tomato, onion and capsicum in layers and finish with a few pats of margarine on top. Pour on the wine (riesling is ideal), and a little oil, and season to taste with salt and pepper. Fold the foil to make a parcel and seal firmly.

If the fish is frozen, cook the parcels in shallow water in a baking dish in the oven or on top of the stove for about 40 minutes. If fish is fresh, cook for about 20–25 minutes. Ensure that the water does not enter the foil as this acts as a 'steamer' for the fish. Serve with lemon and parsley.

Whiting in champagne (recipe page 73).

Barramundi macadamia

This is one of Graham Kerr's attempts at an authentic (but instant) Australian cuisine. He did this on local television. Not long after, I was with him in a taxi. 'Aren't you the cooking bloke?' asked the taxi driver. Kerr modestly conceded he was. The driver went on, 'Thought so. I'm a bit of a cook meself. In fact I tried that dish you did with Barra and nuts. I got no Barra but I did have some frozen fish fingers. And I got no macadamias, but I did have a tin of mixed nuts left over from Chrissie. And I couldn't get parsley stalks but I found some mint in the garden.'

Kerr had listened to this with growing horror. 'Good heavens,' he said. 'How on earth did it turn out?'

'Bloody awful,' said the driver. 'Do you know what you're talking about?'

Tammy Fraser doesn't seem too disappointed. At a fund raising dinner for the Australiana Fund at Rothbury. We bought a painting of Governor Hunter with the proceeds.

2 x 185g barramundi fillets	30g grated macadamia nuts
1 egg yolk	60g clarified butter
juice of quarter of lemon	2 tablespoons sherry
1 tablespoon parsley stalks	15g unsalted butter
white peppercorns, to season	Serves 2
salt, to season	

Slice the barramundi diagonally. Mix the egg yolk and lemon juice. Chop the parsley stalks finely. Season the fish with peppercorns and salt, brush with egg yolk mixture and press the nuts into each side. Melt the clarified butter in a frying pan. When hot, add the fish and sauté 3 minutes each side. Pour in the sherry and light. Add chopped parsley stalks. Place fish on a serving dish. Add unsalted butter to the frying pan. Pour this sauce over the fish.

Matelote of bream with white wine and mushrooms

1kg bream fillets	¼ cup brandy
60g butter	½ bottle white wine
250g mushrooms, sliced very finely	½ cup fish stock (optional)
1 large finely chopped onion	Serves 4–6
2 cloves crushed garlic	

Heat half the butter in a large pan over moderate heat, sweat (sauté very lightly) the mushrooms until they have lost their firmness. Remove. Put the rest of the butter into the pan, add the onions and garlic, lightly sauté, add the fish, add the brandy and flame. Add the white wine, then add the fish stock if you wish for a stronger flavoured sauce. Add the mushrooms. Poach until the fish is tender.

Remove the fish, reduce the remaining liquid by half, thicken with a mixture of a little butter and flour (pre-cooked) or cornflour. Smother the fish with the sauce and serve.

Flathead fry

filleted flathead pieces
for the batter:
self-raising flour

dash of oil
dash of vinegar
beer

To make the batter, combine flour, oil and vinegar. Beat into a smooth consistency with the beer. Cover the fish fillets with batter and deep fry them on a very high temperature for a few minutes or until pieces become golden brown.

———————— ❦ ————————

Stuffed flounder

2 flounders (750g)
90g butter
4 spring onions, finely chopped
1/2 cup plain flour
3/4 fish stock
3 tablespoons white wine
1/4 teaspoon salt
dash cayenne
1 egg yolk

75g crabmeat
125g shelled prawns
6 oysters
2 teaspoons parsley
1 tablespoon paprika
1/2 cup grated Parmesan
1/2 cup fresh breadcrumbs
1/4 cup vegetable oil
Serves 2

Melt the butter in a frying pan and sauté the onions until tender. Add the sifted flour and blend thoroughly. Cook on low heat for 5 minutes, stirring constantly. Remove pan from the heat. Add the fish stock, wine, salt and pepper and stir until smooth. Add the egg yolk and return the pan to a low heat. Cook, stirring constantly for about 15 minutes. Add crabmeat, prawns, oysters and parsley, and mix thoroughly. Heat through and remove from heat.

Cut head from the fish with the fish lying flat, dark side up, then make a slit from head to tail with a boning knife, going through flesh to bone. With the tail section of the fish towards you, take a boning knife and work from the centre slit to fins, loosening the flesh from the bone. Turn the fish so that the tail is now away from you and insert the blade of the knife under the backbone. Work from the centre to the side in a slicing motion to loosen the back of fish from bone. With scissors, cut the bone loose from the fins. Now lift the backbone and break it away from fish near tail. Preheat oven to 200°C/400°F.

Fill the fish with the stuffing and sprinkle with a mixture of paprika, Parmesan and breadcrumbs. Tie up the fish. Place the vegetable oil in a large roasting pan, and when hot sear the fish on each side. Place the pan containing the fish in the oven and cook for about 20 minutes. Serve accompanied by lemon slices and parsley.

'Port Phillip Bay abounds with small flathead, and when staying with Judy and Doug Crittenden, of wine fame, at Mount Martha, we generally manage to catch a few. This is the traditional lunch afterwards. One afternoon, after such a fry, Judy was sunbaking in a bikini, lying on her back. I was drinking a glass of Montrachet, 61 I believe. I couldn't resist the temptation and dropped some into her navel. She didn't move, just opened one eye and murmured, 'Now drink it.' I did, too. Marvellously sexy stuff, flathead fry.'

Jewfish cutlets with tomato purée

6 medium-sized jewfish cutlets	glass white wine (optional)
750g ripe tomatoes	½ cup finely chopped parsley
60g butter	tablespoon finely chopped basil
2 tablespoons olive oil	salt
2 medium-sized onions	cayenne
2 cloves crushed garlic	Serves 6

'This is an easy and attractive way to serve any kind of firm-fleshed fish. Some people like to cook the purée and fish separately, and then put the purée on individual plates and set the fish on each. My method is less good-looking on the plate, but I like the infusion of flavours into the fish.'

Blanch, skin and seed the tomatoes, and chop into small pieces. Heat half the butter and oil, add onions and sauté lightly. Add the tomatoes and garlic and season with salt and pepper. Cook until tender, blend into a purée. Add a touch of white wine if too solid. Put the remaining butter and oil in a frying pan. Fry the cutlets for a couple of minutes each side. Lift from the pan. Add half of the purée, put cutlets back, and smother with the rest of the purée. Let simmer for a few minutes until tender. Remove fish to a warm serving dish. Off the heat, mix the parsley and basil into the purée and season. Cover the fish with it, and serve.

Matelote of jewfish in red wine

6 large pieces of filleted jewfish	2 cloves crushed garlic
100g champignons	¼ cup brandy
100g small onions	½ bottle red wine
100g butter	½ cup reduced fish stock
1 large finely chopped onion	Serves 6

Sauté the onions and champignons in butter until tender. Remove. Sauté the chopped onion and garlic in a large frying pan in a little butter for a minute or so, then add the pieces of fish. Seal the fish. Add brandy and flame. Add the red wine and poach gently. When the fish is cooked, remove the fillets and place on a warmed serving dish. Put the remaining liquid in a saucepan, and reduce by half. Thicken it with 30g butter and the fish stock, then add cooked onions and champignons. Heat, then pour over the fish.

Sometimes, this dish (which looks quite attractive if arranged properly on the serving dish) can be further decorated with croûtons.

Pavé of John Dory and salmon

A Kables special from the Regent Hotel, Sydney.

150g John Dory } cut in long strips	
150g salmon } 2 x 2cm x 12cm long	
for the sauce:	¾ cup cream
½ cup white wine	10g of sorrel in julienne
½ cup fish stock	10g of butter

Plait the strips of fish, alternating the two colours. Set on a small, reinforced square of aluminium paper. Poach in the white wine and fish stock. Drain the fish. Reduce liquid by half. Add cream and reduce by half again. Just before serving, add sorrel and butter. Pour the sauce on a serving plate, and place the fish on the sauce.

Garnish with wild rice and seasonal vegetables.

Soused fillets of John Dory

Anders Ousback, who created this recipe, has a special place in the heart of my wine and food professionalism. I met him at a luncheon given by Dr Bob Smith when Anders was still at school. He professed interest in film and wine. I suggested he talk to me when he left school if he couldn't get a film job. He came for an interview and Ann Tyrrell, who ran the Bulletin Place cellar, asked afterwards, 'We're not going to give *him* a job, are we?'

We did, and he was delightful. Anders, with his fantastic flair, wit and intelligence, was quite one of the clumsiest people I've ever met. He has been the Flying Dutchman of the wine and food business, wandering from place to place, business to business, learning all the time. Now settled, we hope, in Sydney, he has a successful catering business and restaurant at the Barracks in Sydney's Macquarie Street.

Well, it was a beginning.

6 medium fillets of John Dory
salt and pepper
oil
chives
for the sousing liquid:
1 cup water
1 cup white wine
1 cup white wine vinegar

1 tablespoon sugar
1 teaspoon mustard seeds
knob of ginger, peeled and cut into fine julienne
rind of 1 orange, cut into fine julienne
Serves 6

To make the sousing liquid, combine all ingredients in a saucepan, bring to the boil and reduce by a third.

Season the fillets of fish with salt and pepper and fry, flesh side first, in a little oil on high heat. The fish should be coloured on the outside and translucent in the centre. Transfer to a shallow dish and pour on the boiling sousing liquid. Allow the fish to steep, and when cool enough to handle, remove skin and any bones from fillets. Each fillet will then easily separate into three pieces.

Place the fish and liquid, covered with foil, into a hot oven for 1–2 minutes. The fish and liquid should be lukewarm. Arrange pieces of fish on a plate. Spoon a tablespoon or two of liquid on top, allowing a few pieces of ginger, rind and mustard seed for each plate. Cut the chives into pieces the same length as the ginger and rind, and sprinkle half a dozen pieces on each serving.

Kipper pâté

200g can kipper fillets, drained
2 tablespoons lemon juice
½ x 300g carton sour cream
75g melted butter or margarine
¼ teaspoon freshly ground black
    pepper
½ cup chopped fresh parsley

Combine fillets, lemon juice, sour cream, butter and pepper in a processor or blender, or mash thoroughly with a fork. Stir in the parsley. Put in serving bowl, then cover and chill well. Serve with fingers of hot toast.

Lattice wrapped mullet with tomato stuffing

'A fairly laborious process, altogether, yet one which is well worth it when the dish is presented on the table.'

This recipe came from a great bloke, Syd Watt, who opened Cid's at Wharf Street in Forster. He and his wife Edie really love the business and feature lots of fine seafood dishes made from the freshest ingredients.

1 medium mullet, head removed,
    scaled and cleaned
3 cloves garlic, crushed
1 medium onion, finely diced
1 tablespoon oil
2–3 cups roughly chopped and
    skinned tomatoes
½ cup finely sliced mushrooms
1 teaspoon dried oregano
½ teaspoon salt
freshly ground black pepper
2 ready rolled sheets puff pastry
2 egg yolks
Serves 2

To minimise any earthy flavour, pre-soak the mullet in milk for half an hour. Remove the backbone by cutting along each side of it. Remove the fins.

Sauté the garlic and onion in oil, mix in the tomato and mushrooms and allow to heat through slightly. Add oregano, salt and pepper. Mix well. Drain the liquid from the tomato filling, and place it in the mullet.

Cut pastry sheets into strips, approximately 1cm wide. A woven basket cover is to be made to wrap the mullet in. Lay cut strips of pastry from one sheet back together in a square shape. Lift up alternate pastry strips lengthwise towards you, taking them right back. Lay a strip of pastry vertically across these strips. Return the pastry strips as they were before. Now lift up the other pastry strips (the ones you didn't turn back before) and bring them toward you. Continue in this way, weaving strips in a basket-weave fashion until the square is completed. Brush edges with beaten egg yolks. Place the mullet on one edge of the pastry square and fold top over. Trim the edges and curve, cutting into a fish shape. Leave the tail visible but wrap it in foil. Glaze the pastry with egg yolk.

Place on a wet baking slide, and bake at 190°C/375°F for approximately 40 minutes, or until golden brown. Serve hot or cold with a side salad. Slice diagonally to serve.

Fillets des perches meunière

1kg perch fillets
½ cup milk
1 cup plain flour
400g butter
salt

freshly ground black pepper
lemon juice to season
small knob of butter extra
chopped fresh parsley
Serves 6

Season milk with salt and pepper. Sift flour and place on a flat dish. Dip fish into the seasoned milk and then into the flour. Place the butter in a frying pan, and when foaming add fish and fry.

Place the fish on a hot serving dish, sprinkle with lemon juice. Place some butter in a fresh pan and when browned pour over fish. Garnish with parsley. Serve with plain boiled potatoes.

Pearl perch and abalone with tomatoes and onion

1kg pearl perch fillets
2 onions
1 capsicum
1 stalk celery
⅔ cup fish stock
garlic to taste
Tabasco to taste

5 tomatoes
salt and pepper
chopped fresh basil
can abalone
chopped fresh parsley
Serves 4–6

Thinly slice onions, capsicum and celery and poach in the fish stock until tender. Add crushed garlic, a dash of Tabasco, sliced peeled tomatoes, salt and pepper, and cook until done. Add the basil and the fillets of pearl perch cut into chunks and cook for about 4–5 minutes until the fish is cooked through. Add thin slices of canned abalone and fresh parsley, and serve with rice.

Fishing on Lake Taupo in New Zealand. Geoff Harvey, musical director of Network Nine, is in the background.

Salmon Tewantin

This recipe is from John Roe of Brisbane, who says it was the original method for cooking large fish at the old Tewantin Hotel, near Noosa Heads in Queensland. The method is simple, yet tasty, and ideal for bush and beach picnics.

4–5kg fresh sea salmon
250g salt
500g sugar
240g butter
lemon slices
chopped fresh parsley

'This is simple, yet tasty, and ideal for bush and beach picnics.'

Skin and fillet the salmon. Apply salt and sugar in a mixture of one part salt and two of sugar, covering the entire surface of the fish. Let stand for approximately three hours. (Standing time is dependent on the weight and quantity of salmon.) Light the fire and grill the salmon in an open wire griller on coals that are about 8cm deep, constantly turning the salmon and basting it with melted butter on both sides. The sugar will caramelise and turn brown.

The secret of this recipe is that you must cook the salmon slowly and baste it continuously to keep the salmon surface moist. Serve with melted butter, slices of lemon and parsley.

Smoked salmon, trout and potato gâteau

This recipe comes from Peter Jarmer of Adelaide, who has long been my favourite chef in that city. His restaurant, Reilly's, in King William Road, is consistently good and now, with his wife Kathy, he has extended to Jarmer's in Kensington Road. Kathy and Peter are the subjects of an amusing story. They live in the Adelaide suburb of Paradise. A couple of years ago they went to a fancy dress party, Kathy as a good time girl and Peter as an angel. Peter felt unwell during the evening, and since Kathy was having a great time, he decided to go home alone. He called a taxi. It arrived to pick up an angel. 'Where to?' asked the driver. Came the answer, 'Paradise, of course.'

3 large freshwater trout
10 slices smoked salmon
8–10 large potatoes, peeled
3 medium onions
200g butter
3 large eggs
½ cup thickened cream
salt and pepper
fresh dill
Serves 6–8

Slice the peeled potatoes 3mm thick and blanch in boiling salted water until nearly done. Drain off the water and place potato slices on paper towels to dry. Peel and slice the onions and cook in a little butter until soft but not coloured. Fillet and skin the trout, and remove all bones with a pair of tweezers. Mix the eggs and cream together, and season lightly with salt and pepper. Chop the fresh dill roughly.

Butter a teflon-coated, spring-loaded cake tin, then arrange a layer of potato slices in the bottom. Have the potatoes slightly over-lapping, similar to an apple tart. Sprinkle over some sautéed onions, and season lightly with salt and pepper. Cut three trout fillets in half and place over onions. Pour over some egg and cream mixture. Now cover with slices of smoked salmon and sprinkle with chopped dill. Repeat the process until the cake tin is nearly filled to the top. Finish with a layer of potatoes. Pour over the remaining egg mixture and bake in preheated oven for 50 minutes at 190°C/375°F.

Serve with hot butter and fresh dill.

Sole Albert

For overseas recipes mentioning *langoustines* (France) or *scampi* (Italy) I've always used our local bugs. Now Western Australia is producing a deep water version of *scampi*, discovered by the CSIRO. They're delicious.

4 x 360g sole	1 tablespoon beef extract
1½ cups fresh breadcrumbs	6 shelled Moreton Bay bugs
4 shallots	salt, to season
2 teaspoons tarragon	fresh black peppercorns, to season
2 teaspoons parsley	1 cup dry white wine
500g butter	Serves 4
2 cups dry vermouth	

I've had a good life.

Remove the black skin from the sole after removing the heads. Put the breadcrumbs through a sieve. Chop the shallots and the tarragon and parsley finely. Preheat oven to 220°C/425°F.

Place 20g of butter in a saucepan and sauté the shallots. Add 1½ cups of vermouth and the beef extract. Cook until the shallots are tender. Remove the saucepan from the heat and let it cool. Then add 400g of butter a little at a time, beating to form a smooth sauce. Add the tails of the Moreton Bay bugs, the tarragon and season with salt and peppercorns.

Brush the sole with melted butter and coat the side with the skin removed with the breadcrumbs. Place the fish in a buttered oven-proof dish, breadcrumbed side uppermost. Pour the white wine and remaining vermouth over the fish and cook 20 minutes in the oven until the fish are golden.

Just before serving, gently reheat the sauce (preferably standing the saucepan in a pan of water). Place the sole on a warmed serving dish and spoon over them some of their cooking liquid. Serve the sauce in a sauce boat.

Warm fish salad with a sherry vinaigrette

This recipe comes from Brian Turner, the chef of the Capital Hotel, my London home. The Levins, who own the hotel, visited Australia at my behest and had a great holiday here. They even managed to conceive their third child, 14 years after the previous one. I wanted her named Oz, but they reneged and called her Kate.

2 sole fillets
1 snapper fillet
1 small piece (34g) salmon fillet or boned trout
250g button mushrooms
125g cooked green beans
125g tomatoes

250g leaves of lamb's lettuce
for the vinaigrette:
½ cup mayonnaise
dash sherry vinegar
¼ cup cream
chopped chives
Serves 4

Add vinegar, cream and chives to mayonnaise. Season and spread over the centre of a large plate. Decorate the sides of the plate with the sliced mushrooms and place the beans in centre of the plate.

Poach the seasoned fish and then place it on the bed of beans and decorate with tomato and lamb's lettuce. Serve while the fish is still warm.

Casting in New Zealand.

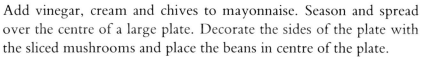

Sole au Chambertin

This delicious dish is ideal for Sunday lunches, for example. You might enjoy a rosé or light red with this.

4 fillets sole
30g butter
2 shallots
salt and fresh black pepper to season

½ cup red Burgundy
2 teaspoons butter extra
2 teaspoons plain flour
Serves 2

Measure 2 portions of butter. Finely chop the shallots. Preheat oven to 180°C/350°F. Place the butter in a baking dish, add the shallots and season with pepper and salt. Lay the fillets of sole on the top and cover with the wine. Poach in the oven until the sauce is reduced by two-thirds. Remove from the oven and set over a low heat.

Thicken the sauce by adding the extra butter kneaded with the flour, stirring all the time. Cover and keep warm until required.

Serve with small boiled potatoes tossed in butter and parsley.

Grilled sole with chives

This recipe is from a dear man, the late Jean Troisgros, co-owner of the famous restaurant of his name in Roanne, regarded by most as among the top five of all the French three star restaurants, and by many as the best. He came to Australia as guest-of-honour at the

Great Chefs of Australia banquet held at Rothbury. An immensely likeable, charming, simple man, he died after playing tennis at the age of 58. He was a great chef, who loved food and wines and people who loved them with him.

4 x 350g sole | *1 shallot, chopped*
100g day-old white bread | *1 teaspoon tomato paste*
100g butter | *2 cups cream*
chives | *juice of half a lemon*
¾ cup fish fumet | *salt and pepper*
5 tablespoons white wine | Serves 4
2 tablespoons dry white vermouth

Rub the bread through a wire sieve. Clarify 75g of the butter. Cut up the chives with scissors. Preheat the oven to 200°C/400°F. To prepare the sole, remove the dark skin from each fish (or have it done by the fishmonger), scale the white side, cut off the head diagonally, and trim the tail. Season with a little salt.

Put the clarified butter in a large, oval, ovenproof fish. Dip the soles in the butter and then coat the white sides with the breadcrumbs. Put a little of the fish fumet in the bottom of the dish and put in the fish with breadcrumbed sides uppermost, being careful not to get the breadcrumbs wet. Cook in the oven for 15 minutes and finish off under the grill to give the fish a nice golden colour. Take out the sole and remove the little bones on either side of the fish.

Boil the white wine, vermouth, the remaining fish fumet and the shallot, together with tomato paste until almost completely reduced. Add the cream and bring to the boil to obtain a lightly thickened sauce. Strain through a fine conical strainer and work in the rest of the butter. Add a squeeze of lemon juice and season to taste with salt and pepper.

Heat the sole in the oven, divide the sauce between four large plates, sprinkle with chives and put the fish on top.

'Jean Troisgrois was a great chef, who liked food and wines and people who loved them with him.'

Soused fish

This recipe came from Ken Caldwell, a retired grazier, who as a young lad used to go fishing with his father (of the old wine firm of that name) and the great Leo Buring (ditto).

500g fish fillets | *2½ cups milk*
1 cup vinegar | *6 cloves*
water to cover | Serves 3–4

Soak cleaned fish fillets in a solution of vinegar and water overnight. Drain and place in a casserole dish, and cover with milk. Dot the top layer of fish with cloves and cook in a moderately slow oven for 2–3 hours. Let everything set after being taken from the oven—this can be done in the fridge. Cut into jellied squares and serve with a salad.

Fillets of sole Christopher Columbus

1kg sole	½ carrot
1 cup plain flour	½ leek
2 eggs, beaten	1 stick celery
125g butter	butter
salt and black pepper	1 crayfish carcass
2 bananas	paprika to season
lemons to garnish	flour
parsley to garnish	1½ tablespoons brandy
for the sauce:	2½ cups fish stock
½ onion	Serves 4

First prepare the sauce. Finely chop vegetables. Place the butter in a saucepan, add the vegetables and sauté till golden. Pound the crayfish carcass into pieces and add to the saucepan with the paprika. Sprinkle the flour in and then add the brandy and flame it. Add the fish stock, cover the saucepan and simmer for 45 minutes.

Season the fish with salt and pepper, then dip in flour and egg and fry in hot butter. Fry whole bananas in hot butter and then split in half. Place banana halves on bottom of casserole dish, then the sole, and cover with the sauce. Serve with parsley and lemon.

Poached snapper with parsley sauce

A part of my childhood, and one of the great fish dishes of the world, this recipe is adapted from the United Kingdom where the best fishes for this are haddock and turbot, though cod is very good.

1kg fresh snapper fillets	½ cup reduced fish stock
court-bouillon	salt and pepper
for the sauce:	½ cup chopped fresh parsley
50g butter	malt vinegar
¼ cup plain flour	Serves 4–6
2 cups milk	

'A part of my childhood, and one of the great fish dishes of the world, this recipe is adapted from the United Kingdom where the best fishes for this are haddock and turbot, though cod is very good.'

Bring the court-bouillon to the boil, in fish kettle or saucepan. Lower the fish into it, preferably on a kettle drainer. If not available use any convenient method of lifting out the fish intact (I've often used a chip basket, for example). As soon as the fish is in the bouillon, switch off the heat. Let stand for 10–15 minutes while you make the sauce.

Heat the butter to foaming, add the flour and cook for 3–4 minutes. Add the hot milk over gentle heat, stirring all the time. Add the fish stock and simmer for a couple of minutes. Add the parsley and season. Correct with vinegar. The vinegar should not be obvious but should lift the sauce from blandness.

Lift the fish from the court-bouillon, drain for a moment, then place on a warmed serving dish and smother with sauce. Serve with boiled new potatoes.

————— ❧ —————

Spinach and snapper mousseline

250g English spinach	*2 eggs*
⅔ cup stock	*chopped fresh basil*
500g snapper fillets	*salt and pepper*
120g cottage cheese	Serves 4

Use real spinach (English spinach) for this recipe, not silver beet; it is available from good greengrocers. Poach the spinach for a few minutes only in a little stock in a covered stainless steel saucepan. Take out and pat dry in clean tea towel. Place the spinach, the chopped snapper fillets, the cottage cheese and the eggs in a Magimix or Robot Coupe, adding basil and salt and pepper. Pour the mixture into an oiled tin mould and poach in a bain-marie in a pre-heated oven for 30 minutes at 180°C/360°F. The mixture must set, but do not overcook it.

Invert and serve with any traditional fish sauce.

————— ❧ —————

Fish stew with onions and mushrooms

2–3kg fish, scaled and cleaned (use firm fish such as gemfish, bream, jewfish)	*250g mushrooms*
	bouquet garni
	salt and pepper
2 tablespoons oil	*red wine*
125g butter	*1 tablespoon flour*
250g small onions, peeled and left whole	Serves 6–8

Cut the fish into equal pieces. Heat the oil and half the butter in a heavy pan. Add the fish pieces and fry. Add the onions, mushrooms, bouquet garni, salt and pepper and enough red wine to moisten the mixture—the fish should be not quite covered. Gently simmer for 15 minutes, or until the fish is tender.

Discard the bouquet garni and drain the fish, mushrooms and onions. Place them on a serving dish and keep in a warm place while preparing the sauce. Boil the fish stock vigorously and reduce it until it is two thirds the original volume. Strain.

Melt the remaining butter in another saucepan. Stir in the flour and cook. Combine fish stock with the flour and butter to make a slightly thickened sauce. Pour over fish pieces and onions and mushrooms. Serve immediately.

'This version of a traditional recipe was put down by Tony Schmaeling, an architect who has had a hand in developing many Sydney restaurants. There are endless variations, and one can add other seafoods— green prawns, squid, scallops, even oysters—though these should be added later to either simmering wine or sauce, depending on the cooking times. Remember, most seafood is served overcooked, so be gentle.'

Truite farcie au riz sauvage

A recipe from Jean Jacques Demoz, the seafood master of Melbourne.

6 fresh rainbow trout	3 egg yolks
for the filling:	¼ cup cream
½ onion, chopped	for the sauce:
1 clove garlic	½ bunch sorrel
2 tablespoons butter	knob of butter
1 cup wild rice	¼ cup dry vermouth
2 cups water	1½ cups cream
salt and pepper to taste	salt and pepper
¼ cup finely diced Granny Smith	lemon juice (optional)
apple	Serves 6
¼ cup diced smoked salmon	

Fishing with Michael Kailis off Carnarvon in Western Australia, I landed a 50 kilogram cod, my biggest fish caught on a hand line.

To prepare the trout, slide a small paring knife along each side of the collar bones from the head to the tail of the fish. Remove the collar bones with a pair of scissors. Now slide the knife between the flesh and rib cage bones on both sides of fish, taking care not to damage the flesh. Remove the side bones.

To prepare the filling, sweat the onion and garlic with the butter in a heavy based 8-cup pot. When soft, add the wild rice and stir for 2–3 minutes before adding water, and salt and pepper to taste. Simmer for about 15 minutes. Add the apple and salmon and simmer for a further 5 minutes, by which time the rice should be cooked but still firm. In a separate bowl blend the egg yolks with cream. Pour this into the wild rice mixture and cook for a further 2 minutes on low heat, ensuring that the mixture does not actually boil. Correct the seasoning and place the filling in a cool bowl.

To fill the trout, lightly salt and pepper the opening you have made in the fish. Spoon the mixture into the trout, using approximately 3 tablespoons of filling per fish and leaving about 2.5 cm along each side of fillet free of filling. Preheat oven to 230°C/450°F. Lightly oil a sheet of greaseproof paper for each fish. Place the trout on the oiled side of the paper and wrap it around the fish, forming a neat parcel. Fill a baking dish to a quarter capacity with hot water. Place the trout side by side in the tray, and poach in the oven for 10–15 minutes.

To prepare the sauce, thoroughly wash sorrel, remove all stalks and chop the leaves. Melt the butter in a saucepan and add the sorrel, cooking it briskly to evaporate the moisture on the leaves. Add the vermouth and simmer to reduce the volume by half. Pour in the cream and simmer for a few minutes until a syrupy consistency is attained. Adjust the seasoning with salt and pepper and a few drops of lemon juice.

Gently unwrap the trout and remove skin, which will pull away easily. Place on a warmed serving dish and coat with the sauce.

Taupo trout

I thought I could cook freshly caught trout fairly well, in various ways, and I must admit that on this particular trip to Lake Taupo I was itching to get started. With Simon Dickie, who runs a sporting service in New Zealand, I caught some magnificent fish, some weighing up to three kilograms, but he insisted on cooking the first for lunch. They were marvellous.

fresh trout   *brown sugar*
butter   *pepper*

Clean trout and butterfly it, so that the halves can be spread wide on a hand-held double-sided grill. Place the grill on the coals of a wood fire, skin side down. Coat the top side with butter and sprinkle with pepper and brown sugar. After 5–7 minutes, the butter on the flesh of the upper side will begin to bubble. When heated right through, turn the trout over and sear the flesh side for a minute or so.

Lake Pedder, Tasmania. The trout are among the biggest in the world.

Whole pan-fried trout with bacon

This recipe was created by Judy and Michael McMahon, together with chef Neil Perry, of the Barrenjoey Restaurant at Palm Beach.

2 x 350g whole trout   *4 tablespoons unsalted butter*
4 slices bacon   *juice of ¼ lemon*
plain flour   *salt and pepper*
2 tablespoons olive oil   *nutmeg*
2 tablespoons butter for frying *1 tablespoon chopped parsley and*
30ml Cognac   *   chervil*
100ml white wine   *Serves 2*
4 tablespoons creme fraiche

Cut heads and tails off the trout and lightly coat with flour. Melt the oil with butter in a large copper frying pan (or heavy pan) until sizzling. Place the trout in the pan. Cook on one side for approximately 5 minutes, then place the bacon beside it in the pan and turn over the trout. Cook for about 5 minutes on the other side. During the cooking, when the bacon browns, lift it from the pan, and place it on top of the trout. (This time will make the trout pink in the middle. It can be cooked longer but the texture and taste of the fish will become dry.) Remove the trout and bacon from the pan and remove the crisp skin from both sides. Place the trout on a warm plate, with bacon arranged on top, and keep warm.

Pour the butter and oil from the pan and make the sauce. Deglaze first with the Cognac, then the wine, reducing by half. Add creme fraiche and reduce until the liquid is thickening. Remove from the heat and whisk in the unsalted butter. Add lemon juice and seasoning to taste and strain the sauce over the trout and bacon. Sprinkle with parsley and chervil, and serve immediately.

Stuffed trout, foil-wrapped

6 x 250g trout
3 cups fresh breadcrumbs
¾ cup cream
250g butter
salt and pepper to season
1 egg

chopped fresh parsley, tarragon,
    chervil and chives to season
½ cup white wine
1 teaspoon lemon juice
Serves 6

Remove the backbone from the trout, leaving tails and heads on. Soak the breadcrumbs in the cream, squeeze out, and reserve the cream for later use. Butter an ovenproof dish. Preheat oven to 150°C/300°F. Cut 6 pieces of aluminium foil in which to wrap each trout.

To prepare the stuffing, season the breadcrumbs with salt and pepper, mix in the egg, 60g butter and the herbs. Stuff the fish with this mixture and place them side by side in an ovenproof dish. Pour the wine over the fish, place it on top of the stove to warm and then put in the oven for 5 minutes. Remove the fish and drain. Reserve the juice. Wrap each fish in lightly buttered foil and return them to the oven. Cook for about 8 minutes and then remove the fish, unwrap them and place on a heated serving dish.

Heat the cooking juice of the fish and add the cream and the lemon juice, stirring all the time. Strain and serve in a sauce boat.

'This is one of the all-time great lunches.'

Trout Sydney Morning Herald, or Age, Advertiser, Courier Mail, Western Australian

1 freshly caught trout (rainbow or
    brown)
4 sheets local newspaper
salt

pepper
200g unsalted butter
sliced Vogel's bread

Light a brush fire. Clean and gut the trout. Soak four sheets of newspaper, one at a time (most important). Sprinkle the trout with salt and pepper and dabs of butter before placing it on the first wet sheet. Wrap this around it. Then wrap the other three sheets one at a time.

Put the long, wet package on the brush fire. The fire does not have to be reduced to coals, since the fish is steamed in the wet paper. If the outside papers char, even better, since the char indicates that the heat is penetrating the layers. After 20–30 minutes, test by sticking a fork through the package. It should find no resistance. Remove the paper, and the skin should come off with it.

Take off pieces of the trout, and place them on freshly buttered bread. Grind black pepper on each slice. This is one of the all-time great lunches.

Sliced tuna à la Grecque

This very easy, simple dish was served by Peter Kailis on a fishing trip to Exmouth, Western Australia. Make sure the tuna is fresh, and if you've caught it, bleed it straight away.

slices of freshly caught tuna fillet   *salt*
olive oil   *black pepper*
vinegar   *1 clove crushed garlic*
lemon juice

Mix together the oil, vinegar and lemon juice. Pour some in a serving dish, add a layer of tuna fillets, more oil, vinegar and lemon, then salt, freshly ground black pepper and crushed garlic. Continue layering fish, the oil, vinegar and lemon mixture, salt, pepper and garlic. Marinate for one hour, then turn to cover any flesh which hasn't changed colour.

Poisson cru

This is my version of the celebrated 'raw' fish dish which isn't raw at all as the marinade changes the character of the flesh. The process of the coconut milk is tedious, but it's worth it!

2kg fresh tuna   *12 spring onions*
salt   *2 capsicums, 1 red, 1 yellow*
4 onions, finely chopped   *2 cucumbers*
lime juice   *4 hard-boiled eggs*
2–3 coconuts   *150g anchovies*
hot water   Serves 12

Fillet the tuna, and cut into pieces about 2.5cm square and 1cm thick. Put into a bowl with salt, finely chopped onions and lime juice. Mix the ingredients well and allow to marinate for about 4–5 hours, turning every half hour or so.

Pierce 2 or 3 coconuts, discard the water inside the shell, break up the shell, remove the hard outside and pare away the brown lining on the white meat. Chop the white meat very finely in a food processor. Add hot water as you go along, until there is a finely granulated loose paste. Let this stand for an hour or so, and then give it another whirl. Hang a clean cloth over a bowl, pour the mixture through, squeezing as much liquid out as possible. Put this in a tall jug and let it stand for a couple of hours. The cream will separate and float to the top. Siphon off the bottom with a tube dropped to the base of the jug. When the fish has changed colour to an opaque white-brown, drain and add the coconut cream.

All that done, add anything that takes your fancy—finely chopped spring onions, spring onion greens, capsicum, cucumber, grated hard-boiled egg, anchovies, almost anything.

'This is my version of the celebrated "raw" fish dish which isn't raw at all as the marinade changes the character of the flesh.'

Fishing at Lake Pedder with Peter Doyle and the Boxall brothers.

Rolled spinach leaves with tuna

I first tried this pleasant dish, suitable for light diets, at Berida Manor, the well-run, get-you-healthy spot at Bowral, in New South Wales.

8 spinach leaves
400g can tuna, drained
1 red capsicum
1 green capsicum
1 medium onion
chives

mixed herbs
400ml can tomato juice
2 tablespoons desiccated coconut
½ cup grated cheddar cheese
Serves 8

Blanch spinach leaves in boiling water for 2 minutes. Remove and allow to dry. Chop capsicums, onion and chives finely and mix with the herbs. Place mixture in bowl with tuna and blend until thoroughly mixed. Place 2 tablespoons of this mixture into each spinach leaf and roll tightly, holding it together with a toothpick if necessary. When ready to cook place rolls in baking tray, pour tomato juice over, sprinkle with coconut and grated cheese and allow to cook in a hot oven for 8–10 minutes. If cheese requires further colouring, place under grill.

———————❧———————

Sugar cured tuna or trout

In Sweden there is a renowned dish called *Gravlax*: fresh salmon soaked in a marinade. Fresh salmon is difficult to get in Australia, so we adapted the dish for both tuna and trout. It works magnificently. Another 'local' touch is to serve it with *washabi*, the exquisite Japanese green-coloured horseradish. Interesting to note that so many national influences can be brought to bear on an Australian variant, which, of course, is also based on availability.

1kg good tuna (sushimi style) or
    fresh trout fillets (must be wild—
    i.e. pink—not hatchery reared)
100g chopped fresh dill

¼ cup sugar
¼ cup coarse salt
¼ cup olive oil
washabi

Mix dill, sugar, salt and oil together. Coat both sides of the fish, building up layers of fillets. Allow to cure for six hours. Remove, wipe clean and cut across to create pieces which are thoroughly cured outside, yet have tender, delicately flavoured centres.

Spread 2–4 pieces on each plate, and garnish with *washabi*.

———————— ❦ ————————

Tuna en papillote

This recipe is an adaption by Anne Marshall of a dish of Freddie Girardet's, the chef who runs a great restaurant at Crissier in Switzerland. (Where did *he* get it from?)

8 fillets tuna (or fresh salmon)
32 sheets filo pastry
250g butter, melted
salt and white pepper
2 shallots, thinly sliced
2 tablespoons chopped fresh ginger
1 tablespoon lime or lemon juice
⅔ cup dry white wine

1 tablespoon olive oil
quartered slices lime or lemon with
   pith removed
julienne strips of lime or lemon rind
parsley sprigs and lime or lemon
   segments for garnish
Serves 8

Trim and wash the fillets of tuna, pat dry with paper towels. Spread two sheets of filo pastry on a damp tea towel, brush with melted butter, place another two sheets on top and brush with more butter. Place a tuna fillet in the middle of the pastry, sprinkle with salt and pepper, one teaspoon of chopped shallot, half a teaspoon of chopped ginger, one teaspoon of lime juice, one tablespoon of white wine, half a teaspoon of olive oil, lime slices and strips of lime rind.

Trim the excess pastry with scissors, and fold the edges to the top to enclose fish neatly. Then fold or gently twist the edges together to seal until the parcel looks similar to a Cornish pasty. Place on a greased baking tray and brush with melted butter. Repeat this process with the remaining fillets.

Bake at the top of a hot oven (230°C/450°F) for 15 minutes until fish is pink and tender. Serve hot, garnished with parsley sprigs and lime or lemon segments.

'Whitebait is the most delectable of fish fry, but it must be cooked when very fresh.'

———————— ❦ ————————

Whitebait one way

Whitebait is the most delectable of fish fry, but it must be cooked when very fresh.

Fried whitebait is extemely simple to prepare. Heat oil or fat until smoking, dredge whitebait thoroughly with flour into which a little salt and pepper has been mixed. Shake off the excess flour and drop the fish into oil one at a time. They cook almost straight away. Do only a few at a time, otherwise the first ones will be overdone. Drain on a grid or heavy paper.

Whitebait a second way

This method is the same as the first way, except that after dredging each whitebait with flour, dip it into a mixture of beaten eggs and olive oil. Hold the fish for a second or two over the mixture after you have done this, since a very thin coating is desired. Then drop the fish into the hot oil for a minute or so.

Whitebait a third way

Cook one cake for each person an an entrée. These can be served with a sauce tartare, but in my opinion they are incomparable just as is.

whitebait	*pepper*
oil	*1 egg*
for the batter:	*milk*
½ cup self-raising flour	*water*
salt	

Mix the batter ingredients in a large bowl and add whitebait. Heat the oil to moderate temperature in a large frying pan. Lift out a portion of whitebait and batter, heaped on a slotted kitchen spoon, and drop it gently into the pan. With a fish slice, pat the spoonful carefully into a cake shape, about 3cm thick. It should hold together. Do not disturb it again until the underside is well-browned. Turn over the cake with the slice and repeat. The outsides should be brown and crunchy and the insides moist, yet cooked through.

Vanuatu baked fish

2 cups coconut milk	*salt*
1 large fish, gutted and scaled	*curry powder*
1 tomato, finely sliced	*rice*
1 onion, finely sliced	Serves 6

To make coconut milk, dig the white flesh out of the coconut (liquid *in* the coconut is not the milk). Put the flesh in the blender with a little water, and reduce to a pulp. Sieve through a cloth. Allow the liquid to settle in two parts. Pour off the clear part, and keep the thick milk. (You can use desiccated coconut mixed with water in the blender; strain it and use the resulting liquid.)

Place the fish in a baking dish and cover with sliced tomato and onion and sprinkle salt over the top. Gently pour coconut milk over the fish. Bake it until half done. Sprinkle curry powder over the fish and finish cooking.

Serve with rice which has been cooked in coconut milk and water.

Whiting in beer batter

This recipe sounds terribly simple, and it is. Once I went fishing with Wolfie Blass, dressed in U-boat commander's hat, off Kangaroo Island. This was in honour of Michael Broadbent, who hates boats anyway. We caught plenty of whiting and then had to wait offshore because Captain Blass had forgotten about the tide. Once ashore, we were ravenous. Primo Caon and I cooked the whiting at once. Years later, Broadbent still remembers this occasion when 'we had the finest fresh fish I've ever eaten in the world'. Which does show that the most sophisticated people enjoy simplicity when the ingredients are the best.

1kg fresh whiting fillets
oil
for the batter:
1¼ cups self-raising flour
2 eggs
milk

salt
pepper
beer
lemon juice
Serves 4

'Michael Broadbent still remembers when "we had the finest fresh fish I've ever eaten in the world".'

Make a fairly stiff batter with the flour, eggs, milk, salt and pepper. Allow to stand for an hour if possible. Make into a thinnish batter with beer. Heat the oil, dip whiting fillets into the batter, and drop in hot oil until golden brown. Remove, drain on thick paper, and sprinkle with lemon juice. Serve immediately.

Whiting in champagne

Another plug for whiting, which is such a good fish when it is fresh. I've enjoyed it straight from the sea many times, especially in South Australia.

6 whiting, scaled and cleaned
250g butter
½ bottle French Champagne
¾ cup reduced fish stock

¼ cup chopped chervil or a pinch
*   dried chervil*
salt
pepper
Serves 6

Heat a little butter in a baking dish until it has melted. Slit the whiting down the back to open them to the heat. Lie the whiting in the pan, add butter, champagne, and stock, and bake in a moderate oven, frequently basting the fish. When the fish are done, remove to a warmed dish and keep warm. Put remainder of liquid into a saucepan over a fierce heat and reduce to a thick sauce. Add the chervil, correct the seasoning and pour sauce over the whiting to serve.

CHAPTER FOUR

Seafood: friendships

AUSTRALIA HAS SOME OF THE GREATEST SEAFOOD in the world, plus freshwater crustaceans, and most of it is within reach, either physically or financially. It is the stuff about which most visitors rave. But this raving becomes even more ravenous, so to speak, if one can serve it fresh. Too much quality is lost in the frozen or pre-treated methods used, however necessary they are in some markets.

Years ago, at Rothbury, I had the pleasure of entertaining Paul Bocuse and Michel Guerard, two great French chefs. What to give them? Any meat dish, galantine, mousse or mousseline, would be instantly compared with their own offerings: ah, but we do it this way, or at best, that's an interesting derivation of the classic. I decided to serve a seafood buffet of the freshest possible variety, and to do this I solicited help from friends all over Australia. Mud and sand crabs were flown from Queensland, scallops from Tasmania, marons from Western Australia, green prawns from Sydney, unopened oysters, mussels and pipis, yabbies from Lake Alexandria in South Australia, Moreton Bay bugs from Brisbane, all arrived alive and kicking amid a mess of meeting times, schedules, phone calls, planes, refrigerated trucks and Eskys in the backs of friends' cars.

Much of the seafood was cooked at the last moment, the yabbies in white wine and dill, for example, and served lukewarm. The oysters were opened without being washed, the pipis purged and gently steamed open, the mud crab body meat, after being cooked at the last moment and taken out of the shell, being mixed with a very light egg mayonnaise and put back in the inverted top shell, surrounded by defiant legs and claws.

The luncheon was a sensational success, everyone gorging themselves in a sort of seafood degustation, chattering away five hundred to the minute. Guerard thought it all marvellous, particularly the sand crabs, bugs and yabbies, while Bocuse said the scallops were the best he had ever had, demanding, finally, that they be served raw, the better that he could taste them.

So often seafood is ruined. The scallops are frozen in blocks and are then overcooked to emerge like smelly ball bearings. Prawns are over-salted and over-boiled, crays have the life frozen out of them or again are boiled to toughness.

The Dreaded Oxenbould, John Rourke, myself, Bob Mayne, Deeta Colvin, Max Lake and Bubbles Fisher at a wine promotion party.

Some years ago in Hobart I tasted the best scallops I've ever had at the Atheneum Club. Charles Bucher was the chef there, and I took the liberty of going behind the scenes to find out why they were so good. It was easy. They were kept fresh and plump, with that soft full whiteness of body, until the moment of serving. Then they were plunged into the hot sauce, which had been prepared beforehand, for seconds only, prior to being carried into the dining room. In fact, they continued to cook while on their way. I'm quite sure this is one of the great secrets of serving seafood—to make sure that it is not overcooked. The Chinese and Japanese, for example, have known this for centuries, and that is why both serve outstanding seafood.

Scores of delicious and delightful occasions have confirmed this principle. During the 1960s, Burleigh Marr in Brisbane used to serve the simplest of great seafood: oysters freshly opened and sand crabs and mud crabs boiled that morning and allowed to cool, offered with bread and butter and not much else.

On a sparkling spring day on a visit to Brooklyn on the Hawkesbury River, we opened massive four-year-old oysters on the spot to present to a visiting American gourmet writer. She sank her oysters, sipped her Hunter semillon, looked up and down the river with boats bobbing and said, 'This must be the best kept secret in the world.' Still later, on an impromptu but idyllic visit to Forster on the New South Wales coast, I was told to visit the oyster squire of the area, Graham Barclay. I asked for him at his vast shed piled high with stacks of oysters. 'That's him over there, mate, the only one in the clean overalls.'

'I don't think I ever enjoyed anything better than a succulent oyster at the peak of condition, taken off it's stick, opened with care, unwashed.'

Graham took us out for lunch, on a boat, with halves of lemon only. He moved up and down the beds, inspecting the various stages and ages before tying up at a particular spot. I don't think I ever enjoyed anything better than a succulent oyster at the peak of condition, taken off it's stick, opened with care, unwashed. One cannot better such an original flavour, though, on one occasion many years ago, someone tried.

When the late André Simon, the founder and father of the International Wine and Food Society, visited Australia in the early 1960s he was presented with a dish containing 12 huge oysters, garnished with grapefruit pieces, topped with cream on which was piled caviar. Rather over-elaborate, he said, though I noticed he ate the lot.

I've never been quite so fond of sea-water crayfish as some, though I love the maron, the freshwater cray which inhabits Western Australian waters, whenever I've been lucky enough to find some. The sea-water crays can be very good, if caught and consumed on the spot, though this is difficult most of the time. Consequently, the frozen variety, which is mostly our lot, are simply tougher and less juicy, however carefully they are thawed and cooked. Sydney crays can be quite fine, if obtained uncooked, and I've had some from Coff's Harbour which were delicious straight from the sea. But the best I've ever had were enjoyed at Robe in South Australia, and once again, simplicity and freshness were the the keynotes.

Fishing with a group of mates off Exmouth in Western Australia. Michael Kailis is at the rear in a dark shirt, while Evans, Peter Doyle and Laurie Brereton play with the fish.

We were showing Josie Wilson, food professional and writer, the best of Australian food on behalf of Qantas. At the time she was working for James Beard, one of the most prominent gastronomes of the United States. We were to travel on a cray boat from Robe, which is not far from the wine district of Coonawarra, and return with live crays which were to be cooked at the local hotel. Everything went well until the presentation of the cooked crays. The charming young couple in charge of the small hotel had taken the whole thing very seriously, including the preparation of a sauce based on scotch whisky, while the crays 'stood' after cooking. I could see that Josie was not impressed. With considerable tact—at least for me who forever charges down the paths of imagined truth with the delicacy of a rutting elephant—I asked the couple if they would mind if I tried an experiment with some remaining fresh crays. Not at all, they replied. I killed the crays by cutting them in half, then liberally basted the meat with melted butter before putting them under the salamander. Using moderate heat and frequently basting with more butter, I cooked the flesh, just through, before removing it and pulling it into strips rather than cutting it into medallions. Very quickly I then scraped out of the shell all the butter and 'coral' from the head, mixed and seasoned it and poured it over the strips. This tasted so marvellous that I became an instant grand master, but any fool can understand just how easy it was. All we needed were great ingredients, treated gently and simply and not over-embellished.

I wonder, however, if even at their best the warm-water crays of Australia equal, for example, the flavours to be found in an Atlantic lobster. I enjoyed one in Ireland, which was served in a very intelligent way. We ordered the rather high-priced item on the recommendation of the waiter, since it was 'fresh that minute'. It arrived at the table, half each for my friend and I. Except that *his* had a huge claw attached while mine had none. I was incensed. 'That's all right, sir,' said the waiter. 'Your's will be a-coming when you get your second half.' So, after enjoying this most magnificent half of lobster, the chef cooked the second half while we paused for breath. A splendid idea, since the lobster arrives piping hot at maximum succulence—except that the waiter had switched plates and my mate got the second claw.

Which reminds me of the story of the bloke who was served a lobster with one claw. 'Why is this?' he asked the waiter. 'Well, sir, they sometimes lose a claw in a fight,' he was told. The customer pushed the plate away. 'In that case, then,' he said, 'please bring me the winner.'

There are many different kinds of prawn in Australia, some of which are almost as big as small crays. My favourite prawn is almost the smallest, the school prawn which is often so much cheaper than any other. I don't really go too much on those huge cooked prawns one finds at markets, over-salted and overcooked to hardness and dryness. I prefer the large ones green and preferably alive, to be cooked in the shell in herbs, wine and garlic or whatever, using more flavour than is apparently needed, since not all of it penetrates the shell. But again, the idea is in speed of cooking so that the flesh remains tender and succulent.

I've thought always that the humble clam, or pipi, is very much underestimated in Australia; often the diligent people one finds searching from them on the beach just want them for bait. I think it's great fun finding pipis, and I've spent many happy hours on the beach with my family, in summer and winter, squirming toes in the sand as the water flows and ebbs. Pipis must be purged before they are cooked; a little sand in the mouth can ruin any flavour. I put them in a bucket of fresh water, and add oatmeal or sugar, the idea being that the pipis suck in the nutrient and expell the sand. Others claim it works as well if you just stand them in water.

'I think it's great fun finding pipis, and I've spent many happy hours on the beach with my family, in summer and winter, squirming toes in the sand as the water flows and ebbs.'

Fishing with Peter Doyle off Sydney. Dinner for two?

The pipis can be steamed with a few shredded vegetables and a little garlic in the water, and the juices drunk as a broth when they are opened, or you can tear off the empty side of the shell and cover the others, using various toppings (I use one of garlic, finely chopped parsley and breadcrumbs mixed with wine and butter). Cover each clam with topping before heating under the grill or in the oven. Pipis are also delicious in a soup, or as part of a seafood stew, or with tomato and basil in pasta. Whichever way you use them, they have a delicious flavour, and they should not be kept in such a humble position.

Yabbies, which the French call *les écrevisses*, were not highly regarded by the majority of Australians until a few years ago, and now really good fresh ones are becoming increasingly hard to find. Again, I prefer to buy mine alive, then cook them in a court-bouillon of wine and vinegar and vegetables, using plenty of dill. Yabbies were appreciated years ago, by some. The great Maurice O'Shea, one of the most famous of all wine makers, used to cook billycans of them in his white wine. The French, Swedes and Danes have had a passion for these freshwater crayfish for centuries, though most of theirs now come from Central Europe.

When the kids were young I used to enjoy yabby hunting expeditions with them, though these excursions were as much for my benefit as theirs. I would like to farm yabbies commercially, one day, since this is being done successfully here and there.

'Maurice O'Shea, one of the most famous of all wine makers, used to cook billycans of yabbies in his white wine.'

One of my delights has been to make seafood stews, chowders and clear soups thick with fish and seafood. The Tasting Room used to feature Sydney Seafood Stew, which was loosely based on the famous French dish, bouillabaisse. One cannot really repeat that dish with local ingredients, though there are many versions of it. I did try one Australian version, which turned out to be a near disaster, for the Wine and Food Society of New South Wales.

We obtained the various ingredients, going to a great deal of trouble to find counterparts of the French varieties used. Came the day, a fantastic stock was brewed and taken to the kitchen to be used. Unfortunately, the stove in this kitchen had a will of its own and the stock took a long time to heat up because the electricity supply kept fading. As soon as we added the cold ingredients, the stock took more time to reheat. On top of this, I was told there would be about 40 guests. Trouble was, 70 turned up, and about 20 of these showed up when I had served over half the food. So latecomers were not served a meal that they could get excited about.

It seems to me that Australian seafoods are best served as chowders, based on a good fish stock and including plenty of vegetables as well as seafood, with cream being added at the end. Though these do not have the sharp piquancy of saffron and tomato fish soups, they have a rich smoothness and mouth filling flavours aplenty.

I've promised the Wine and Food Society I shall cook one of my chowders for them instead of trying to emulate the dish of another country.

Abalone with Chinese vegetables

650g tenderised abalone slices
cider vinegar
plain flour
pepper
2 tablespoons oil
2 cups diced white onions
1 green capsicum, sliced

2 cups celery, sliced lengthways
2 cups tomato wedges
1 tablespoon soy sauce
long grain rice
½ teaspoon salt
Serves 4

To tenderise the abalone meat, pressure-cook for up to 45 minutes or more if necessary. Marinate the abalone in cider vinegar for two days. Toss the abalone in flour and pepper, then fry in oil until brown. Add the onion, capsicum, celery and tomato, simmer for 5 minutes, then add the soy sauce. Serve piping hot with boiled, salted long grain rice.

'To tenderise abalone meat, pressure-cook for up to 45 minutes or more if necessary.'

Baby abalones in oyster sauce

Alfred Lai, the owner of the Imperial Peking Harbourside Restaurant, Sydney, thinks this is one of his greatest offerings. Simple, yet absolutely delicious.

8 baby abalones
½ teaspoon salt
½ teaspoon sugar
8 pieces broccoli
1 teaspoon oil

4 teaspoons oyster sauce
1 teaspoon soya sauce
touch of ginger
1 tablespoon cornflour
Serves 4

Cover the baby abalones with water, add salt and sugar. Soak for 10 hours or overnight. Stir-fry broccoli flowers in a wok or saucepan and place on a plate for later use. Simmer soaked abalones with oil, oyster sauce, soya sauce and ginger for ½ an hour. Add cornflour and water, stir and serve.

Cold Balmain bugs with lemon sauce

I found this one in *The Great Australian Shellfish Cookbook* written by Grant Blackman. It's simple and effective. However, I must say I prefer the dish warm. But others insist it's better cold.

16 green bugs or bay lobsters
2 tablespoons vegetable oil
1 cup white wine
1 cup basic court-bouillon
2 cloves minced garlic

3 tablespoons lemon juice
salt and pepper
parsley to garnish
Serves 4

Heat the oil in a large frying pan or saucepan, split the bugs lengthways and sauté them in the oil for 3–4 minutes over a high heat. Add the wine, court-bouillon and garlic, reduce the heat, and simmer for 4–5 minutes. Remove the bugs and strain the cooking liquid. Add the lemon juice to the cooking liquid and reduce by one-third. Season. Pour the sauce over the bugs and garnish with parsley. Leave to cool and serve at room temperature.

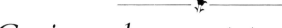

Caviar and new potatoes Stanford Court

This is a favourite 'starter' (we call them entrées) at the famous Fournou's Ovens, the main restaurant of the Stanford Court Hotel of San Francisco. It's often served as a drinks accompaniment (of a very special kind). Once I rushed to the Stanford Court after a week of gastronomic disasters in other parts of the United States. Pure bliss was a couple of these and a glass of champagne, enjoyed minutes after arriving.

250g tin fresh caviar or less
12–14 very small, red, waxy
   potatoes, 500g or less
4–5 cups rock salt

oil for deep frying
½ cup sour cream
Serves 6

Preheat the oven to 230°C/450°F. Wash and dry the potatoes. Arrange them on a bed of rock salt and place in the oven. Bake for 30 –35 minutes or until tender. Slice the potatoes in half. Scoop out the centre pulp with a melon-ball cutter or small spoon; reserve both the pulp and skins. Mash the pulp slightly and keep warm.

   Heat the oil for deep frying. The proper temperature is 190°C/ 375°F. Drop the potato shells into the oil and cook quickly until golden brown and crisp. Drain well. Fill the shells with the mashed potato mixture. Top with a spoonful or so of sour cream. Then add a teaspoon or more of caviar to the top. Serve on a bed of hot rock salt, if desired.

Crab meat timbale

250g crab meat
1 capsicum
4 anchovies
½ cup mayonnaise

3 teaspoons gelatine
1 cup vinegar
pepper and salt
Serves 2

Finely chop the capsicum and anchovies. Dissolve the gelatine in the vinegar. Mix together the mayonnaise, capsicum and anchovies. Season with salt and pepper. Add the crab meat. Combine the gelatine and vinegar with the crab mixture. Place in a mould which has been rinsed out with cold water and refrigerate for 1 hour.

Crab meat and soft egg

From Matthew Chan of the Peacock Gardens. Matthew also has a fortune cookie business. On one occasion we were farewelling Bartholomew Broadbent, son of the great English palate, and now an emerging wine man himself. We have reason to believe he lost his virginity in Australia, having been smuggled into the Nurses Quarters of Adelaide Hospital for ten days. When he emerged, beaming, we asked him about his experiences. 'Actually,' he replied, 'the food wasn't at all bad.'

So, at this farewell, there were all sorts of statements from my somewhat forward children regarding his return, shot-gun marriages, paternity suits, and so on. Bartholomew protested there would be no problem. Came the end of the meal and fortune cookie time. Mine read, 'Middle age is when you're sure you'll feel better in two weeks time', which I thought more than apt. Finally, it was the turn of our guest. 'Oh, I say,' he exclaimed. 'Mine's rather peculiar. This insert has a protective coating.'

90g Alaskan king crab meat	1/6 teaspoon sesame oil
7 eggs	pepper
1/4 teaspoon salt	Serves 6

Mix eggs and crab meat with salt and stir well. Heat the oil, put the whole mixture into the pan, and stir-fry until it is 80 per cent cooked. Sprinkle with pepper and serve.

———————— ❧ ————————

Cooking seafood flambé at Rothbury. We can cook enough for 250 people in 15 minutes.

Tropical crayfish

1 crayfish	1 teaspoon mild curry powder
1 1/2 cups coconut milk	2 teaspoons arrowroot
90g onion	2 tablespoons brandy
1 garlic clove	1 banana
250g pineapple	2 tablespoons cream
parsley	Serves 2
30g clarified butter	

Make coconut milk by pouring 1 1/2 cups of water over 1 1/2 cups of coconut. Allow to infuse for 20 minutes and then strain off the milk through muslin. Slice the onion thinly. Peel the garlic clove. Cut the pineapple into chunks. Remove the head of the crayfish and reserve. Make two cuts down either side of the inside of the tail, remove the meat and reserve the tail shell. Cut the crayfish meat into chunks. Chop the parsley.

Place the clarified butter in a pan and when hot sauté the onion until it is soft and golden. Add the crushed garlic and the curry powder. Cook for a few minutes. Add the coconut milk to the onion mixture and simmer for 10 minutes. Mix the arrowroot with the brandy and pour slowly into the hot sauce to thicken it. Add the banana in slices, the pineapple and the crayfish and then stir in the cream.

On a serving dish lay the crayfish head with the tail shell turned upside down to form a receptacle. Fill the tail shell with the crayfish curry and decorate with finely chopped parsley.

Crayfish souffle Ernie's

One of the great dishes of the world, adapted from one first tasted in 1967 at Ernie's, the restaurant on Montgomery Street, San Francisco, run by Victor and Roland Gotti. Years later, after many top meals there, I remembered that it was no longer an item on the menu. Roland wandered off, and half-an-hour or so later it was on the table. 'It's good,' he said, 'to be reminded about the great things.'

1.2kg green crayfish	*1 clove garlic, peeled and crushed*
¼ teaspoon paprika	*¼ cup brandy*
salt, freshly ground black pepper	*1 cup white wine*
2 tablespoons shallots	*1 tablespoon tarragon*
2 tomatoes	*pinch thyme*
1 tablespoon flour	*1 bay leaf*
60g mushrooms	*2½ cups fish stock*
75g butter	*3 egg yolks*
½ cup oil	*4 egg whites, stiffly beaten*

Split the crayfish in two lengthwise. Season both halves with paprika, salt and fresh pepper. Finely chop the shallots. Skin and seed the tomatoes and cut into quarters. Sift the flour. Finely dice the mushrooms and sauté in a little butter till dry. Preheat the oven to 230°C/425°F.

Pour the oil in a large pan over a medium heat, place the crayfish in the pan and sauté until the shell turns red. Add the shallots and garlic. Pour in the brandy and set alight. Add the wine, tomatoes, tarragon, thyme and bay leaf, then fish stock or consommé. Season lightly. Cover and cook for 20 minutes. Remove the pan from heat and remove the crayfish. Strain the poaching broth through muslin. Let liquid and crayfish cool.

Melt the remaining butter and add the flour to form a roux. Cook over a low heat for 3 minutes. Add 1½ cups of poaching broth and whisk to form a smooth sauce. Bring to the boil and when it starts to bubble, remove the pan from heat; add egg yolks and stir well. Dice the lobster meat and add the mushrooms and the lobster to the sauce. Season and lightly fold in the stiffly beaten egg white. Place soufflé mixture in cleaned crayfish shells and place on a heated oven tray. Bake for 15 minutes.

'One of the great dishes of the world, adapted from one first tasted in 1967 at Ernie's, the restaurant on Montgomery Street, San Francisco.'

Crayfish with mangoes

This recipe comes from Jean-Luc Lundy, of the Bagatelle Restaurant, Darlinghurst, who served it at one of the Great Chefs Dinners at Rothbury. I have watched the progress of Jean-Luc since he came to Australia. He is extremely hard-working, innovative and deserves his successes, which include one selection in a national guide as the top restaurant of Sydney.

With Michael Parkinson and his wife at the Hunter.

2 small live crayfish, about 600g each
1 carrot
1 onion
8 cups water
2 glasses white wine
1 bouquet garni (parsley, bay leaf, thyme)
3 tablespoons rock salt
10 black peppercorns
for the sauce:
3 tablespoons tarragon vinegar
9 tablespoons olive oil
40 large basil leaves
salt and pepper
for the garnish:
2 mangoes
Serves 4 as an entrée

Peel carrot and onion, slice finely and bring to the boil in the water and white wine. Add the bouquet garni, salt and pepper. When the water is boiling put in the crayfish for 10 minutes.

While the crays are cooking, peel the mangoes, slice finely and put to one side. To make the sauce put all the ingredients in a blender and blend on and off.

When the crays are cooked separate the head from the tail by cutting behind the head. Peel the tail and slice into 1cm pieces. Divide between four plates, arranging the crayfish neatly in the centre; surround it with mango slices and finish with a circle of sauce around the outside.

Paupiette de truite au mousse d'homard truffee

Rolled trout fillets with truffled crayfish mousse

From the famous Two Faces Restaurant in South Yarra, Melbourne, run by Hermann and Faye Schneider.

4 trout, each about 230g
1 raw crayfish, about 750g
1 egg white
1¼ cups cream
1 tablespoon fine Brunoise of truffle
salt and pepper
fish aspic
quail's eggs
Russian caviar
For the sauce verte:
⅔ cup mayonnaise
⅓ cup sour cream
1 tablespoon 'chlorophyll'
Serves 8

To make the chlorophyll remove stems and wash well 500g spinach, 100g parsley, 50g chives, 50g chervil and 25g tarragon. Put into a vitamizer or vegetable blender with 4 cups of cold water and pulp very fine. Pour into muslin cloth stretched over stainless steel saucepan and press until all juice has passed through. Discard pulp. Heat green juice gently, stirring with wooden spatula until ingredients have coagulated, but do not boil. Gently pour liquid through clean muslin cloth and retain the herb purée. This can be stored with a few drops of oil in refrigerator for 2–3 weeks.

Fillet and skin trout. Remove any centre bones with pincers or pliers. Gently flatten each fillet between two sheets of plastic wrap.

Cut both sides of belly of drowned crayfish with heavy scissors, remove shell from belly and lift out flesh carefully. (If crayfish is chilled for 12 hours beforehand flesh is easier to remove.) Remove crayfish entrail. Grind coarsely chopped meat in food processor with egg white to fine mousse, then pass through very fine sieve. Chill well over ice then vigorously stir in cream bit by bit. Season with white pepper and salt and add truffles.

'If crayfish is chilled for 12 hours beforehand, the flesh is easier to remove from the shell.'

Spread equal quantities of mousse on each fillet and gently roll from tail end. Wrap each fillet individually in foil and seal firmly. Poach in bain-marie for 8–10 minutes in medium oven. Cool, preferably overnight.

Remove foil and slice each roll into 4. Place slices on wire grill and gently coat with fine layer of aspic.

Serve with halved boiled quail's eggs topped with Russian caviar and a sauce verte.

Crayfish julienne

One of those recipes which are actually adaptions. In this case we were fishing at Mount Martha in Victoria and someone brought along a large cray. But there were too many of us to cut it into medallions. Hence the on-the-spot improvisation.

1 large crayfish	*oil*
whites of 2 leeks	*butter*
6 spring onions	*60ml sherry*
1 celery stalk	*vinegar*
2 carrots	*salt and pepper*
1 capsicum, or ½ red, ½ green	*250g bean sprouts*
2 peppers	

Separate the crayfish tail into strips. Cut the vegetables into long, thin strips. In a large pan or wok put oil and a touch of butter. Add the vegetable strips and work around the pan for only a few minutes. Add a touch of sherry and another of vinegar, salt and pepper, and the crayfish pieces. Add the bean sprouts at the last moment. When the crayfish pieces are hot the entrée is ready to serve.

Lobster wrapling

Loong Har Sung Choi Bao

From Gilbert Lau of the Flower Drum Restaurant, Little Bourke Street, Melbourne. This is a delicious way to eat fresh local crayfish (often misnamed lobster).

'This is a delicious way to eat fresh local crayfish (often misnamed lobster).'

1.2kg fresh (green) lobster (equivalent to a whole lobster)
1 whole lettuce
4 cups peanut oil
75g bamboo shoots, sliced
50g diced water chestnuts
50g sliced celery
2 stalks spring onions, chopped

1 teaspoon cornflour dissolved in 1 tablespoon water
for the seasoning:
½ teaspoon salt
½ teaspoon sesame oil
1 teaspoon Chinese wine or sweet sherry

Separate the tail from the lobster and remove the meat. Steam the shell and the claws (lightly cracked) for 10 minutes. Dice the meat from the body. Separate and wash the lettuce leaves, trim the edges neatly and chill in the refrigerator to crisp.

Heat the peanut oil in the wok over a moderate heat and 'blanch' the lobster pieces until the colour changes—about 2–3 minutes. Remove and drain the lobster. Drain off the oil, leaving about 2 teaspoons in the wok. Turn up the heat to high and stir fry the bamboo, chestnuts, celery and spring onions for 30 seconds, then add the blanched lobster pieces. Toss quickly to combine, add seasoning, and stir in the cornflour paste to lightly glaze the ingredients.

Serve on the centre of an oval plate, replace the body shell over the top, and arrange the tail and claws around. Serve with a platter of crisp lettuce leaves. The diner spoons a portion of the lobster into a leaf, rolls it up, and eats with the fingers. Towels should be provided by the thoughtful host.

———————— ❦ ————————

Oysters Madelaine

From Fanny's in Melbourne, consistently chosen among the best restaurants of this country. Two-time winner of the best food section of the *Bulletin*/Quelltaler Quest and recipient of numerous awards. The service is outstanding, the ambience 'antiquely romantic'. Opened by Gloria and Blyth Staley who run the restaurant with the assistance of their son Daniel.

32 oysters
2½ cups pure cream
juice of oysters
¾ cup white wine
½ cup grated Gruyère cheese

⅓ cup grated Parmesan cheese
1 lemon
chopped parsley
Serves 4

Reduce cream, oyster juice and white wine for 2 minutes. Add Gruyère cheese and half the Parmesan. Allow cheese to melt. Add lemon juice and parsley. Season to taste. Bring the mixture to the boil. Add the oysters. Remove from the heat as soon as the oysters are warm, do not cook them. Remove the oysters from the mixture and carefully place them back in their shells. Spoon the mixture over the oysters, pouring as much of the mixture in the shell as possible. Sprinkle over each oyster the remaining Parmesan. Glaze under a salamander or heated grill and serve.

Oysters Rockefeller

4 dozen oysters
125g shallots
30g parsley
375g spinach
2 garlic cloves
1 x 50g can anchovies, drained
rock salt

250g butter
½ cup flour
1 cup oyster liquor
½ teaspoon salt
¼ teaspoon cayenne
¼ cup Pernod
Serves 6

Finely chop the shallots, parsley and spinach. Finely chop the garlic cloves. Finely chop the anchovies. Place a layer of rock salt in an ovenproof dish and put it in an oven heated to 200°C/400°F.

Melt the butter in a saucepan and then add the sifted flour to form a roux. Cook slowly for 5 minutes. Add the oyster liquor, garlic, salt and cayenne and then the spinach, parsley, shallots and anchovies. Simmer covered for 20 minutes. Remove the lid, add the Pernod and cook until the sauce has thickened.

Place half oyster shells (6 per person) on the hot rock salt. Fill each shell with an oyster and cover each oyster with some sauce. Place the oysters in the oven for about 3 minutes.

Ian McNee, Margaret Levin, myself, Bobby McNee (Patterson), David Levin and Trish at the Capital Hotel, London.

Oysters in Champagne sauce

4 dozen fresh Sydney oysters in their
*   shells*
1¼ cups French Champagne
⅓ cup reduced fish stock
pinch cayenne pepper

salt and pepper
¾ cup cream
2 egg yolks, beaten
½ cup parsley, chopped
Serves 4

Put Champagne, fish stock, cayenne, salt and pepper in a pan, bring to the boil and reduce by half. Add the cream and bring to the boil, stirring all the time. Take off the heat and gradually add the beaten egg yolks to the mixture. Add the chopped parsley. Fill each shell (still containing its oyster) and place under the grill until it browns.

Oyster tartlets

2 dozen fresh oysters
30g butter
¼ cup flour
⅔ cup reduced fish stock
⅔ cup dry white wine
¼ cup milk
salt and pepper
vinegar

parsley
for rich short pastry:
1½ cups plain flour
pinch salt
90g firm butter, cubed
1 egg yolk
1–2 tablespoons cold water
Serves 4

'This is one of our standards, which is very popular at home and in the Tasting Room.'

First make the pastry. Sift the flour and salt into a bowl. Rub the butter into the flour until the mixture resembles fine breadcrumbs. Mix the egg yolk and 1 tablespoon of water and stir into the flour with a spatula or round-bladed knife to form a firm dough, adding more water if necessary. Form into a ball. Wrap and chill for at least 30 minutes. Roll out the pastry very thin and cut into 4 deepish single tart moulds. Bake until almost golden brown.

To make a sauce heat the butter, add the flour and cook for a few minutes. Remove from the heat, and add, a little at a time, the reduced fish stock which has been mixed with dry white wine and a little milk. Continue adding and stirring until a smooth custard-like consistency is obtained. Add salt, pepper, a dash of vinegar and chopped parsley. Fill tarts with oysters. Pour in the sauce and bake until hot. Grated cheese may be added to the top before baking.

Feuilleté of oysters

2 dozen oysters (bottled will do)
¾ cup dry Champagne
4 egg yolks
2 tablespoons cream
salt and pepper
1 tablespoon chopped chervil

for the pastry cases:
½ packet puff pastry or 1 sheet
    Pampas ready-rolled pastry
1 beaten egg
Serves 4

Roll out the puff pastry to about 4mm thick and trim to a rectangle 24cm x 14cm. Cut into four smaller rectangles each 6cm x 14cm. If using the ready-rolled pastry cut it into a 14cm wide strip and then cut across into four rectangles each approximately 6cm x 14cm. Brush a baking tray lightly with water. Turn the pastry rectangles upside down and place on the baking tray. Glaze the tops with beaten egg, being careful that none of the egg trickles over the sides as that would prevent the pastries from rising. Bake at 220°C/425°F for 12–15 minutes. When done, keep the pastries warm in the oven, with the door open and the temperature turned down to 140°C/250°F.

Heat the champagne in a shallow pan. When bubbling and reduced by one-third add the oysters and simmer for 30 seconds only. Remove the oysters carefully to a dish. Beat egg yolks, cream, salt and pepper until thick and a pale lemon colour. Tip the hot champagne onto this and return it to the pan. Stir until thickened but do not allow to boil. Keep hot in the top of a double boiler.

Split each pastry case horizontally using a serrated knife. Put lower halves onto a hot serving plate and arrange the oysters along each half. Pour the hot champagne sauce over, sprinkle with chopped chervil and top with upper halves of pastry. Serve immediately.

Oysters in green waistcoats

From Carolyn Divjak, chef of the Tasting Room.

3 dozen plump oysters in their shells	*1½ cups dry white wine*
2 bunches English spinach	*250g unsalted butter*
250g butter, melted	*125g salted butter*
for the beurre blanc:	Serves 6

Remove the stalks from the spinach. Plunge the leaves into boiling water, and remove immediately and refresh in cold water. Lay 1 leaf lengthways and a smaller piece about 8cm long across it. Place an oyster in the centre and bring the smaller leaf across oyster to cover both ends. Roll it up neatly. Place the oysters on a baking tray. Put the oyster shells into another baking tray. About 10 minutes before service cover the oysters with melted butter, and bake in the oven at 175°C/350°F for 5 minutes. Put the shells in the bottom of the oven.

To make the beurre blanc, reduce the wine in a saucepan to about ½ cup. With a Bamix or a whisk beat in small pieces of butter over a low heat until all is incorporated. If the sauce is too thin add a little more butter. The sauce may be reheated, but do not boil.

To serve, pat excess butter off each oyster before you place it in the shell. Arrange six oysters on each plate and ladle beurre blanc over and around the oysters. Serve immediately.

Pipis Isobel

uncooked pipis	*pepper and salt*
breadcrumbs	*black or Worcestershine sauce*
butter	*Tabasco or chilli sauce*
parsley	*oregano or marjoram*
garlic	

Drop the pipis in boiling water for a few seconds, drain, leave the shells open and pull out the slightly cooked clams. Place in small ramekins. On top, sprinkle some breadcrumbs. Blend together butter, chopped parsley, crushed garlic, pepper, a dash of black or Worcestershire sauce, a drop of Tabasco or chilli sauce, a few flakes of oregano or marjoram, and some salt. Place a blob of this mixture on top of the breadcrumbs. Put the ramekins under a very hot grill or an overhead oven for three or four minutes, or until the tops brown.

'An invention of mine named in honour of Isobel Davidson, who helped me dig for the pipis when Trish and I visited Crescent Head, New South Wales, which must be one of the greatest spots in the world.'

Prawn moska

1kg unpeeled king prawn tails
¼ cup olive oil
1 pinch oregano
1 pinch rosemary
1 pinch coarse black pepper

3 bay leaves
6 garlic cloves, chopped finely
1 pinch salt
¼ cup dry white wine

Serves 6

Heat the oil in a frying pan and add the prawns, oregano, rosemary, coarse black pepper, bay leaves, garlic and salt. Sauté 5 minutes, then add the white wine and cook another 2 minutes until wine is nearly reduced. Place the prawns on a serving dish and pour the aromatic sauce over.

Early judging days in 1964 at the Chevron, with Peter James, Dave Allen and Lorrae Desmond.

King prawns in garlic sauce

Alfred Lai, the proprietor of the Imperial Peking Harbourside in the Sydney Rocks area is an architect. This is reflected in the handsome decor of his large restaurant. He is also a highly determined young man, quite sure that he owns the best Chinese restaurant in Australia, yet quite determined to make it 'better and better'. He frets and worries and works like a demon to make it so. His food is admirable, especially the seafood. His banquets, when he has a chance to cater for many and when he is supported by the price the customer is prepared to pay, can be quite extraordinary.

10 green king prawns
1 teaspoon baking powder
¾ teaspoon salt
¼ teaspoon sugar
10 crushed garlic cloves

1 piece shredded ginger
1 stick shredded spring onion
few dashes Chinese wine

Serves 4

Remove the shells from the prawns, devein them and remove all pink skin. Rinse, drain and soak the prawns in water with one teaspoon of baking powder for 2 hours. Boil 5 cups of water, add salt and sugar, and cook the prawns for ½ minute. Remove, drain and place the prawns on a plate. Heat oil in a saucepan or wok, add garlic, ginger and shallot, then add prawns with dashes of Chinese wine. Serve.

School prawns and melon

2 rock melons
4 cups cooked school prawns, shelled
30g toasted shredded coconut
for the dressing:
1½ cups mayonnaise

½ cup tomato sauce
½ cup red wine vinegar
⅓ cup sweet pickle, finely chopped
salt and pepper

Serves 8

Cut the rind off each rock melon and slice four 8mm thick rings. Remove the seeds and place each ring on a plate. Divide the prawns into 8 portions and pack each portion into an ice cream scoop, gently squeeze to extract a little liquid. Place the mound of prawns on top of the melon.

Combine the mayonnaise, tomato sauce, vinegar and pickle in a small bowl and blend. Add salt and pepper. Spoon the dressing over each serving. Sprinkle toasted shredded coconut on top of each portion.

Fricassee of asparagus, prawns and chervil

Peter Doyle, (the *other* one, nothing to do with my fishy friend), is a totally dedicated cook, enthusiastic yet very serious, extremely attentive to the nuances of flavour, and very involved in wine and food marriages. With his wife Beverley he runs Reflections at Palm Beach.

24 green prawns	*for the sauce:*
48 thin green asparagus spears	*¼ onion, chopped*
3 eggs	*150ml white wine*
1 cup cream	*200g unsalted butter*
salt and pepper	*lemon juice to taste*
chervil sprigs	*salt and pepper*
1 tomato, peeled, seeded, diced	Serves 6

Cook asparagus in boiling salted water, keeping them *al dente*— firm and green. Refresh in cold water. Drain well and reserve 18 spears. Blend remaining 30 spears to a smooth purée, place in a fine strainer and leave to drip-drain for 1 hour. Return purée to blender and blend well with the eggs and cream. Season. Pour purée into six well-buttered moulds and cook in the oven in a bain-marie at 150°C/300°F for 1 hour or until set. Remove from oven, keep warm and leave to rest for 5 minutes.

To make the sauce put the chopped onion into a stainless steel saucepan, add white wine and reduce over a medium heat to 2 tablespoons. Whisk in the butter in pieces over a low heat and when well incorporated finish with lemon juice and season. Strain and keep warm (but not too hot).

Place the prawns, shelled and deveined, onto a buttered tray. Butter the prawns and grill them under a very high heat until just cooked.

Steam the reserved asparagus spears to heat through with the tomato pieces.

Unmould the asparagus flans onto the middle of each warmed plate and surround with the asparagus spears and prawns. Carefully moisten with the sauce, sprinkle with the tomato dice and chervil and serve immediately.

Creole Jambalaya

There are many variations of this. Having been exposed to the Wine and Food Society mentality at a fairly tender age, with the inherent pedantic assertions that a certain dish *must* contain this and *must* contain that, I firmly believe that *any* dish can be changed or adapted at the cook's whim or in relation to availabilities. Just as there are endless variations of the classic French cassoulet, so there are variations of jambalaya. In New Orleans the dish is often served with slices of ham and even pieces of chicken. I also had a 'hot' jambalaya, with red chillies very much in evidence. That fantastic jazzman, Louis Armstrong, once stayed at the Chevron Hilton when I was there and all he wanted was 'that old Creole cooking'. This was one of the dishes we prepared for him.

'That fantastic jazzman, Louis Armstrong, once stayed at the Chevron Hilton when I was there and all he wanted was "that old Creole cooking". This was one of the dishes we prepared him.'

60g spring onion
60g white onion
60g green capsicum
60g celery
1 clove garlic
75g butter
250g raw prawns, peeled and cleaned

24 oysters
250g tomatoes
1 cup water
1 bay leaf
½ teaspoon salt
¼ teaspoon cayenne
1½ cups rice
Serves 4

Finely chop the spring onion, white onion, capsicum, celery and garlic. Wash the rice. Melt the butter in a large saucepan. Add the onion, capsicum, celery and garlic and sauté till tender. Add the prawns and oysters and cook for 5 minutes. Then add the remaining ingredients except the rice and cook over a low heat for 10–15 minutes. Finally, add the rice, stir and cover tightly. Cook for 25–30 minutes over a low heat or until the rice is done.

Honey king prawns

500g green prawn meat
marinade of salt, sugar, pepper and peanut oil mixed together
½ cup flour
salt
1 beaten egg

⅓ cup honey
⅓ cup water
one fresh chilli, finely chopped
½ teaspoon chilli sauce
sesame seeds
Serves 4

Marinate the prawn meat for 1 to 1½ hours. Mix flour, egg and salt with enough water to make a light batter. To make a honey sauce bring the honey and water to the boil and stir in the chilli and chilli sauce. Coat the prawn meat in the batter and deep fry in hot oil until crisp. Re-heat the honey sauce in a wok, add the fried prawn meat and toss until the sauce is evenly coated over the prawns. Sprinkle with sesame seeds before serving.

Green prawns with rosemary

In the garden of Angela and Bob Raymond. The painter John Olsen is on my left.

1kg unpeeled green prawns
¼ cup olive oil
6 cloves garlic, crushed
6–8 stalks fresh rosemary
½ cup soft white wine

½ cup chopped parsley
dash Tabasco
salt
pepper
Serves 6

Heat oil in heavy frying pan. Cook garlic for ½ minute, then add prawns. Add rosemary and cook for 2–3 minutes until prawns are done. Add white wine, parsley, Tabasco, salt and pepper and serve as soon as everything is hot.

School prawns in sour cream with mushrooms

From the Stanford Court Hotel's Fournou's Ovens Restaurant.

250g school prawns, peeled and deveined and cooked
12 tablespoons sour cream
4 teaspoons horseradish
Cognac to taste

100g mushrooms, finely sliced and lightly cooked
chopped parsley
Serves 4

Toss the school prawns and sour cream together in a stainless steel bowl. Add the horseradish, a dash of Cognac and add the mushrooms. Serve in a fluted white ramekin dish underlined with lettuce leaf. Sprinkle with finely chopped parsley.

Prawns in Pernod sauce

1kg fresh green prawns, peeled
100g butter
2 tablespoons Pernod
¾ cup dry white wine
1 cup fish stock

20g finely chopped white of spring
   onion
¾ cup cream
salt and pepper
Serves 6–8

Use small school prawns if you can get them green. These are by far the best in Australian waters, the meat being much sweeter and more tender than the larger species. Sauté the prawns in some of the butter for a minute, flame with the Pernod, add the white wine and fish stock, and bring to near boiling. Remove the prawns and keep them warm. Add the chopped onion to the pan. Reduce the liquid over a fierce heat, add the cream and season. Add more butter, heat, pour over the prawns and serve.

Prawn and potato fritters

500g large potatoes
500g peeled prawns (preferably
   uncooked)
2 eggs
2 onions
parsley

chives
salt and pepper
Tabasco or chilli powder
oil
butter
Serves 4

Peel large potatoes and boil them for 6–8 minutes. Cool and grate. Mix with finely chopped prawns, eggs, finely chopped onion, parsley and chives, plus salt and pepper and a touch of Tabasco or chilli powder. Heat oil and a touch of butter in a large skillet or heavy pan and fry the mix until golden brown on both sides. Serve with salad or a slice of bread and butter.

Prawns Rothbury

'Another of the standards of Rothbury flambé cooking. There are many variations on this theme. The secret? The prawns must be fresh and uncooked, and must be cooked quickly, since it's necessary only to heat them through.'

1kg green prawns, peeled and
   deveined
90g butter
1 large onion
1 celery stalk
1 capsicum or ½ green, ½ red
garlic

lemon peel
salt and pepper
parsley
basil
chives
60ml brandy
Serves 4–6

Foam butter in a pan. Add finely sliced onion, celery and capsicum, crushed garlic, lemon peel, salt and pepper; cook for a couple of minutes only until vegetables are translucent and *not* browning. Add plenty of parsley, basil and chives. Add the green prawns, flame with brandy and serve.

Dartois of fresh king prawns

First tasted at the Yellow Book, a restaurant of superb ambience run by Graham Gibson and David Rice. The chef at the time was Rolf Widmer, who now runs his own place.

1kg green king prawns
2 cups cream
4–5 eggs
fresh ginger
salt and pepper
fish soy
dill
500g unsalted butter
4 cups flour
1 tablespoon sugar
1 teaspoon salt
1¼ cups water
2 tablespoons brandy
2 cups cream
2 cups champagne vinegar
1 egg
Serves 6

To make the filling, peel prawns, keeping the shells. Put flesh into the food processer, add cream and eggs and blend until fluffy. Add grated ginger, fish soy, salt, pepper, and dill to taste.

For the puff pastry cut butter into cubes, add flour, sugar, salt and mix together lightly with wooden spoon. Add water. Roll out in a rough square (there will still be lumps of butter visible) on a cool, floured surface. Pick up each corner and fold back towards centre. Repeat rolling out and folding process 3 more times. Refrigerate for 15–20 minutes.

To make the sauce heat a heavy pan containing a touch of olive oil. When really hot add prawn shells. Flambé with brandy and cook until brown. Add cream and vinegar and boil for 30 minutes. Strain through a sieve.

To assemble, roll out puff pastry. Cut 12 crescent shapes; place 6 on a lightly buttered tray. Pipe the prawn mixture on the crescents to within 5mm of the edge. Top with remaining crescents, brush with egg wash and press edges together with a fork. Bake at 240°C/425°F for 15 minutes.

To serve place each crescent on a plate with a small amount of sauce. Garnish with watercress.

Potted prawns

500g cooked school prawns
90g unsalted butter
¼ teaspoon each of mace, nutmeg,
  cayenne
clarified butter to seal
Serves 4

Shell the prawns. Melt the butter; add the mace, nutmeg and cayenne. Stir in the prawns and coat them in butter. Pack into a pot and when cooled seal with a little clarified butter. Refrigerate. Turn out on to a lettuce leaf and serve with thin slices of brown bread and butter. Garnish with lemon wedges.

Prawn and scallop mousseline

From Carolyn Divjak, chef of the Tasting Room.

for the mousseline:
500g fresh green prawns
250g scallops
1 egg
1½ egg whites
1½ cups cream
salt, pepper
for the bisque base:
1 carrot
1 onion
prawn heads and shells
oil

75ml brandy
1 cup white wine
75ml port
3 tomatoes
1 tablespoon tomato paste
600ml cream
parsley and thyme
for the vin blanc sauce:
1½ cups dry white wine
250g unsalted butter
300g prawn bisque base
Serves 8

First prepare the bisque base. Peel and finely dice carrot and onion. Peel prawns and reserve for mousseline. Wash out prawn heads under running water. Heat two tablespoons of oil in a large saucepan. Add heads and shells and colour slightly. In another saucepan, heat two tablespoons of oil and sweat off vegetables. Combine vegetables with prawn heads and shells. Add the brandy, white wine and port and reduce by one third. Add the roughly chopped tomatoes, tomato paste, cream and herbs. Simmer gently for about 1½ hours. Add a little more cream if necessary. Blend and then pass through a strainer or Mouli.

To make the vin blanc sauce, reduce wine to ⅔ of a cup. Using a Bamix preferably, or a whisk, mix in the butter, small pieces at a time until all is incorporated over a low heat. Whisk 300g prawn bisque base into the vin blanc sauce. Strain through muslin.

For the mousseline, peel and devein the prawns and remove the coral from the scallops. Blend together in a food processor and add the egg, egg whites, salt and pepper and re-blend. Transfer to a bowl and gradually whisk in 1½ cups of cream. Pass the finished mousseline mixture through a fine strainer or Mouli and refrigerate. When the mousseline has set, fill 8 pots with the mixture and cook in a bain-marie for about 20 minutes at 200°C/400°F.

When turning out, place a cloth over the pot and invert, draining off any excess liquid. Quickly slide onto a plate and surround with bisque sauce. Garnish with coriander or watercress.

With the Brand family and Gino Merlo (right) at Coonawarra in 1977. Nancy Brand's father, Bill Redman (centre right), did his first vintage in Coonawarra in 1902.

Scallops with leek purée

16 plump fresh scallops
250g leeks
½ cup reduced fish stock
⅓ cup white wine
salt

pepper
½ cup cream
25g butter
Serves 4

Chop up the leeks finely, making sure all dirt has been washed out from between the layers. Heat the leeks in a pan with the fish stock, white wine, salt and pepper until soft. Blend into a smooth paste in a blender. Return the leak paste to the pan, add the cream and heat a smooth purée. Spread a layer of purée on entrée plates. Quickly toss the scallops into foaming butter and cook for one minute; drain and place in the middle of the purée. Grind black pepper on top.

Prawn and scallop mousseline in pastry

This is a very successful variant of a recipe I first tried at the Yellow Book. The chef used a shorter pastry cover. The filo works better, I think. Serve with one of the classic seafood sauces, or with Hoi Sin, the Chinese sauce, to give the dish an altogether different character. This dish is very popular in the Tasting Room. Once I served it to the Wine and Food Society of New South Wales. Later, it was voted entrée of the year.

'This dish is very popular in the Tasting Room. Once I served it to the Wine and Food Society of New South Wales. Later, it was voted entrée of the year.'

500g green prawns, peeled weight
500g fresh scallops
1¼ cups cream

2 egg whites
1 packet filo pastry
200g melted butter

Combine prawns, scallops, cream and egg whites in a blender for seconds only. The resultant paste must be quite firm. Butter a sheet of filo pastry, fold over twice put a spoonful of paste near the fold, wrap the sides and roll into portions about 2.5cm thick and 7.5cm long. Cook for about 15 minutes in a high oven. Serve with any seafood sauce (I use nantua).

Moulded smoked salmon with tomato coulis

325g smoked salmon
6 teaspoons lumpfish 'caviar' or
  salmon roe
pinch cayenne
½ cup cream

4 large tomatoes
salt and pepper
chilli
Serves 4

Line the moulds with salmon and trim off the excess: purée this in a food processor. Combine puréed salmon, caviar and cayenne. Beat cream until soft peaks form and fold into purée. Divide the mixture between the moulds and chill for 1 hour. Skin, seed and chop the tomatoes. Purée in blender and pass through a sieve. Season with salt and pepper and chilli. To serve, unmould and serve decorated with chives and tomato coulis.

Scallops with snow peas

A delicious dish, easy to prepare and very easy to cook. If you're not adept at holding food to one side of the pan, remove to a warm dish for the little time needed. Do *not* overcook.

250g scallops	2 teaspoons cornflour
2 leeks	¼ cup water
125g snow peas	1 teaspoon light soy sauce
2 tablespoons peanut oil	½ teaspoon salt
½ teaspoon finely grated fresh ginger	Serves 2–3

Wash the scallops and dry well. Wash the leeks thoroughly to get rid of all sand and grit. Cut the white part of the leeks into thin diagonal slices. Remove the strings from the snow peas. Heat the oil in a wok or frying pan and fry the leeks and ginger for 2 minutes over medium heat. Add the scallops and fry on high heat, stirring, for ½ minute. Add snow peas and toss with other ingredients for just ½ minute longer. Push to side of pan, add cornflour, mixed with water and soy sauce, and stir until thickened, about 1 minute. Stir in scallops and vegetables, sprinkle with salt and serve immediately.

Scallop sticks

This makes an acceptable entrée, but we use it as a barbecue special when entertaining lots of people and serving various things. The joy is that the skewers can be prepared beforehand, leaving time for your guests.

500g fresh scallops	chopped marjoram
250g bacon, cut very thin	cayenne
60g butter	

Gently fry the bacon, cool and cut into 3cm squares. Impale on wooden skewers, alternating scallops and bacon pieces. Sprinkle with marjoram and dust lightly with cayenne. Grill quickly, basting with melted butter.

'A recipe from the accomplished young chef, Greg Doyle. I've watched his career carefully through the few restaurants at which he worked prior to his establishment of Puligny's in Neutral Bay, Sydney.'

Scallop mousseline with coral and champagne sauce

400g scallops (retain roe)	for the sauce:
2 egg whites	2 cups champagne
1 egg	½ cup vinegar
salt and pepper	½ onion finely chopped
300ml cream	250g butter
	Serves 4–6

To make the sauce, reduce the champagne, vinegar and onion by two-thirds. Poach the roes in this mixture. When cold, purée, and add to the beaten butter. Heat gently to serve.

Purée the scallops in a blender with seasoning until fine. Add the egg and egg whites and purée once again. Fold in the cream, place in buttered moulds and cook in a bain-marie in the oven at 200°C/400°F for 20–30 minutes.

To serve, tip each mousse out onto a plate and serve the sauce on the side. Garnish with a yabbie or a piece of chive.

Quenelles of scallops

500g scallops   *can of lobster bisque*
1 egg white   *pepper*
¾ cup cream   *Tabasco*

Remove the coral from the scallops and set aside. Blend the scallop whites, egg white and most of the cream into a thick, stodgy paste. Blend the lobster bisque and coral into a thickish sauce; heat it, add a touch of cream, pepper, and a drop of Tabasco.

Using a hot spoon, place little moulded rounds of the scallop paste into a pan of salted boiling water. When the spoon-shaped chunks hit the water, they set and then take about five minutes to cook through. Serve two or three on a hot entrée plate and smother with the sauce.

Plugging Rothbury wines in London. Myself, Michael and Daphne Broadbent, Serena Sutcliffe MW, and David Peppercorn MW, two of the wine stars of the world.

Scampi with nantua sauce

16 fresh scampi   *125ml (1 glass) white wine*
60g butter   *pinch thyme*
30g finely chopped onions   *300ml cream*
30g finely chopped carrots   *pinch salt*
1 clove garlic, crushed   *pinch cayenne*
60ml brandy   Serves 8

To make the sauce, which can be made in advance and stored, devein the scampi. Then heat the butter in a saucepan until foaming, add the onions, carrots and garlic and simmer until nearly tender. Add the scampi, cook until they turn red, add the brandy, heat for a moment and flame, add the white wine, thyme, and season with salt and cayenne pepper. Heat, then simmer for five minutes. Remove and let cool.

Shell all the scampi, retaining the shells and liquid separately. Put the scampi tails to one side. In a large mortar, pound the shells until they become a paste. Alternatively, this may be done in a blender. Put this paste into the cooking liquid and heat. Add the cream and work well together. Then rub this sauce through a fine sieve.

To serve, reheat the nantua sauce, correct seasoning, add the shelled scampi tails and serve. Alternatively, you may wish to present the scampi in their shells, as shown on the cover. To do this you will require an *additional* 16 fresh scampi and 60g butter.

Prepare nantua sauce as shown, discarding the shelled scampi tails. Devein the extra scampi. In a pan, heat butter until foaming, add scampi and cook until the shells turn red and the skin is opaque. Add nantua sauce, heat, correct seasoning and serve.

———— ❦ ————

Coquilles St Jacques persillées

Very quick and very easy. Do not overcook the scallops.

20g butter
250g scallops
touch of crushed garlic
1 teaspoon chives and parsley, finely chopped

one tablespoon white wine or sherry
dash of cream
salt and pepper
Serves 2

Scampi with nantua sauce being sampled by Michael Parkinson. Recipe page 99.

Sauté scallops in hot butter for a minute. Remove the scallops from the pan and place in a bowl. Put the garlic, chives and parsley in the pan, then the wine and cream. Reduce the sauce on a slow heat for a few seconds. Add salt and pepper to taste. Return the scallops to the pan for a few seconds and serve.

———— ❦ ————

Marinated squid

From a luncheon party given by Bob and Barbie Sanders. Excellent as an appetiser, entrée or main luncheon dish with salad.

whole squid
1 clove garlic, crushed
½ cup olive oil

½ cup white vinegar
½ cup lemon juice
salt and pepper

Mix together the garlic, olive oil, vinegar, lemon juice and salt and pepper to taste. Clean and prepare the squid. Grill whole at a fairly high temperature for a couple of minutes only. Slice up and leave overnight in the marinade. Serve cold in the marinade.

———— ❦ ————

Squid with sprouts in tomato sauce

500g squid
dash olive oil
2 cloves crushed garlic
200g champignons, sliced in half

¾ cup tomato paste
100g fresh bean sprouts
salt and pepper
Serves 4

Heat the olive oil, and lightly sauté the garlic. Add the squid, cut into strips 5cm x 5mm, the tomato paste and the halved champignons. Season. When the dish is hot the squid is done. Stir in the bean sprouts and serve.

Frozen squid and canned vegetables make a highly acceptable 'caught-short' substitute.

Calamari ripieni

8 large squid
2 large cloves garlic
12–15 sprigs Italian parsley
2 slices white bread

½ cup olive oil
salt and freshly ground pepper
1½ cups dry white wine
Serves 4

Clean the squid without cutting the stomachs. Remove the tentacles from the bottom part of the heads and soak them, along with the stomachs, in cold salted water for 10–15 minutes. Be sure that nothing remains in the bottom of the stomachs. Chop the tentacles finely, together with the garlic and parsley, remove the crusts from the bread. Heat ¼ cup of the oil in a saucepan and, when it is warm, add the chopped ingredients and the bread. Sauté on a medium flame, mixing very well until the bread is completely incorporated with the other ingredients (about 12–15 minutes). Season with salt and pepper, then cool. Preheat the oven to 190°C/375°F.

Stuff the squid stomachs with the contents of the pan, but not too full or they will split. Fasten the open end of each with a toothpick, then place in a rectangular Pyrex baking dish 35cm x 20cm. Combine the wine and the remaining ¼ cup olive oil and pour over the calamari. Sprinkle with salt and pepper, then place in a preheated oven and cook for 25–35 minutes or until the squid can be pricked with a fork. Transfer the squid to a serving dish, and serve hot.

The finished scampi with nantua sauce. Recipe page 99.

Scrumptious squid

10 medium squid
350g abalone, when trimmed
250g mushrooms
150g chopped shallots
2 eggs
1½ cups cream
¼ grated nutmeg
salt and pepper

for the stock:
abalone trimmings
1 onion
2 garlic cloves
1 bay leaf
1 carrot
1 glass white wine
Serves 8

'A really good and innovative dish from chef Peter Szymanski, which I tried when he worked for Ned Manners at Glenella in Blackheath. Peter now has The Richmond in Richmond, New South Wales.'

Cut the tentacles off the squid; clean and skin. Put the tentacles aside. Trim the abalone, retaining the trimmings. Fry the mushrooms over high heat for 5 minutes to remove moisture. Purée abalone, tentacles, mushrooms and shallots in a food processor. Add the beaten eggs and 1 cup cream slowly with salt and pepper and grated nutmeg. Pass the mixture through a fine Mouli or sieve. Make a stock with the abalone trimmings by boiling the onion, garlic cloves, bay leaf, chopped carrot and white wine with water to cover.

Three quarters fill the squid tubes with the abalone purée. Wrap them in individual foil packets and bake in the oven, with a little water in the bottom of the dish, for 45 minutes at 120°C/250°C. To make the sauce, strain the stock, add remaining cream and reduce gently by half. To serve, slice squid and pour sauce over.

Squid with marjoram

500g squid
salt
freshly ground black pepper
lemon juice

marjoram, chopped or dried
3 garlic cloves, crushed
oil
Serves 4

Clean and bone the squid. Cut the tentacles into long pieces. Slice the tube into thin rings and then cut each ring so that it becomes a strip. Sprinkle the strips with salt, black pepper, lemon juice, marjoram (not too much) and crushed garlic. Heat the oil and pan fry the strips for seconds only.

———————❦———————

Yabbies in whisky

The yabby is a great local food item, and it's essential to buy them fresh or catch your own. There are many ways to cook them but whichever way, don't overdo.

12 yabbies
60g mushrooms
60g green tomatoes
¼ cup cream
2 egg yolks

60g butter
salt and fresh white peppercorns
1 tablespoon lemon juice
2 tablespoons Scotch whisky
Serves 2–3

Remove the heads from the yabbies and the meat from the tails, reserving the tail shells. Plunge the tail shells into boiling water for 1 minute or until they turn red. Finely slice mushrooms. Dice green tomato finely. Combine cream and egg yolks. Remove the yabby claws. Melt 30g butter in a pan and throw in the claws. Sauté until they turn to red, remove and take out the meat. Add the rest of the butter to the pan and add the uncooked yabby meat, seasoning with salt, pepper and a squeeze of lemon juice. Add the mushrooms and green tomato. Cook for 1 minute. Add the cooked meat from the yabby claws. Flambé with the whisky and remove from the heat. Allow to cool for 1 minute, then pour on the combined egg yolks and cream all at once and stir over a very low heat until thickened. Serve surrounded by the tails and accompanied separately by lemon wedges.

'The yabby is a great local food item, and it's essential to buy them fresh or catch your own. There are many ways to cook them but whichever way, don't overdo.'

———————❦———————

Yabbies with nantua sauce

24 fresh yabbies
60g butter
30g finely chopped onions
30g finely chopped carrots
1 clove garlic, crushed
¼ cup brandy

½ cup (one glass) white wine
pinch thyme
pinch salt
pinch cayenne
1¼ cups cream

Devein the yabbies. Heat the butter in a saucepan until foaming; add the onions, carrots and garlic and cook gently until nearly tender. Add the yabbies, cook until they turn red, then add the brandy, heat for a moment and flame, add the white wine, thyme, and season with salt and cayenne pepper. Heat, then simmer for five minutes. Remove, and let cool.

Now the hard work begins. Shell all the yabbies, keeping the shells and liquid separate. Put the tails to one side. In a large mortar pound the shells to a paste. This takes a fair bit of energy and patience. Keep at it. Put this paste into the cooking liquid and heat. Add the cream and work well together. Then rub this sauce through a fine sieve, re-heat, correct the seasoning, add the yabbies and serve.

If you don't want to go to all this trouble (you should, at least once, because there is a considerable glow of self-esteem when it comes off), there are some excellent packets of powdered soups from Norway which can be used with fish stock and cream added to make excellent sauces of this nature. (That's one of my professional secrets which is one no longer.)

With Jan Oxenbould and Trish at one of our Christmas revues. The Dreaded Oxenbould is on the left.

Fresh yabby entrée

Yabbies have become much better understood in Australia over the past few years. Regarded as a great delicacy overseas, here they were simply fun for the kids, caught by them with string and a bit of meat and then, more often than not, boiled. Maurice O'Shea, I'm told, had a little more style. He boiled his in a pail of Hunter white. Now yabbies are available commercially, both green and cooked. This is a simple way to prepare green (can be live) ones.

24 yabbies	*salt and pepper*
100g butter	*½ bottle white wine*
60g of chopped shallots or spring onions, some green included	*½ cup reduced fish stock*
pinch thyme	*Tabasco*
bay leaf	*parsley*

Devein the yabbies by taking the middle part of the three-part tail segment between thumb and forefinger and pulling gently. The intestine should come away easily. Foam some of the butter in a large pan and toss in the yabbies. Turn them until they redden. Add the shallots or spring onion, the thyme, the bay leaf crumbled into pieces, season with salt and pepper and add the wine. Let all this heat up for a few minutes, then remove the yabbies to a warm serving dish and keep warm. Add to the residue in the pan the rest of the butter, the reduced fish stock and a dash of Tabasco. Reduce to a smooth liquid, pour over the yabbies and serve.

'Should the yabbies be already cooked when they are obtained, they may be served this way.'

Cooked yabby entrée

24 cooked yabbies, shelled
½ bottle white wine
1¼ cups reduced fish stock
malt vinegar
30g finely chopped carrot
30g finely chopped onion

1 clove garlic, crushed
pinch thyme
pinch cayene papper
salt
½ cup fresh cream
Serves 4

Put all ingredients except the cream into a saucepan, bring to the boil and simmer for a minute or so. Remove the yabbies onto a warm serving dish and keep warm. Reduce the liquid by half, add the cream, pour over the yabbies and serve.

Jo Bugner, the former heavy weight champion, Lyn Redgrave, Peter Doyle, Dave Allen and myself after a hot day on the Harbour.

Marinated yabbies

Ideal for fresh yabbies gathered when visiting friends. When our family visited the Roberts at Mudgee we use to go on yabby expeditions, sometimes cooking them straight away and sometimes preparing them like this for the next day.

20 yabbies
1 tablespoon brown sugar
1¼ cups wine vinegar
¼ teaspoon dried fennel or several
    fronds of fresh fennel

6 peppercorns
shredded lettuce leaves
lemons or limes
Serves 4–6

Simmer yabbies and shell when cooked. Dissolve brown sugar in wine vinegar and add fennel and peppercorns. Bring to the boil, remove from heat and allow to cool to infuse the mixture. Pour over the yabbies. Cover and refrigerate for 24 hours. Drain the yabbies and serve on shredded lettuce leaves. Garnish with thinly sliced lemons or limes.

Ciuppino alla ligure

From Beppi Polese of Beppi's, one of Sydney's leading Italian restaurants.

1½kg mixed fish (rock fish, squid,
    whiting, fresh prawns, small
    mussels, small baby clams or
    pipis, 3 small crabs cut into pieces,
    1 small lobster cut into pieces,
    Tasmanian scallops)
8 cups water
2 stalks celery
2 carrots
1 bay leaf

salt and pepper
1 onion, finely chopped
3 cloves garlic
4 anchovy fillets, finely chopped
6 tablespoons olive oil
150ml dry white wine
6 slices stale bread
chopped parsley
Serves 6

Clean and wash the fish, then cut into pieces. Remove the heads, tails and bones and use them to make a stock with the water, celery, carrots, bay leaf, salt and pepper. Brown the onion, 2 cloves of garlic and the anchovies in a deep pan with the oil. Then add the wine, tarragon, squid and, 5 minutes later, the other fish. Stir in the stock. Boil the soup gently for 15 minutes. Taste for seasoning. Rub the slices of bread with the remaining garlic, sprinkle with a few drops of olive oil and toast lightly in the oven.

Put a slice of bread in each plate and pour the hot soup over it. Sprinkle a little chopped parsley over each plate of soup and then serve immediately.

Fish stew with saffron

One of my favourite dishes when fishing with my friends.

3–4kg fresh seafood
  cooked mud crab pieces, fish pieces, pipis in shell, mussels in shell, jewfish, pearl perch, green prawns, crayfish pieces, cooked blue swimmer crabs, squid, scallops, oysters, or whatever is available)
turmeric, to taste
saffron, to taste
4 potatoes
2 stalks celery
3 onions
6 tomatoes

6 cloves garlic, crushed
to make strong fish stock (3 litres):
2kg cheap fish
2kg fish heads and bones from the better fish, crayfish shells, prawn heads and tails
6 ripe tomatoes
4 onions
3 stalks celery
bay leaves
herbs
salt and pepper
water

'Line up seafood ingredients in order of cooking time. Use whatever ingredients are available from the catch or the fish markets. The blue swimmer crabs, squid, scallops and oysters are put in the bubbling soup for seconds only, and even the first lots take a few minutes only to heat the cook through.'

Prepare the fish stock in the normal way, combining the fish, fish heads and bones, crayfish shells, prawn heads and tails together with the tomatoes, onions, celery, bay leaves and herbs, salt and pepper and water. Skim and sieve.

Add turmeric and saffron to taste. Add chopped potatoes, celery, onions, skinned tomatoes and garlic. Cook until tender. Correct seasoning. The soup is ready.

Line up seafood ingredients in order of cooking time. Use whatever ingredients are available from the catch or the fish markets. The blue swimmer crabs, squid, scallops and oysters are put in the bubbling soup for seconds only, and even the first lots take a few minutes only to heat and cook through.

Serve with fresh crusty bread on two plates, one for the seafood pieces and the other for the soup.

Paella—an Australian version

John Olsen, the great Australian artist now living in South Australia, serves the best paella I've ever tasted, but he always avoids giving away his secrets by singing another song or drinking more wine or something.

1kg live crayfish	1 red capsicum, sliced
12 green prawns	2 large tomatoes, blanched, skinned,
300g garlic sausage	seeded and chopped
12 pipis, uncooked	1kg rice
12 mussels, uncooked	salt and pepper
olive oil	1 level teaspoon saffron
8 chicken drumsticks	300g squid tubes, cut in circles
100g bacon, diced	50g peas
1 large onion, diced	lemon slices
1 green capsicum, sliced	Serves 6–8
4 cloves garlic, chopped	

Cut the crayfish tail—with the shell on—into medallions, using a heavy chopper. Shell the prawns and devein them. Cook the sausage and slice it. Make sure the pipis are free of sand. Clean the mussels.

Into a paellera, the traditional iron cooking pan, or a heavy frying pan, heat plenty of olive oil. Brown the chicken drumsticks and cook nearly through; remove. Cook the crayfish medallions for 1–2 minutes; remove. Cook the bacon and add the onion, capsicums, garlic and tomatoes. Add the raw rice, salt, pepper and saffron. Pour in boiling water to cover. Bring to the boil. Correct the seasoning. Remove from the heat and let the dish stand for 10 minutes.

In the rice arrange the chicken, crayfish, prawns, pipis, mussels in their shells, sliced squid and sausage. Scatter the peas over. Put the pan, uncovered, in a preheated, moderately hot oven, or if you are doing it outside, put on a part of the barbecue or fire which will keep the rice cooking. Cook for 30–40 minutes until rice grains are *al dente*, i.e., just prior to becoming soft. Remove from the heat, cover with a large, clean tea towel and leave to stand for 10 minutes.

Place lemon slices around the pan and put in the middle of the table. Traditionally, paella should be eaten straight from the pan. Hygienic-minded Australians may prefer to be served individually.

Doyle's paella

Alice Doyle's paella is popular at Doyles, Watson's Bay. Our family and friends eat there often and we have platters of seafood—oysters, mussels in white wine sauce, stuffed prawns—and paella brought to the centre of the table for a first course of random selection. Afterwards, platters of fried fish and chips and lashings of their chilli jam sauce.

After the Doyles won yet another award for their fabulous location and honest, simple, fresh food, I received a letter from a woman complaining that the 'Payola' was greasy. So I sent Peter Doyle a copy asking why his payola was considered more greasy than anyone else's.

50g squid, cleaned and cut into rings
¼ cup Spanish olive oil
1 tomato, skinned, seeded and chopped
2 tablespoons tomato paste
½ brown onion, chopped
1 clove garlic, finely chopped
3 bay leaves
50g green prawns, shelled
1½kg green mud crab, cut in 3 pieces
200g white fish fillets, cut in pieces
50g mussels, cleaned

4 shallots, chopped
¼ cup water
¾ cup dry white wine
1 tablespoon chopped parsley
pinch thyme
½ teaspoon paprika
salt and freshly ground pepper
3 cups cooked rice
saffron
Serves 2

As a large squid can take a long time to cook, I suggest you boil it first for an hour. In a deep serving/cooking saucepan heat the oil, add the tomato, tomato paste, onion, garlic and 2 bay leaves, stir well and add the prawns, crab pieces, squid and fish. Wash the mussels, remove their beards, tap the shells hard and if they do not close discard. In separate pan, gently fry the shallots and garlic in a little olive oil and butter. Add the wine, water, parsley, thyme, a bay leaf, pepper and mussels. Cover the pan, bring to the boil and steam over a high heat for about 4 minutes, shaking the pan. The shells will open as the mussels cook. Combine both mixtures, adding paprika, salt and pepper and stir. Cook slowly for 10 minutes after the ingredients have come to the boil. Serve in the pot you cooked it in, with a dish of hot fluffy rice lightly dusted with paprika or saffron and finely chopped parsley.

With my good friend David McNicoll.

Seafood rolls

180g scallops
180g prawns, peeled
pork net (caul)
salt
½ teaspoon sesame oil

⅙ teaspoon pepper
4 tablespoons self-raising flour
    mixed with 15 tablespoons water
Serves 6

Clean and dry the scallops and prawns. Mix with salt, sesame oil and pepper. Cut pork net into 10cm squares and sprinkle some flour on top. Place one portion of the filling in the middle of pork net square and fold the pork net so that it encases the filling in the form of a roll. Coat each seafood roll with batter. Drop rolls into hot oil and deep fry for 7 minutes over medium heat until golden. Remove and drain. Serve.

With Tony Bilson and Robyn Roux.

Seafood casserole Côte d'Azur

185g mahimahi or jewfish
185g prawns, green
185g scallops
1 garlic clove
2 teaspoons arrowroot
½ cup chablis or other dry white
    wine
2 teaspoons Dijon mustard
1 tablespoon clarified butter

1 tablespoon olive oil
1 tablespoon lemon juice
2 tablespoons parsley
salt, black peppercorns
1 tablespoon cream
sprinkle of dill
sprinkle of cayenne
2 large servings

Slice the fish into slivers; cut the prawns into collops; cut the scallops into halves. Peel the garlic clove. Mix the arrowroot with a little white wine and mustard. Place the clarified butter and oil in a pan and add the fish, scallops and prawns. Sauté quickly, then cover, remove from the heat and leave for 5 minutes. Stir in the crushed garlic clove, chablis and lemon juice. Thicken with the arrowroot mixture. Add the parsley. Season. Add the cream. Sprinkle dill and cayenne over.

Seafood fondue

Clean a variety of local seafood and fish and prepare it in pieces. Present the seafood raw on a platter. Cook in a bubbling pot of hot oil at the table. Dip each piece into a choice of three sauces, using whatever sauces appeal to you.

A terrific idea from the Restaurant de Champenoise on the west coast of France. Lucien Fleury, the chef-proprietor, lets his customers get on with it, using the finest seafood ingredients available. The beauty of it is, they can never complain about the cooking.

Timbales des fruits de mer

Jean-Jacques Demoz, together with wife and partner Susan, runs Jean Jacques which won or shared first place for three consecutive years as the best seafood restaurant in Australia in the *Bulletin/Quelltaler* quest.

16 mussels, freshly opened
12 prawns, shelled, gutted and
   halved
12 scallops, cleaned and halved
   horizontally
4 ripe tomatoes
2 cloves garlic, chopped finely

½ teaspoon basil, chopped finely
¼ teaspoon oregano, chopped finely
¼ teaspoon thyme, chopped finely
salt and freshly ground pepper
olive oil
2 medium size zucchinis
Serves 4

Blanch, peel and seed the tomatoes; chop them finely. Add garlic, herbs and season to taste. Brush the insides of 4 dariole moulds with olive oil. With a vegetable peeler cut strips of zucchini about 4cm wide and 14cm long. Line the moulds with the zucchini, placing the strips lengthwise from the bottom to the top, leaving 4cm overhanging at the top. Overlap the strips. Place one and a half tablespoons of the tomato mixture in the bottom of each mould. Evenly disperse the seafood on top of the tomato mixture, until the moulds are full. Fold the zucchini strips over the filling and press down with your hand. Brush with olive oil. Bake at 190°C/375°F for 15–20 minutes.

Délices des fruits de mer

8 pancakes
3 cups cream
500g Alaskan crab
1 cup dry white wine
2 teaspoons shallots, finely chopped
2 teaspoons Worcestershire sauce
2 teaspoons Dijon mustard

4 tablespoons roux (60g butter and
   ⅓ cup plain flour)
salt, m.s.g., cayenne, to season
the juice of ¼ lemon
60g Parmesan cheese, grated
Serves 4–8

Make the pancakes. Whip ¾ cup of the cream. Preheat the oven to 180°C/350°F. Cut the crab into small pieces. Butter an ovenproof dish. Place the wine in a saucepan, add the shallots and reduce the liquid to half. Blend in the Worcestershire sauce and mustard. Add 2¼ cups of cream to the roux, salt and msg and bring to the boil. Add the lemon juice. Add a dash of cayenne. Taste to correct seasoning. Reserve half this sauce. Place the crab in half the sauce and bring to the boil.

Place the pancakes on the overproof dish and fill each with 2 tablespoons of the seafood mixture. Roll up the pancakes, making sure that the pancakes don't touch each other. To the sauce that you have reserved add the whipped cream. Pour the sauce over the pancakes and sprinkle with the Parmesan cheese. Place under the grill on a medium heat till golden. Accompany with asparagus and rice pilaf.

The two biggest bums in the business: myself with Michael Broadbent on his property near Bath. He is considered to be one of the finest palates and best wine writers in the world.

CHAPTER FIVE

Entrées: the Tasting Room

WHILE WORKING AS A GLASS WASHER at the Ship Inn at Sydney's Circular Quay during the late 1950s, I was aware that the Quay was not regarded as the most shining part of the city. It seemed to me then that the north end of the city really ended at Bridge Street, the southerly extent being Anthony Hordens Store in Liverpool Street. Over the intervening years there has been first a subtle, then a dramatic shift to the Quay end. I think I understood this would happen, for one of my earliest endeavours was an attempt to take over Ye Olde Crusty Cellar in George Street. In my time off I used to wander the area, wondering what could be done with some of the great old buildings that have now been torn down. I used to wander up Bulletin Place where there was still an old sandstone building arching one end, a right-of-way that remains. There was a wine merchant in the cellar of a grand if rather dilapidated old warehouse. I think his name was Ken Berger and he dealt in his own bottlings and bits and pieces. I can remember wanting to examine the premises but not doing so, because I had no money and was shy about taking up anybody's time.

My hesitance reminds me of the story of a villager to whom I talked some years ago when I was staying in a cottage in Surrey for a few days. 'How far away is Australia?' he asked. I told him. 'Oh I can't understand that,' he replied. 'It's outside my comprehension.' Changing the subject, he asked me where I had been locally. Fittleworth, I told him. 'Oh, that's a nice place,' he said. 'They've got shops and all that. I go there sometimes.' (Fittleworth was about six kilometres away.) 'Where else you going?' he asked. I told him we were going next day to Petworth, about 16 kilometres away, a country town of 4000 dominated by a magnificent mansion, Petworth House. His eyes shone. 'Petworth! You going to Petworth. Oh, that's a grand place. I went there once but I didn't go right in.'

So there I was in Bulletin Place, hovering but not going right in, looking at a building that would eventually mean so much to me.

After nearly five years at the Chevron Hilton, followed by another three years as Director of the Wine Bureau for Australia, by the end of 1967 I was looking for a job. I had written the book *Galloping Gourmets* with Graham Kerr after a gastronomical trip round the

An early tasting of great wines at Bulletin Place. Oliver Shaul and Tony Albert are to the left.

world, but I was uncertain of the future. So like many people in that situation, I set myself up as a consultant.

Harry Alce of Millers Brewery, who became boss of Tooth and Co., gave me a start, QANTAS decided to pay a small fee for what had been an honorary position as wine consultant, then both the Summit and Coachman restaurants wanted help, followed by Travelodge. I thought I was doing very well indeed, grossing $19,000 in my first independent year, which was almost three times my Wine Bureau salary and therefore justified the move.

In 1968 we started to talk of the commencement of Rothbury, and then one day I was accosted by Richard de Salis, who berated me for not being more ambitious. 'Why not set up as a wine merchant?' he said. 'I believe the wine and spirit licence of Ye Olde Crusty Cellar is available [coincidence!] and there's an old building in Bulletin Place which is available. The previous tenant has done a bunk.'

Enquiries revealed this was so, for the wine merchant I knew had vacated the premises, and the lease had gone to a gentleman who ran the nearby Old San Francisco Restaurant. But he had disappeared, the lease had lapsed and the landlord, Bill Rubenson, was quite firm about my right to move in if I could find the money. So much for those people who have claimed that I am intensely ambitious; they have never understood just how much, as was said to have occurred with the British Empire, that it's been a case of muddling through!

I had wine stocks in my cellar at home, some of it 20 cases of this and that, but I had little money. The bank helped, so did friends like Dr Ray Healey, and a loan from Lindemans allowed me to buy the licence from them. The renovation of Bulletin Place began.

It was in a terrible mess. There were few windows, and only a couple of the swing doors that are a feature of old warehouses. Floors needed replacing and strengthening, and the lower floors were full of old rubbish; altogether we carted away over 50 tonnes. But there were compensations. Peeling away over 20 coats of paint from the walls, we found old Scottish sandstock bricks. My builder told me they would fret; I insisted they be exposed. One day he arrived triumphant. 'I know the look you want, and I know how to get it for you. I'll render the wall and use this paper.' And he held up a sample of 'colonial-style' wallpaper featuring faithful copies of sandstocks. Fortunately, I had my way, and the bricks have never fretted. I sometimes think they are glad to have been exposed, to be part of all the 'goings-on'.

There was one scare along the way, when the cellar was almost completed and the framework for the housing of the stairs, which now acts as a bar on the floor above, was half-finished. I took the family to see what was happening and lowered them through this framework into the cellar. After a good look around I picked up my three-year-old son, Toby, and pushed him to the floor above, then turned to reach for Jodie, my daughter. Suddenly we heard the high whine of the exposed circular saw the builders were using on that floor. Visions of Toby cut to pieces. I seemed to rise vertically

My father and Ann Tyrrell outside Bulletin Place cellars, 1969.

through the opening, taking the skin off my shins. I bear the scars today. And there was Toby, fortunately backing away from the electrical switch he'd pressed to start the saw. I love my kids more than anything in the world, and I don't know what would have happened to our lives if Toby had been damaged.

Soon the cellar was completed, and Graham and Treena Kerr and Trish and I symbolically opened it on the day man first stood on the moon, on July 1969. But the floor upstairs remained a problem. It was an area for tasting, since consultancy was still the major part of my business. I had to have lavatories installed, and it seemed a good idea to have a little kitchen as well, for when I wanted to entertain. There were only three staff: Mary McDiarmid, Ann Tyrrell and myself, with Ann downstairs in the cellar.

We decided to use the first floor as a luncheon club as well as a tasting room. So, the Tasting Room was born, open to those people interested in wine who wanted to taste plenty of samples before they bought, fee $5 per year, and luncheon, all inclusive, for $5. For this the member received drinks before lunch, a main course followed by cheese, up to about seven wines on the table and as much as he or she could eat and drink. Needless to say, it was popular, and often we were booked out for weeks ahead.

Greg, an Englishman, was the first cook, and Margaret and Chrissie the first waitresses. I would select the wine, start proceedings with a bang of the gavel, give a talk on the food, wines and prices, and generally misbehave for the next two hours. Sometimes lunch went on all afternoon, once until after 7 pm, with nearly everyone

'Sometimes lunch went on all afternoon, once until after 7 pm, with nearly everyone staying. People sat at three huge tables, each with two three-seater pews to each side and chairs at the ends; hence 42 was our maximum seating.'

The beginning of the Tasting Room, 1969. Mary MacDiarmid, the first manager, is on the left.

staying. People sat at three huge tables, each with two three-seater pews to each side and chairs at the ends; hence 42 was our maximum seating.

At the beginning of each lunch, there was often shyness or restraint caused by groups having to sit together. But this soon disappeared with the passing around of the wine and food, and the discussions that followed. At times the atmosphere became very informal. On one occasion, two Taswegians were brought along by a member. They wanted to know what it was all about, and I explained that there was only one main course, and therefore no choice. 'What's on today?' asked one. I told him and he appeared satisfied. They sat down next to two charming girls, one of whom was a member. The lunch went on, they had a great time, the host eventually departed, and his two friends were left with the girls. Later on still, I saw them walking out, hand in hand.

One of the Taswegians rang the next day. 'Hey, that was one of the greatest days of my life. The food was great, the wines were great and the girls! We went out for a drink and then dinner and then dancing and then they took us back to their place. They cook a great breakfast ... What's on today?'

The mid-1970s recession hit us. People no longer had time for three-hour lunches; the heady days of the mining boom were over and most people were working harder. So the tables were cut in half before being finally replaced by other tables more suitable for business use. Today the only remnant of the old days is my table, which is half of one of the originals, and a solitary pew that provides seating at one side.

But we did have some funny moments. On the occasion of the 1000th lunch, I proposed a Russian toast, demonstrating how the glass should be smashed after the toast. A jeroboam of Pol Roger was poured and the glasses handed around. Fifty gasses hitting the deck at the same time makes an impressive noise, and the guests were

'As Anders decanted the 1727 Rudesheimer Apostelwein, there was an expectant hush around the room. The hush deepened to silence after the fearful crash in his corner. Everyone stared agonisingly at him. He looked up, paused and then said, "I say, shall I decant the 1728?"'

The menu for the original Single Bottle Club dinner held in 1977. Special glasses were blown for the 1727, which opened splendidly!

An irreverent comment on one of our dinners.

elated, many doing something for the first time that they'd always wanted to do. The mood was flattened slightly when my friend Tony Albert leaned over and said, 'I didn't know you had so many chipped glasses.'

Both the Tasting Room and the Beef Room, which was on the floor above, were always available for functions, but I think some of the best dinners were those we put on ourselves. At three successive dinners, for example, we enjoyed 27 different vintages of Château Latour. There were Lafite, Haut-Brion and Margaux dinners, and we tasted all the great vintages of Max Schubert's celebrated baby at the Grange dinner. Indeed, on the following day I announced, 'Today we are tasting all the great Granges (pause—cheers and gasps of delight) in the gravy.'

The dinners culminated in the 1977 epic, the menu of which is reproduced on page 116. It was in honour of Michael Broadbent of Christies Wine Department, who possesses an impeccable palate and who followed André Simon as the President of the International Wine and Food Society. This dinner, attended by the then Prime Minister Malcolm Fraser, is now recognised as the first dinner of the Single Bottle Club, perhaps the most indulgent of all small wine and food clubs. The 1977 dinner was not without its moments.

Anders Ousback, who started his career at Bulletin Place, was good enough to act as chief butler for the night. As he decanted the 1727 Rudesheimer Apostelwein, there was an expectant hush around the room. The hush deepened to silence after the fearful crash in his corner. Everyone stared agonisingly at Anders. He looked up, paused and then said, 'I say, shall I decant the 1728?' Anders, maladroit as ever, had dropped an empty bottle to the floor but just couldn't resist the moment.

Brioche filled with bone marrow and topped with meat glaze (recipe page 123).

The New South Wales Tasting team, which was beaten by the cunning Victorians in the mid-1970s. Wantirna South will never be forgotten! At the front, Neville Baker, myself, Tony Albert, and behind, John Beeston and James Halliday.

Another major feature of the Tasting Room was the Options Game, which had been invented, in rough form, during a tasting at Greenwich, in the mid-1960s. The Options Game, which has now become highly sophisticated, was played on Mondays when the few members of it were in town. But it can be played at any lunch or dinner party.

Each person brings a masked bottle, which is decanted out of sight. The decanters, each bearing the initials of the donor, are brought to the table, mixed up and then put in some order. Each donor in turn asks five questions of their own wine. When we started we would ask questions of this nature: 'Is this local or imported?' 'Is it Burgundy or Bordeaux?'

Now we've all realised every question is precious, so this could be a typical game: 'Is this Côte des Nuits or Côte de Beaune?' recognising that every member would know it was a French Burgundy. They answer in turn; it is revealed to be a Nuits. Those who answered Beaune put 20 cents in the middle, everyone starting with exactly four dollars of 20 cent pieces. Next question: 'Is it a Tête de Cuvee, a Premier Growth or a Commune wine?' Answer: a Tête, those answering incorrectly again putting 20 cents in the middle. Three questions are asked and answered in turn: 'Is it from Vosne Romanee, Chambolle Musigny or Gevrey Cambertin?' Answer: Vosne Romanee. 'Is it Richebourg, la Tache, or Romanee St Vivant?' Answer: Richebourg. Finally, 'Is it 1962, 66 or 69?' Answer: 1966.

Each wrong answer costs players 20 cents. In this way they can lose from nothing up to a dollar on each wine. However, the money isn't important, for the score is the thing. At the end of the day, usually tasting great wines, each player's losses are counted up: 13 mistakes, 11 mistakes, 9, 9, 10, may be a typical result of tasting six wines. (People obviously do not score with their own wine.) The winner is congratulated, the loser buys champagne and the scores are entered into a leather-bound book. Every ten meetings count as a sort of Vardon trophy. In golf, a Vardon trophy, named after British golfer Harry Vardon, is awarded for a series of rounds rather than for one tournament. So far there have been 35 such series, and I have a slight lead on the other players. However, the tightness of the scoring is such that over 15 years, of the original players I've made 4007 mistakes, James Halliday 4062, Tony Albert 4119, and John Beeston 4186. Just 181 mistakes cover the range of errors, representing only 2 per cent of all questions asked.

The game has spread and is now played all over Australia and in some parts of the United States. There have been Options championships and the originals still have a trophy for winning in 1979.

In 1976 I had a mild heart scare. One of my arteries was diseased and blocked (and still is) and I was put into hospital. During that time my great friend Peter Fox lent some money to the business, which was suffering one of its periodic cash flow crises, on three conditions:

there was to be no security, no interest fee and I wasn't to know about it. Unusual terms, to say the least. I finally found out about it some six months later, and since by then Peter had become a fixture, I offered him 49 per cent of Bulletin Place. This evolved into the Evans Wine Company, with two châteaux in Bordeaux and a vineyard in the Napa Valley in California. Peter was killed in a car crash in December 1981, and we still miss him. The Evans Wine Co. was dissolved, but Peter's widow, Jenny, still retains her shares and interest in Bulletin Place.

The food of the Tasting Room has always been good, and sometimes it's been outstanding. Greg served traditional English fare of very high quality. John Ewen then took over after a stint at the Paternoster, and his cooking really developed. When John left, he was replaced with Carolyn Divjac, who had joined John straight from the Ryde Food School. Carolyn, in turn, has developed marvellously and I believe she is now quite outstanding in her work. During her time in office she helped to train Alex Roser, who came to Bulletin Place as an apprentice and qualified with distinction. He is now working for Anders Ousback in the latter's restaurant and catering business.

Goose liver salad (recipe page 131).

It's always gratifying to see Bulletin Placers do so well. Over the years some remarkable people have worked in the place: Ann Tyrrell, who went on to run the marketing of Tisdall's; John Hennessey, New South Wales Manager for Bailey's; John Raven, now with Lindemans; Anders Ousback; Alex Roser; Chris Shannon who has a restaurant in Queensland; Michael McMahon who is now part-owner of two restaurants with his wife Judy, who also started at Bulletin Place; Peter Morse and Michael Bright, who are both wine consultants; plus others no less worthy. I must say I am very proud of my 'kids', many of whom now know so much more than I do about various aspects of our industry.

Bobby Paterson, a teacher who just wanted a break from her job, began as a waitress, then became a leading hand, then took charge of the food. She went on to become general manager and eventually managing director before leaving to get married. Since Bobby left in 1980, Sally Cleaver, who began as my secretary before becoming Bobby's assistant, has been in charge. Sally, who is totally loyal to me and the business, will take even greater responsibility as I tend to stay away from headquarters more and more, looking after my interests at Rothbury and Petaluma and living on my farm in the Hunter.

I sold out a majority interest in the wine shop part of Bulletin Place in 1984. I no longer had the time and enthusiasm or could spare the money to develop it. The wine shop received those qualities in good measure from Chris Hayes, who has a good palate and who is in business with the McMahons and also at Terrigal.

Thus pass 16 years and maybe more of a man's life.

I love those great old restaurants overseas, which have been there for years and have developed so much style and character. I also

Sweet revenge. The triumphant New South Wales Tasting Team of 1979. Left to right: John Beeston, Peter Fox, self, James Halliday and Tony Albert.

adore great restorations: old mills, châteaux and mansions that are made into comfortable places with great charm and atmosphere. I don't have that feeling about my place when I'm there more or less constantly, but when I return from an absence I am sharply reminded that 16–18 Bulletin Place, and particularly the Tasting Room, has become an institution in its own right. It's never made much money, it has had its ups and downs, yet it has provided great enjoyment for thousands of people, and for me, a hell of a lot of fun.

The Bulletin Place style, today, stresses simplicity and the highest quality ingredients. There are only one or two main courses offered, plus cheeses and a sweet selection from a trolley, but three or four entrées are always available. Among these are some of the most interesting dishes I've enjoyed over the past few years, and many are included among the following recipes.

Blinis with smoked trout

4 cups plain flour
30g yeast
2½ cups milk
1 cup flour

1 cup milk
salt
white pepper
6 eggs, separated

Make a thin batter of 4 cups of flour, yeast and 2½ cups of milk and leave in warm area for an hour or so. Then add the yolks, then the remaining ingredients except the egg whites. Add the egg whites last, well whisked, and let stand for another hour. Spoon the mixture onto a hot griddle wiped with oil and make little savoury cakes about 6cm across, cooking each side until brown. Top with fillets of smoked trout or eel, cut diagonally into thin slices, cream and horse-radish sauce. Mix a little cream and horseradish together. When the blinis are taken, piping hot, off the griddle, coat one side thinly with the creamed horseradish and then pieces of smoked trout or eel.

'Hermann Schneider served something of this nature at an outstanding dinner he gave for the Single Bottle Club. The secret is to serve them at once, the contrast in texture, temperature and taste being outstanding.'

Brioche filled with bone marrow and topped with meat glaze

I first came across this dish at Tony's Bon Gout, run in the old days by Tony and Gay Bilson. It was a great place and the enthusiasm of those two was contagious. Gay used to make fabulous brioche pastry, but I don't think you really should bother. There are some excellent pastry shops around now.

1 brioche per person
3 pieces of bone marrow per person

½ cup thoroughly reduced meat
* glaze per person*

Heat the glaze, poach the marrows in it until done, and pour the marrows into the hot brioche and surround with glaze. Perfectly simple and absolutely delicious.

Brains in black pepper butter

500g brains (calves, lambs, sheep)
60g butter
1 chopped onion
1 chopped carrot
chopped celery
1 cup white wine

1 cup veal stock
100g clarified butter
lemon juice
salt
black pepper
Serves 3–4

Heat the butter for poaching liquid in a pan, add chopped vegetables and sauté. Add white wine and veal stock and bring to the boil. Skin the brains, soak until clean, and poach in the liquid gently for an hour. Remove and slice into pieces 1cm thick. Heat the clarified butter until it achieves a rich colour. Add the sliced brains, a squeeze of lemon juice, salt and plenty of freshly ground black pepper.

Calves liver with herbs and onions

This is for those people with a herb garden or access to one.

600g calves liver	*sprig rosemary (stalk removed)*
500g onions	*chopped chervil*
oil	*chopped chives*
chopped parsley	*60g butter*
chopped basil	*salt*
chopped oregano	*black pepper*
chopped marjoram	Serves 4

Fry the sliced onions in oil until browned and well done. Set aside. Gather all the green herbs, wash them and chop coarsely together. Slice the liver thinly. Sauté one side in the heated butter, heap the other side with the chopped herbs, turn and cook the second side. Smother with onions and serve with mashed potatoes.

Stuffed cabbage Vinding-Diers

'*This was served fairly often at Château Rahoul as the main course at lunch when we were picking. Frankly, I used to enjoy this kind of food, especially when really hungry, more than the rather elaborate meals of the evening.*'

1 large green cabbage, preferably Savoy cabbage	*2 sets sheep's brains, skinned and chopped*
3 cups stock	*2 tablespoons oil*
1 bottle white wine	*1½ cups cooked rice*
2 chopped carrots	*5 cloves garlic, peeled and crushed*
2 chopped onions	*2 teaspoons fine herb mix*
10 spring onions, sliced	*2 eggs beaten*
for the stuffing:	*salt and pepper to taste*
1kg pork and veal mince	

Trim any tired outer leaves and hard bottom stalk from cabbage. Bring stock to the boil in a large saucepan and drop in the cabbage. Boil for a few minutes, remove and run under cold water straight away. This retains the colour and makes the leaves manageable. When cool enough to handle, cut out the heart and separate the leaves.

Prepare the stuffing by lightly frying the pork and veal mince and chopped brains in hot oil. Add rice, garlic, herbs and beaten eggs. The mixture should be malleable but not too wet. Season with salt and pepper. Spread a layer of the stuffing inside the cabbage, then a layer of inside leaves. More stuffing and more leaves until all the stuffing is used. The whole should resemble a slightly opened flower lined with layers of stuffing. The form is retained by the cabbage being tied with string.

Add wine, chopped carrots and onions to the stock in the pot, bring to the boil, add stuffed cabbage and cover with a lid. Simmer gently for 3–4 hours. The cabbage must be basted frequently. Other vegetables may be added to the pan towards the end of cooking to be served with the dish.

Platter poulet avec Grand Marnier pâté

A recipe from Katherine Bunton, who was then a student at East Sydney Technical College. The recipes were devised for a Pernod and Grand Marnier promotion and had to use either. The ingenuity shown is typical of the catering revolution among young professionals in Australia.

100g can peaches
120g raw chicken livers
2½ tablespoons Grand Marnier
2 eggs
1 teaspoon mixed herbs
¼ teaspoon black pepper
10 slices wholegrain bread
1.5kg chicken
cooking oil for basting

for the sauce:
3 tablespoons sugar
3 tablespoons white wine vinegar
2 cups chicken stock
2 tablespoons cornflour
2 tablespoons Grand Marnier
1 tablespoons Grand Marnier extra
Serves 4–5

With my great friend Peter Fox at a Bulletin Place function.

Place peaches, livers, Grand Marnier, eggs, herbs, pepper and bread in a food processor and blend well, making a moist mixture. Cover.

To prepare the chicken, place it on it's breast and cut along the backbone using poultry shears or scissors. Open the chicken with the breast side up. Firmly strike the chicken on the breast to break the bone structure. Free the chicken skin from the flesh by placing your fingers between the skin and flesh at the neck and working them towards the other end. Sew up any tears. Beginning at the neck, work the stuffing into the chicken between its flesh and skin, settling it into the natural shape of the chicken. When this is completed pull the neck flap over the opening and tuck it underneath. Make a small slit in a flap of skin and pass the drumstick end through this to keep it from moving—otherwise it will tend to spread outwards during cooking. Rub a little oil into the chicken skin, place in a roasting pan with a small amount of water and a little oil, and place in a preheated oven of 200°C/400°F for 10 minutes. Reduce temperature to 180°C/350°F for another 60 minutes or until cooked. During cooking, baste every 20 minutes.

While the chicken is cooking prepare the sauce. Place sugar and wine vinegar in a saucepan over a low heat until the sugar has dissolved. Then bring to the boil until the mixture turns golden brown in colour. Add the stock followed by cornflour blended in 2 tablespoons of Grand Marnier. Boil the mixture until the sauce thickens and the cornflour is cooked.

When the chicken is cooked, remove from oven, place on a plate and allow it to stand for 10–15 minutes before carving.

To complete the sauce, remove as much fat as possible from the roasting dish, add the sauce to the dish, heat and then add 1 tablespoon of Grand Marnier. Arrange the chicken on a serving plate and put the sauce in a sauce boat.

Carpaccia

I first encountered this classic at D'Arcy's in Paddington, owned and run by Aldo Zuzza.

fillet steak   *ground black pepper*
olive oil   *lemon*
salt (mineral salt is best)

Slice fillet steak extremely thinly—as fine as possible. Lay out on an entrée plate. Sprinkle on drops of good olive oil, such as Olio Sassa, salt, and plenty of ground black pepper. Add a squeeze of lemon and serve.

———————————————

The opening of Bulletin Place in 1969. Daughter Sally pours in the grapes.

Sautéed duck livers with blackcurrants

Michael McMahon has caused me many headaches in the past. He worked for me for five years. Then, just as he was becoming knowledgeable and worthwhile, he left to run his own business. Such is fate. Michael and his wife, Judy, (who also started at Bulletin Place and met Michael there) and chef Neil Perry share the lease of Barrenjoey House Restaurant at Palm Beach, to the north of Sydney. They've made a success of it, which is a tribute to their hard work and dedication. One of the great delights is to take the little seaplane from Rose Bay to Palm Beach in the evening, wander to Barrenjoey, have a glass of champagne or two, then dinner, then have a hire-car drive you back. I did this with a party of four once and had a marvellous and reasonably priced evening for such a treat. This is one of their great dishes.

6 perfect duck livers   *1 cup demi-glaze*
50g blackcurrants, fresh or thawed   *1 tablespoon butter*
2 tablespoons sherry vinegar   *pepper*
sprinkling of sugar   Serves 2

Clean the livers and remove fat, veins and sinews. Pat dry with kitchen paper. In a heavy pan heat 1 tablespoon oil until just smoking. Place livers in, presentation side down. Cook for one minute. The outside must be crisp and very well sealed. Turn livers and cook for a further 1½ minutes, then remove and rest, while making the sauce. (The livers can be cooked longer if you prefer them slightly more on the well-done side, and also, slight variations of cooking times will occur, according to the size of the livers. Never be afraid to trust your own judgement.)

De-glaze the pan with vinegar and sugar. As it caramelises, add demi-glaze and reduce by half. Add blackcurrants. Reduce for a further 30 seconds. Remove from the heat and add butter. Throw in livers, and toss around in the pan, completely coating in sauce. Add pepper, and taste for further seasoning. Then place livers on warm plates. Spoon sauce over and serve immediately with a glass of good aged Sauternes.

———————— ❦ ————————

Terrine of fresh duck liver pâté with pistachio

2 slices white bread, crumbed
¼ cup milk
500g thinly sliced pork fatback to line the terrine
500g duck livers
500g pork fatback
500g lean pork shoulder
½–1 teaspoon salt (or to taste)
½ teaspoon cinnamon
½ teaspoon ground allspice
¼ teaspoon nutmeg

⅛ teaspoon ground cloves
¼ teaspoon ground cardamon
½–1 tablespoons flour
½ teaspoon white pepper
4 tablespoons brandy
4 tablespoons pistachios
1 tablespoon black truffle, finely minced (optional)
6 bay leaves
2 teaspoons dried thyme
Serves 8

Preheat the oven to 190°C/375°F. Line a terrine or standard loaf tin with the sliced pork fatback so the bottom and sides are completely covered with one layer and there is enough fatback overhanging the top to cover the top when filled with the forcemeat. There should be several extra pieces to place over the top to cover the bay leaves and thyme which are on top of the fatback covering. Put the bread crumbs in a small bowl and cover with the milk to soak.

Finely grind the duck livers, 500g pork fatback and pork shoulder together twice. Combine the livers, fatback, pork shoulder, salt, cinnamon, allspice, nutmeg, cloves, cardamom, flour, pepper and brandy in a bowl or food processor. Beat or process until the mixture is a paste. Heat a small skillet and cook a spoonful to check seasonings, add more salt, spice or brandy if the mixture is a paste. Heat a small skillet and cook a spoonful to check seasonings, add more salt, spice or brandy if the mixture is too bland. Add the pistachios and truffles (if using) and mix well. Pack the forcemeat mixture into the lined tin, pat and pound with your hand to rid the mixture of air. Dampen your hands and fold the overhanging fatback over the top. Pat and smooth to make a neat loaf. Sprinkle the thyme over the top and place the bay leaves in a row across the top. Put the extra pieces of fatback on top. Put the terrine into a pan of hot water that comes half-way up the sides. Bake for about 2 hours or until a metal skewer inserted in the centre and held for 10 seconds comes out hot. Remove from oven and discard the top fatback. Let cool. Weight down with heavy object and refrigerate. Should mellow for a day before serving. Serve with cornichons (tiny gherkins). This keeps for 2 weeks.

Duck liver with turnip

600g fresh duck livers	4 tablespoons port
4 cups water and 15g coarse salt	2 tablespoons water
16 baby turnips, trimmed	40g butter, extra
25g butter	1 tablespoon flour
1 tablespoon sugar	1½ tablespoons oil
1 tablespoon wine vinegar	Serves 4
4 tablespoons sherry	

'There is still much anti-pathy in Australia towards using offal. Chicken livers seem to have made the grade, yet the fine duck livers and fabulous goose livers are seen but scarce-ly. Well, keep quiet about it, as they remain among the greatest bargains in this country.'

Bring the salted water to the boil, throw in the baby turnips and cook, uncovered, for 15 minutes. Drain. Heat the 25g butter in a sauté pan until golden, put in drained turnips and brown lightly all over. Sprinkle with sugar and shake gently over the heat for three minutes until they turn amber in colour. Add the wine vinegar to the pan and boil for 10 seconds or until the liquid has almost completely evaporated. Then add the sherry, port and water and simmer gently for one minute. Add 40g butter in pieces. Allow to melt in the sim-mering liquid and give the sauce the desired silkiness. Leaves the pan on a low heat, covered until needed.

Prepare the liver by scraping away all green traces left by the gall bladder from between the lobes and trim. Season with salt and pep-per and roll each in flour, shaking off any surplus. Heat oil in a frying pan, and as it begins to smoke put in the livers. Fry 2–3 minutes on each side. Arrange on individual hot plates and cover completely with the turnip sauce.

Delicieux Rouanaise
Duck liver mousse in port aspic

From Two Faces Restaurant, South Yarra, Melbourne, run by Hermann and Faye Schneider.

500g duck livers	½ cup port
4 egg yolks	2 egg whites, beaten with egg shell
1 cup lard	¼ cup chopped spring onions
4 tablespoons port	1 tablespoon wine vinegar
2 teaspoons salt	2 tablespoons gelatine
½ teaspoon four spices	few tarragon leaves
¼ teaspoon white pepper	for the four spice mixture:
1 cup cream	½ cup white pepper
¼ cup peeled pistachio nuts or	¼ cup nutmeg
blanched almond slivers	2 teaspoons ground coriander
for the port aspic:	4 teaspoons ground basil
3 cups reduced chicken stock	Serves 8

Remove all nerves from duck livers and purée in blender. Strain through a fine sieve into mixing bowl, add egg yolks one by one plus pepper, salt and four spice mixture, then slowly pour in melted but cooled lard and port. When thoroughly blended, whisk in cream and divide mixture into 8 buttered porcelain ramekins. Place these into a baking dish half-filled with hot water and bake in preheated slow oven (175°C/325°F) for approximately 20 minutes. Let cool and garnish with pistachio kernels or almond flakes before covering with 6cm of port jelly.

To make the port aspic, in a saucepan combine the chicken stock (cold) with port, egg whites, spring onions, wine vinegar, gelatine and a few tarragon leaves. Bring slowly to the boil while stirring gently. Then let simmer undisturbed until completely clarified. Carefully strain through a double thickness of cheese cloth and let cool before pouring over duck liver mousse. Leave to set.

To make the four spice mixture, mix white pepper, nutmeg, coriander and basil. Store in a well-sealed jar.

Scrambled eggs with mushrooms and herbs

6 eggs
100g champignons, finely sliced
60g butter
salt and pepper
¼ cup cream

parsley, chopped
chives, chopped
tarragon, fresh if possible otherwise
 dried
Serves 2–3

At the Lodge with David McNicoll and the then Prime Minister, Malcolm Fraser. 1982.

Sweat the champignon slices in a little butter over a low heat. Beat the eggs lightly. In a medium saucepan put half the butter and heat lightly. Add the eggs plus a little salt and pepper. Work with a wooden spoon, until the eggs are soft and creamy. Add the rest of the butter in small pieces and the cream. Add the champignons and the chopped herbs.

Serve on toast or with toast while still piping hot. The point of this recipe is that while it's delicious, it's only one of the endless things you can do with scrambled eggs, which are nearly always served by themselves. However, when imagination is used (chopped prawns, yabbies, smoked salmon, crayfish pieces, brains, kidneys, herbs, different mushrooms and so on), marvellous flavours result.

Sherried eggs

12 eggs
peel of an orange
⅔ cup good dry sherry
¼ cup Grand Marnier
2 tablespoons tomato paste
½ cup cream

½ teaspoon paprika
2 pinches saffron
salt
pepper
60g butter
Serves 4–6

'Vary this egg dish by adding diced onion, capsicum, parsley, chillies and so on.'

Slice the orange peel very finely. Break the eggs in a mixing dish, add peel and other ingredients and mix well. Heat the butter in a large omelette pan, pour in the mixture and cook as scrambled eggs.

Eggs Benedict

2 rusks or rounds of thick toast
2 large thin slices of ham
2 eggs
¾ cup hollandaise sauce
truffle slice to garnish
parsley to garnish

for the hollandaise sauce:
4 egg yolks
2 tablespoons lemon juice
250g butter
¼ teaspoon salt
Serves 1

'One of the richest breakfast or brunch dishes there is. Some use it as a restorative, claiming all sorts of magic properties. I find it lasts me for most of the day.'

To make hollandaise sauce, in double boiler beat the egg yolks and stir in lemon juice. Cook very slowly over low heat till it thickens slightly. Never let the water underneath boil. Add the butter a little at a time, stirring constantly with a wooden spoon. Season with salt and pepper and cook till thickened.

Grill the ham and gently poach the eggs. Cover the rusks with ham, then eggs and coat with hollandaise sauce. Garnish each egg with a slice of truffle and a sprig of parsley. Serve immediately.

Gnocchi verdi di ricotta

For almost as long as I remember, Beppi Polese has been running Beppi's on the corner of Yurong and Stanley Streets, East Sydney; one of the greatest of our many Italian restaurants. At times he says he wants to retire, with mock gloomy air, but I think that at heart he is too much of an enthusiast.

90g melted butter
125g creamed spinach
250g cottage cheese
125g ricotta
2 eggs, lightly beaten
½ cup flour

¾ cup grated Parmesan cheese
¼ teaspoon nutmug
¼ cup cream
60g chopped basil
salt and freshly ground pepper
Serves 6

Mix all ingredients thoroughly. Place in the refrigerator for 30 minutes until mixture is quite firm. Flour hands lightly and pick up about one tablespoonful at a time, shaping into small balls. Bring a large pan of salted water to the boil. Drop in gnocchi three or four at a time. Simmer gently until gnocchi rise to the surface. Remove from pan with slotted spoon. Melt 125g of butter in a pan and add gnocchi. Sprinkle with Parmesan cheese and cook until it melts.

Goose liver with raspberry vinegar sauce

One of the great gourmet secrets of Australia is, or was, the ready availability of goose liver. It used not to be expensive, and still isn't too expensive. The French make nearly all their goose livers into *pâté de foie gras*. But wonderful things can be done with it hot.

Anders Ousback, Gay Bilson and myself at the launching of his book *Words on Wine*.

300g goose liver, uncooked
butter
30g chopped spring onions,
    including green rings
½ cup red wine
dash good raspberry vinegar
½ cup brown veal glaze

15g chopped chives
dash lemon juice
walnut oil
salt
pepper
Serves 3–4

Wash and cut the liver into thin slices. Put a scrap of butter in a heavy frying pan. Add spring onions, red wine, raspberry vinegar and glaze. Reduce over a fierce heat. Add the chives and lemon juice. Into another pan put a scrap of butter and some walnut oil, heat and add the slices of liver, turning quickly. Do not overcook. Place on a warm serving dish. Add a scrap more walnut oil to the pan and work in. Add the reduced sauce, heat quickly, season with salt and pepper, pour over the liver and serve.

Warm goose liver salad

200g goose liver, uncooked
150g raw champignons
40g fresh watercress
40g green beans, sliced lengthwise
    and blanched
40g carrots, sliced lengthwise and
    blanched

40g bean sprouts
olive oil
8 crisp lettuce leaves
salt and pepper
Serves 3–4

Wash liver and slice into julienne strips 5mm thick. Heat some olive oil in a frying pan, add liver and champignons and toss together, cooking very quickly. Take off the heat, add watercress, beans, carrots and sprouts. Season. Simmer for a moment only before pouring onto the middle of fresh lettuce leaves which have been sprinkled with sauce vinaigrette.

I've written regular columns for the *Bulletin*, the *Sun-Herald*, *Rydges*, the *Sunday Mirror*, the *Weekend Australian* and the *Australian Women's Weekly*, plus hundreds of others for all sorts of magazines and newspapers; plus hundreds of radio broadcasts and TV appearances; plus 12 books. And you still don't drink enough wine!

Now—it's Len Evans in the Sunday Mirror

Len Evans appraising a wine.

One of Sydney's most colorful personalities joins the Sunday Mirror on Sunday.

He is Len Evans, writer, wit, bon vivant and expert on everything there is to know about food and wine.

A former director of the Australian Wine Bureau and a wine merchant, Evans is famous for his Tasting Room in Bulletin Place.

Food and wine lovers clamor for invitations to his luncheons because Evans knows what's what about food and wines.

And now he has agreed to pass on his knowledge to Sunday Mirror readers.

Evans will write in down-to-earth language that will make a hit with everyone from budget-conscious housewives to jet-setters with wallets full of credit cards.

Full details of Evans' plans will be announced in the Sunday Mirror this weekend.

So watch for the big announcement.

Life will be a whole lot brighter once you've met Len Evans in the Sunday Mirror.

Kidneys and leeks in mushrooms

This is a Tasting Room special devised by Sally Cleaver and Carolyn Divjak. I've never seen anything like it in cookbooks. I believe it will become a classic.

1 veal or 4 lamb kidneys per person
1 leek (white part only), per person
1 large cup-shaped mushroom, 8cm diameter, per person
1 cup Campbell's beef consommé
1 cup red wine
2 tablespoons butter
chopped parsley

Boil the consommé and wine together in a saucepan until reduced by half. Remove the stalks from the mushrooms, and replace with a knob of butter. Arrange in a greased baking dish and bake in a medium oven until cooked but still firm (approximately 10 minutes). Take out of the oven and put aside. Wash, clean and trim the kidneys. Chop roughly. Wash the leeks thoroughly under running water. Cut into rings. Drain well. Place two tablespoons of butter in a pan. When hot, sauté the kidneys and leeks until the kidneys are cooked but still pink inside (or longer if you prefer, but be careful not to let them get tough). Remove to a warm place.

Pour off the excess butter from the pan and de-glaze with the reduced wine and consommé mixture. Sieve this sauce if you require a clear mixture, otherwise the crusty bits from the bottom of the pan probably add a bit more flavour. Place each mushroom on a warm plate and cover with the kidney and leek mixture. Pour a little sauce over. Sprinkle with a little chopped parsley.

Lotus leaf rice

A recipe from the Flower Drum in Little Bourke Street, Melbourne, which most consider the top Chinese restaurant in that city, and many the best in Australia. Gilbert Lau is another great enthusiast (all the top ones are) and he is forever trying to better his product, never content with what many consider perfection. The care shown with this dish exemplifies his attitude.

2 lotus leaves
120g fresh chicken fillet from breast or leg
120g fresh prawn meat
100g champignons
3 tablespoons peanut oil
3 dried scallops—soaked in warm water 2 hours
1 egg, lightly beaten
2 cups cold cooked rice
1 stalk spring onions, chopped
½ teaspoon salt
½ teaspoon soy sauce, preferably mushroom soy

Cover lotus leaves with cold water and soak approximately 30 minutes. Remove and pat dry gently. Dice chicken, prawns and champignons. Heat the oil in a hot wok and when oil is smoking slightly, add chicken and prawn pieces, stir-frying over high heat until colour changes, 1–2 minutes. Add dried scallops and champignons to the meats, then make a space in the centre of the wok and stir in the beaten egg. Allow a few seconds for the egg to set slightly, then quickly scramble through for a few more seconds before adding the cooked rice.

Move the rice vigorously through the wok, combining all the ingredients well. Add spring onions, salt and soy sauce. Place half of the rice mixture into each lotus leaf and wrap up like a parcel, envelope style. Place on a lightly oiled plate and steam gently for 30 minutes. Serve hot, garnished with ribbons made of ½ carrot strips. The lotus leaf wrapping must be cut from the top with a pair of scissors at the table, thereby resembling the opening of a lotus flower. (The dried scallops and lotus leaves are available at Chinese supermarkets.)

Omelette Jennifer

This dish was invented on the spur of the moment for Jenny Fox, widow of my great mate Peter Fox. She wanted something 'very light and fresh'.

3 eggs
4 champignons
15g butter
½ cup bean sprouts
lemon juice

Tabasco
salt and pepper
2 lettuce leaves
Serves 1

Finely slice the champignons and sweat them. Take off the heat, and add bean sprouts. Add a squeeze of lemon, a drop of Tabasco, salt and pepper. Put the two lettuce leaves together and lie flat. Put mixture on one half and fold over. Steam lightly in a steamer for a few minutes until the lettuce is soft. Make the omelette in a normal way, place the folded lettuce on one side and fold the omelette over.

Smoked salmon pinwheels

These are highly successful with pre-dinner drinks.

400g smoked salmon, thinly sliced
90g butter
chopped dill

whole loaf unsliced brown bread
whole loaf unsliced white bread

Blend together the butter and dill in a food processor. Whip slightly. De-crust the loaves. Slice loaves lengthwise about 1cm thick. Roll each slice with a rolling pin. Butter the pieces thinly. Cover the bread with thinly sliced salmon, roll tightly, wrap in plastic and freeze. Remove plastic and slice thinly (2mm). Arrange alternate bread colours on a platter. Allow 10 minutes to thaw after cutting.

Pickled salmon

1kg fresh salmon, completely boned
1 tablespoon caster sugar
3 tablespoons salt
1 tablespoon sugar
fresh black pepper
1 tablespoon dill
3 tablespoons fresh chopped dill

for the mustard sauce:
250g mild mustard
¾ cup brown sugar
4 cups tarragon vinegar
5 cups maize oil
salt and ground black pepper
fresh chopped dill
Serves 8–10

Cut the salmon in half and leave skin on both sides. Mix the caster sugar with the salt, sugar, black pepper, dill and plenty of chopped dill and rub it on the meat side of the salmon. Place the salmon on a flat dish with a weight on top in the refrigerator for 12 hours. Remove from the dish and eat within 3 days. To make the sauce, mix mustard with the sugar and then add the vinegar and maize oil. Season with salt and pepper to taste and add plenty of fresh chopped dill.

'Two old friends, Nick and Brigitte Tripiano used to own the pizza bar at Thredbo. Without any doubt, they made the best pizzas I've ever tasted, here or abroad.'

Pizza Leonardo da Vino

Two old friends, Nick and Brigitte Tripiano used to own the pizza bar at Thredbo. Without any doubt, they made the best pizzas I've ever tasted, here or abroad. Use plenty of dough for the base, and really heap the ingredients on.

mozzarella cheese
firm tomatoes
lean bacon
green olives
capers
tinned anchovy fillets
oregano
Parmesan cheese

for the pizza base:
1 cup lukewarm water
30g compressed yeast
3 tablespoons olive oil
3¼ cups plain flour
1½ teaspoons salt
¼ teaspoon pepper
Serves 6

Measure the water into large warm bowl. Crumble yeast into the water and stir until smooth, stir in the olive oil. Add flour and blend thoroughly with a wooden spoon. Turn onto a lightly floured surface and knead until smooth and elastic. Return to a greased bowl, turn dough to grease all over. Cover with a clean tea towel and leave in a warm place for about 2 hours or until double in bulk.

Take off 6 round pieces something less than tennis ball size, flatten, roll and shape. Don't knock the stuffing out of the risen dough. Place on greased baking trays. Add thick grated mozzarella cheese all over. On top of this, thin sliced firm tomatoes, thin sliced lean bacon, split green olives, capers and anchovy fillets. Sprinkle oregano and fine grated Parmesan cheese on top. Pop in the oven at 200°C/400°F for 15 minutes.

Fricassee of rabbit with garlic

2 rabbits (boned, only the saddle and
    thighs are used)
125g butter
salt and freshly ground pepper

2 cloves garlic, crushed
½ cup cream
1 bunch chives, chopped

Serves 4–5

Preheat the oven to 180°C/350°F. In a heavy-bottomed pan melt half the butter and brown the rabbit pieces. Add garlic, salt and pepper. Place the covered pan in the oven and cook gently for 1–1¼ hours, allowing the rabbit to cook in its own steam.

When the rabbit is cooked, prepare the sauce by melting the remaining butter in a saucepan, adding the juice from the casserole, and finally the cream and the chives. Carve the saddle of rabbit into escalopes lengthwise. Cover the pieces with the sauce.

'A basic recipe. You can try variants. I flame the pieces and add port to the butter before baking. Other herbs (oregano, tarragon, basil or thyme) may be used. Recipes should be flexible, depending on the availability of ingredients and your taste. An appreciation of cooking times, so that nothing is overcooked, is often more important than exact ingredients.'

Sang choy bow

This has become almost a standard in top Chinese restaurants. Of these, I like the Flower Drum in Melbourne, the Choys restaurants and the Imperial Peking in Sydney particularly. Not forgetting our great 'local', Matthew Chan's Peacock Gardens in Crow's Nest. I've known Matthew since he was a young waiter.

1 lettuce
4 Chinese dried mushrooms
125g bamboo shoots
1 Chinese sausage
3 tablespoons peanut oil
250g minced pork
1 tablespoon oyster sauce
1 tablespoon soy sauce

sprinkling of sugar
salt and pepper to taste
2 tablespoons dry sherry (or Chinese
    rose wine)
3 teaspoons cornflour
½ cup water
1 chopped onion

Serves 4

Trim lettuce leaves to about 8cm x 10cm. Cut mushrooms into fine slices, put into warm water to soften. Cut bamboo shoots and Chinese sausage finely. Heat peanut oil in a fryng pan. Put mushrooms, onions, bamboo shoots and Chinese sausage into the pan and stir-fry for about 2 minutes. Add minced pork, stir-fry on high heat for about 7–8 minutes until cooked. Now add oyster sauce, soy sauce, sugar, salt and pepper and 2 tablespoons of dry sherry (pouring sherry onto the hot side of the pan, letting it run into the meat). Keep stirring for one minute then add cornflour which has been mixed with half a cup of water to make a smooth mixture. Stir for another minute until the mixture thickens.

To ensure crispness of the lettuce, plunge into iced water for one minute before serving. To serve this dish use two large tureens—one for fresh lettuce and one for *sang choy bow*. Then place the mixture on lettuce leaves and serve on individual plates. Guests then roll mixture in their own lettuce leaf and eat with fingers.

Hot vegetable salad

This looks very attractive and tastes very good. Lovely as an entrée or single luncheon dish.

Ham and vegetable terrine (recipe page 142).

2/3 cup chicken stock
120g thick sliced leeks (white)
120g cauliflower heads
120g broccoli heads
60g sliced red capsicum
60g sliced green capsicum
60g champignons cut in half

salt
cayenne pepper
3 hard-boiled eggs
chopped parsley
fried croûtons
Serves 4

Heat stock in saucepan to boiling. Add leeks and cook for three minutes, add all other vegetables, season, cover and cook until tender. Remove and drain. Add chopped boiled eggs, chopped parsley and piping hot fried croûtons, mix lightly and serve.

'This is actually a potato dish which accompanies any grilled meat. I prefer it with barbecued or grilled sausages. It can be eaten on its own.'

Sausage with potatoes

6 medium-sized well shaped potatoes
olive oil
1 large onion
3 cloves garlic, crushed
1/2 cup parsley, chopped

salt
pepper
brown veal stock
Serves 6

Cover a heavy frying pan with oil, and heat. Add sliced potatoes and cook until both sides are brown. Mix the onions, garlic, parsley, salt and pepper together and sprinkle over the potatoes. Add veal stock diluted with water which has been heated until boiling. (About a good cup full.) Cover the pan and simmer for 15 minutes or so until the potatoes are tender, and the liquid has almost gone. Serve with sausages or other meat.

Sellouts

2 avocados
4 cups chicken stock
2 teaspoons arrowroot
60g chicken breast

60g crab
salt and fresh black pepper, to season
Serves 4

To make the stock, cover a chicken carcass with 1 litre of water, add 1 finely sliced onion, 1 sliced carrot, bouquet garni (sprig thyme, bay leaf, 3 parsley stalks and 1 small piece celery), 6 black peppercorns and 1 chicken stock cube. Bring to the boil and simmer for 1 hour. Bring the chicken stock to the boil again, season to taste and thicken with the arrowroot mixed with a little of the cold stock. Peel and stone the avocados. Shred the chicken and crab meat. Place the avocados in a liquidiser, pour over the hot chicken stock, and purée. Serve garnished with the chicken and crab meat.

Slivered steak with rice

1½ cups rice
500g meat (grilling quality steak or
   pork fillet)
soy sauce
1 crushed garlic clove
1 large onion
oil

crushed pineapple and juice
1 tablespoon cornflour
1 cup water
sliced chillies
chopped parsley or shallots
Serves 4–6

'Another "caught short" recipe, when there's only a scrap of meat to go around. Start to finish in less than 20 minutes.'

Put the rice on to cook in salted boiling water. In the meantime, thinly sliver the meat and toss in a small amount of soy sauce and crushed garlic clove. Sauté the sliced onion in hot oil in a frying pan. Remove the onion when transparent (2–3 minutes). Add more oil to the pan and sauté the meat, stirring until cooked (about 3 minutes). Remove the meat to the onions, reduce the pan heat and add crushed pineapple and juice. Combine the juice with the rich red meat residue in pan and bring to the boil gently. Thicken mixture with cornflour and water and cook for two minutes. The meat and onions are stirred into this sauce.

When rice is cooked, strain and press into a greased basin, just large enough to be completely filled with rice. Press the rice flat and invert the basin on to a silver plate or other suitable serving dish. Decorate simply with sliced chillies. Place the meat on an attractive serving platter, sprinkle with chopped parsley or shallots and serve at the table.

Pigeons and peas (recipe page 174).

Snails in clay pots

375g butter, unsalted
45g shallots, finely chopped
4 garlic cloves, crushed
1 tablespoon parsley, finely chopped

6 hazelnuts, peeled and finely
   chopped
36 snails
puff pastry (optional)
Serves 6

Mix all ingredients, except the snails, and whip to a cream. Place snails in clay pots. Stuff each pot generously with finished snail butter. Fill each metal dish with white rock salt and arrange six snail pots by partially immersing in salt. Bake in 190°C/375°F oven, about 12 minutes, until done. Cover each snail pot with a cap of puff pastry and bake until golden brown.

Soufflé Suissesse
Soufflé with Swiss cheese

I first met Michel Roux, the outstanding French chef who has done so well in the United Kingdom, when I walked into the kitchen of Le Gavroche as it was then. I had been immensely impressed with the food and wanted to meet 'who-did-it'. Michel has since told me that this hadn't happened before. The new Le Gavroche, run in conjuction with brother Albert, has the only Michelin three star award in the United Kingdom. They have also the Waterside Inn (a three-star restaurant) at Bray on the Thames as well as Le Poulbot, Le Gamin and Gavvers. Michel married an Australian girl, Robyn Joyce, who used to host Le Café in Paddington.

140g butter	*6 egg whites*
65g flour	*200g grated Gruyère or Emmental*
700ml milk	*cheese*
5 egg yolks	*salt*
4 cups thickened cream	*freshly ground white pepper*
	Serves 4

Preheat the oven to 200°C/400°F. Melt the butter in a small saucepan over low heat. Using a small wire whisk, stir in the flour. Cook gently for 2–3 minutes, stirring continuously. Take the pan off the heat and leave the roux to cool slightly. Bring the milk to the boil, then pour it over the cooled roux, whisking all the time. Set the pan over high heat and, stirring continuously, bring the mixture to the boil and cook for 3 minutes. Take the pan off the heat and stir in the egg yolks. Season to taste with salt and pepper. Dot the surface with a tablespoon of butter, cut into small pieces, to prevent a skin from forming. Set aside at room temperature.

Meanwhile, chill 8 round, 8cm tartlet tins in the refrigerator or freezer for a few minutes. Remove and immediately grease them generously with softened butter and arrange on a baking tray.

Pour the cream into a gratin or bimetal dish. Lightly salt the cream, then warm it gently without letting it boil. Beat the egg whites with a pinch of salt until they form stiff peaks. Pour the soufflé mixture into a wide-mouthed bowl. Using a whisk, quickly beat in about one-third of the beaten egg whites, then, using a spatula, carefully fold in the remainder. Using a tablespoon, heap the mixture in the tartlet tins to form 8 large moulds.

Bake soufflés in the preheated oven for 3 minutes, until the tops begin to turn golden. Remove from the oven and, protecting your hands with a cloth, turn out each soufflé into the dish of warm cream. Sprinkle over the Gruyère or Emmental and return to the oven for five minutes. The soufflés must be taken immediately to the table; serve them with spoon and fork, taking care not to crush them.

Spaghetti carbonara

A lovely rough dish from one of my Italian friends, Gino Merlo of the Milano Restaurant, Brisbane. He is one of my greatest friends. He arrived in Australia virtually penniless, worked extremely hard as a cane cutter and finally opened a small espresso bar in Queen Street, Brisbane. This developed into an eating house featuring pasta, which

begat a larger place, which became the Milano. Gino is the ultimate enthusiast, worrier, perfectionist and professional. He has won the Best Cellar in Australia in the *Bulletin*/Quelltaler Quest three years in a row. None deserves it more. Milano, to me, is a sort of Italian brasserie, with people taking an hour or five over dinner.

Murray Tyrrell, Simon Seward, Ray Healy, Max Lake, Rudy Komon, Peter Fox, James Halliday, Hermann Schneider, Dan Murphy, Michael Broadbent, and self at the 1977 dinner. Malcolm Fraser came later.

2 rashers of bacon, do not remove fat
2 cloves garlic, crushed
2 eggs

2 tablespoons Parmesan cheese,
  grated
spaghetti
Serves 2

Dice rashers of bacon. Pan-sauté until cooked through and add a squeeze of garlic. Add cooked spaghetti straight from the pot into the pan, not overdone and claggy, and mix into the bacon. Break over a couple of eggs and stir around until cooked through. Sprinkle Parmesan over and serve.

Spaghetti con salsa di vongole

500g spaghetti
for the sauce:
750g shelled pipis
3 tablespoons olive oil
1 tablespoon chopped capers
1 clove garlic, crushed

500g tomatoes, skinned, seeded and
  chopped
3 tablespoons chopped parsley
salt and fresh black pepper, to season
Serves 6

'You must be sure to clean the pipis first. This is an excellent way of using the wondrous local clam, which is so often ignored or used just as bait.'

Cook the spaghetti. Place the oil in a saucepan and when hot add the capers and crushed garlic clove. Sauté but don't brown. Add the tomatoes and parsley and cook for 30 minutes. Add the pipis to the tomato sauce and season with salt and fresh black pepper. Cook uncovered until the sauce has thickened.

Spanish omelette

12 eggs
salt and pepper
2 rashers bacon, cut into small pieces
50g onions, sliced
2 medium tomatoes, skinned, seeded
   and chopped
½ red capsicum, sliced

½ green capsicum, sliced
50g mushrooms, sliced
Tabasco
50g butter
chopped parsley
Serves 4

Beat the eggs lightly with salt and pepper until yolks and whites are melded. Fry bacon for two minutes, add onions, tomatoes, capsicum mushrooms and a dash of Tabasco and cook until done. Try to avoid getting this mixture too wet.

Into an omelette pan put a spot of butter, and when it foams add a part of the egg mix to cover the bottom of the pan. Let this cook until the bottom has set. Then push part to one side and work rest of liquid mixture to base of pan. In this way a fluffy, soft, thick omelette is obtained. Spread a spoonful of the mixture across the thick half and turn the other part over. Invert onto a warm plate. Sprinkle with chopped parsley.

The size of the omelette depends on the pan size. I have cooked the above quantities as one omelette, serving at the table in one piece to be cut up into required portions.

With wine judging friends in the Tasting Room.

Ham and vegetable terrine

250g green beans
6 bottoms fresh artichoke (can be
   replaced by fresh asparagus or
   turnip)
300g young, whole carrots
300g fresh shelled peas
a little salt
vine leaves

for the stuffing:
250g ham
1 egg
salt and pepper
½ cup peanut oil
½ cup lemon juice
Serves 8

Cook peas and beans separately, cook artichoke separately and whole carrots must also be cooked separately. Cook gently so that they retain their crispness, then drain and let all vegetables cool.

For the stuffing remove the skin of the ham, cut into tiny cubes and place in a blender. Remember the mixing bowl must stay very cold. Then put egg white, salt and pepper with the ham in the blender and put on high speed. Then slowly incorporate the oil and lemon juice together. This must be done quickly to avoid the mixture heating.

Line a mould approximately 30cm long 22cm wide and 15cm deep with a layer of vine leaves. Put one layer of stuffing, one of carrots, artichoke, peas and beans, then a layer of ham. Keep layering until the mould is filled. Ultimately the vine leaves become the skin of the pâté. Cover the mould with greaseproof paper to seal and put into a bain-marie and place in the oven at 150°C/300°F for 30 minutes. When cooked, remove and leave for 8 hours till very cold. Serve with Jean Yanne Sauce.

Jean Yanne sauce

1kg tomatoes	1 cup olive oil
2 teaspoons tomato paste	pinch of tarragon
salt and pepper	parsley
½ cup wine vinegar	

Lightly cook the tomatoes, then skin and sieve. Mix with tomato paste, salt, pepper, vinegar, olive oil and tarragon. This makes a coulis.

To serve, take the coulis of tomatoes and pour onto individual serving plates then slice the terrine, take out of the mould and place terrine on top of each tomato coulis. Garnish with parsley.

Tongue in cheek

From Gay Bilson of the famous Berowra Waters Inn Restaurant.

2 pickled ox tongues	onion, diced
4 pairs of whole ox cheeks	thyme
2 pigs trotters	bay leaf
light beef stock	peppercorns
celery, diced	5 red capsicums, grilled and peeled
carrot, diced	

Rinse the tongues. Poach tongues in unsalted water with the celery, carrot, onion, thyme, bay leaf and peppercorns. When tender, peel and trim. Poach the cheeks in beef stock with trotters, vegetables and herbs until tender. Trim cheeks and use only the fat meaty parts.

Clear and reduce the stock until it will set hard. Pour a layer in a mould and allow to set. Arrange tongues, with cheeks nestled around them, and with pieces of grilled, peeled capsicum between the cheeks and the tongue. Pour more jelly around and over them. Allow to set; thus, tongue in cheek.

Serve thickly sliced with perhaps a thick dressing using virgin olive oil, pitted black olives and fresh herbs such as basil, parsley and chives.

Ox tongue with cumberland sauce

A recipe from Louis Vaudable, who used to own the famous Maxim's in Paris before selling out to Cartier. Graham Kerr and I met
him in 1967, and thereby hangs a tale. We were doing some work for
Pan-American Airways in return for a round-the-world flight. I had
spotted on the plane an oxidised wine, a Santenay from the southern
part of the Côte d'Or, Burgundy, and was told to pursue the matter
with the owner of Maxims, who prepared the menus and selected the
wines in those days for Pan-Am. M. Vaudable asked me if I was
prepared to taste the wine 'blind'. The next day, with Pommier, their
celebrated *sommelier*, we went to Bercy where nearly all their wines
were stored. The exercise was not a difficult one. Among the 10 wines
or so shown to me there was one with quite brown tinges which I
correctly surmised to be the Santenay. But I went through it all,
supposing the other wines were Pan-Am offerings and so it was.
Hence I did fairly well, and much excited discussion followed in
French. Finally, M. Vaudable looked at me, and with great dignity
said, 'You have done well. We agree that the wine is slightly
oxidised. Please inform your principals in New York it will be
withdrawn from service and a credit will be passed.' I couldn't help
myself. 'And what will you do with it?' I asked. 'Who knows?' he
replied. 'Probably sell it to another airline.'

'A recipe from Louis Vaudable, who used to own the famous Maxim's in Paris before selling out to Cartier.'

1 small cured ox tongue	for the cumberland sauce:
2 large onions	*1 orange*
2 medium carrots	*1 lemon*
1 cup chicken or pork fat	*6 tablespoons redcurrant jelly*
1 clove garlic	*1 cup port*
½ bottle dry white wine	*1 teaspoon mustard*
10 cups bouillon blanc	*red pepper*
bouquet garni	*powdered ginger*
salt and pepper	Serves 6

Slice the onions and carrots and brown them in the fat in a shallow
pan. Remove and keep hot. Brown the trimmed tongue lightly on all
sides. Put the onions and carrots back in the pan with the garlic and
cut off the tongue root. Lay the tongue on top, pour over the dry
white wine, bring to the boil, and simmer until the liquid is almost
completely reduced. Pour in the bouillon, covering the tongue entirely, add the bouquet garni and season with salt and pepper. Bring
to the boil, cover, and cook in a moderate oven (175°C/350°F), turning
often, for about 3 hours. In the meantime, make the cold cumberland
sauce. Cut tiny thin strips of peel from the orange and the lemon, 1
tablespoon of each. Blanch them in boiling water for 3 minutes,
drain, and leave to cool. Melt the jelly; transfer to a bowl, stir in the
port, citrus peels, and the juice of the whole orange and half the
lemon. Add the mustard, a pinch of red pepper, and one of powdered ginger. Mix well. This sauce may be served either hot or cold,

but is usually served cold. When the tongue is done, the liquid should be reduced to about 1½ cups. Place the sliced meat on a serving platter; strain the juice through a cheesecloth and pour over the tongue. Serve the sauce separately in a gravy boat.

Tortellini palermitana

8 dozen tortellini
60g butter
60g Parmesan cheese
30g butter
for the sauce:
60g butter
1 clove garlic, chopped
2 medium onions, chopped
4 tomatoes, skinned and chopped

1 tablespoon tomato paste
1 tablespoon plain flour
1 cup beef stock
¼ teaspoon thyme
½ bay leaf
1 teaspoon salt
black peppercorns
2 medium mushrooms, chopped
Serves 4

Grate the Parmesan. Preheat the oven to 220°C/425°F. Place the tortellini in a shallow baking dish, pour butter over them and cook over a moderate heat, stirring to coat them with the butter. Cook 3 minutes.

To prepare the sauce, place 60g butter in a saucepan, add the garlic and onions and cook until the onions have softened. Add the tomatoes to the sauce together with the tomato paste, flour, beef stock, thyme, bay leaf, salt and pepper. Bring to the boil and simmer for 15 minutes, stirring occasionally. Add the mushrooms and cook 5 minutes longer. Keep the sauce hot. Pour the tomato sauce over the tortellini, and add half the Parmesan cheese and stir in gently. Place 30g butter cut into small pieces on the top of the dish and then sprinkle with remaining Parmesan cheese. Bake in a hot oven for 10 minutes.

The Tasting Room today.

Veal kidneys in mustard sauce

500g veal kidneys
20g butter
dash of vegetable oil
1 small clove of garlic, crushed
shot of brandy
100ml veal glaze
200ml cream

100ml dry sherry
Dijon mustard to taste
chopped parsley
salt
pepper
Serves 3

Slice the kidneys very thinly (5mm or less); cut out the white centres. Heat the butter, add garlic and sauté for 30 seconds. Add kidneys, turning quickly, add brandy and flame. This takes very little time. Remove to a serving plate and keep warm. Into this pan, add the veal glaze and sherry, bring to the boil and mix; add mustard to taste (this is very much a matter for the individual). Add the chopped parsley, meld and pour over the kidneys. Serve.

Gordon Bedson's veal, ham and egg pie

Gordon Bedson was a great character, a true eccentric. A racing car driver, Surfers Paradise restaurateur and trade consul, he retired to northern New South Wales to concentrate on developing his invention—a light aircraft. After considerable success, he was killed in a crash, early in 1984. His dear wife Celia wrote to me that he went exactly as he would have wanted it.

750g fillet of veal	1/4 cup medium sherry
500g leg of ham	5 hard-boiled eggs
black pepper, freshly ground, to season	for the hot water crust:
	3 cups plain flour
1/2 teaspoon chopped parsley	2/3 cup water
1 teaspoon mixed herbs	125g lard
1 teaspoon gelatine	1 teaspoon salt

Remove fat and skin from veal and chop into 2.5cm cubes. Chop ham into 2.5cm cubes. Cover meat with water and add seasoning, parsley and mixed herbs. Cook until meat is just 'on the tooth', in other words, firm to the bite. Remove meat from stock and reduce. Add gelatine and sherry. Leave to cool. At this stage there should be approximately 2½ cups of stock. Preheat the oven to 200°C/400°F.

To make pastry, place the flour in a basin in a warm oven. Boil the water. Add lard and allow to dissolve. Add salt. Remove warm basin from oven and add the hot liquid slowly, mixing the pastry with the hands. Work quickly and do not allow the pastry to get cold. Roll out portions of pastry to approximately 1.25cm thick. Cut into shapes to fit sides, base and ends of a rectangular cake tin. Allow 1.25 cm shrinkage in length and width. Assemble the shell by cutting the sides first, setting down dish and laying on pastry. Turn the free edge of the pastry over the top of the sides. Having covered sides cut a piece for the bottom and drop into place, pressing lower edges together to join pastry. Then cut the ends and position, blending intersections of sides and ends together with finger. Try to avoid any holes in pastry, particularly at joins, also make sure that the sides and ends are long enough to fold over top of dish, otherwise, due to the softness of the pastry, they will tend to slide down into the dish.

Fill the pastry case to a depth of 2cm with meat. Trim off ends of the eggs and place end to end along the length of the dish on top of the meat. Make sure the eggs are located centrally. Cover the eggs with the remainder of the meat to within 1.25cm of the top of the dish. Do not pack tightly, otherwise jelly will not fill properly.

Cut pastry top to fit the cake tin, and lay on top of the meat. Join to the ends and sides and pinch together. Indent all around with the side of a spoon. Decorate the top with three pastry flowers. Make 3 holes, one in the centre and one in each end, 2.5cm from the end of the tin. Brush the top with the yolk of an egg. Bake in the oven for

1½ hours at 200°C/400°F until pastry is deep golden brown. While the pie is still warm, drill out holes previously made to accept the funnel. Pour warm stock through the funnel, placing it in each hole to ensure stock is evenly distributed. Allow to settle, and then top up several times. Refrigerate.

Serve accompanied by potatoes roasted in their jackets until crisp, served with parsley and butter, and a green salad and a brown spiced pickled onion.

Veal kidney flambé

1 large veal kidney	1 egg yolk
45g shallots	½ cup Sauternes
30g mushrooms	¼ teaspoon salt
75g butter	⅛ teaspoon cayenne
¼ cup flour	⅓ cup brandy
1 cup milk	Serves 3

Clean, parboil and slice the veal kidney into 1.2cm slices. Chop the shallots and mushrooms finely. Preheat the griller. Place butter in pan, add the shallots and sauté, being careful not to brown. Add flour and cook 3 minutes. Add milk into which the egg yolk has been beaten, and whisk till smooth. Add mushrooms, wine, salt and pepper. Continue cooking 10–15 minutes, stirring occasionally.

Brown kidney slices under the griller. Remove to a metal serving dish. Pour over brandy and set alight. Baste the kidney slices whilst brandy is flaming. Be careful not to flame too long or the kidneys will toughen. Arrange kidney slices on plates, spoon warm brandy over top and cover with the sauce. Serve the remaining sauce in sauce boat.

'Pour over brandy and set alight. Baste the kidney slices whilst brandy is flaming. Be careful not to flame too long or the kidneys will toughen.'

Rognons de veau Antonin Carême

4 veal kidneys	¼ cup cream
1 tablespoon Cognac	1 teaspoon port
60g butter	black peppercorns and salt
2 teaspoons Dijon mustard	Serves 2–3
75g foie gras	

Remove fat from the kidneys and core. Heat the Cognac. Place the whole kidneys into hot butter and sauté for 1 minute. Add the Cognac and set alight. Remove kidneys from the pan and place on a dish to cool. To the sauté pan add the mustard and the foie gras and mash with a fork. Add the cream and stir to combine.

Slice the slightly cooled kidneys into thick slices and add them to the sauce together with their juice and the port. Season with salt and pepper and place on a serving dish.

CHAPTER SIX

Poultry and game: the Wine Bureau

D URING THE LATTER PART OF 1964, I had become restless working at the Chevron Hotel. As assistant to Frank Christie, the General Manager, I still ran the food and beverage departments, a job which included supervising all banquets and conventions. There was much to do, and we were certainly kept very busy. But my three-month tenure as boss while Frank was overseas had given me a taste of higher authority, and I was anxious to find a position as General Manager of a major hotel. There weren't many such establishments. The Menzies had been built and the Wentworth was under construction, but at both establishments the position of General Manager went to long-time employees. There were some discussions with Harry Sebel, who was just completing the Town House, but nothing came of them. Frank Christie was against this prospect, and I think he was right. Harry and I were both fairly volatile characters at the time. Even now, over 20 years later, we sometimes wonder what would have happened should I have applied for, and received, the job. The two of us, as owner and manager, might have made a truly top hotel; or the job could have lasted less than a month.

Then came an offer in which I was very interested. Ken Reid of McWilliams and John Addison of Hamiltons were both leading identities of the National Advertising Committee of the wine industry. Though the Wine Board was centred in Adelaide, this committee operated from Sydney on the basis that this was where the 'selling', rather than the making, took place. The industry wanted a new public relations man. The chief duty of the previous PR man had been to form a strong bond with editors and the like to make sure the industry was regarded in a good light, rather than to promote it. This was an era when little table wine was consumed and the infamous wine saloons dominated. So if a fracas was reported, 'and so-and-so was hit over the head with a wine bottle', it was my predecessor's job to get the 'wine' reference deleted.

Now the National Advertising Committee wanted a more positive approach. Since I had been writing about wine in the *Bulletin* since 1962, Australia's first regular wine column, I seemed a likely lad. Frank Christie was encouraging, and I left the Chevron on the

Rudy Komon, Frank Margan, Murray Tyrrell and Keith Dunstan in 1966, at a 'vertical' tasting at Greenwich.

last day of 1964. My new title, National Promotions Executive, was a strange one, and the job seemed even stranger. No one directed me except the two Committee members who had hired me, and their advice was casual to say the least. I was given a tiny, glass-partitioned office among the main rooms of the Wine and Brandy Producers Association of New South Wales. The rest of the staff regarded me as a curiosity and left me to my devices.

The files revealed very little. The clippings scrapbook from the previous year contained about 20 major stories from newspapers and magazines, about 14 of which I had written. So I remembered that aged dictum of idleness in the Army: when in doubt write a report.

There was already some promotional activity taking place among the various State Associations, mainly conducted wine tastings given free to charity, social and sporting gatherings. These were successful promotions, though they were limited in their scope. I charged around talking to the people running the industry, as well as those who one day would, and wine makers and salesmen who never would. In the meantime, I found it very easy to lodge any story I could write about wine. There seemed to be a need for them, and editors were receptive to the idea of a regular columnist, though they had no idea where to find one. When I got to my fifth pseudonym I decided enough was enough. I presented a submission to form the Australian Wine Bureau. This would incorporate and expand the tasting role, would employ managers in each State to develop promotional activities, and would find top journalists who liked wine and who would be happy to write about it every day and find others to do so. The money for this would come from the National Advertising Committee's inadequate budget. Instead of buying space to promote wine, we would buy people who would get the space free.

It wasn't long before Frank Margan in New South Wales, Frank Doherty in Victoria and Jack Ludbrook in South Australia were part of the team, plus Arthur Moore, Fred McKeever and John Stanford who ran the public promotional side.

The job wasn't without its problems. There were jealousies about positions, and there was little understanding of what promotion was about. For example, one wish of the Committee was that no particular wine should be mentioned. It was all right to promote Hunter Valley white and Barossa red, but not by actual name. Today, when newspapers and magazines are full of wine recommendations, such reticence seems strange, but at the time it was extraordinarily difficult to insist that actual wines and companies be written about. 'But what if you favour one company more than another?' 'What happens if the Hunter gets more publicity than Coonawarra?' Few people seemed to appreciate that everyone would benefit from the promotion of wine, whatever wine. Finally, sheer persistence and lots of noise won the day, and we were able to give editors the copy they wanted, instead of the copy the industry thought would be most suitable.

'Few people seemed to appreciate that everyone would benefit from the promotion of wine, whatever wine. Finally, sheer persistence and lots of noise won the day, and we were able to give editors the copy they wanted, instead of the copy the industry thought would be most suitable.'

In no time at all we were all writing busily, finding contributors for various weeklys and monthlys, arranging promotions, giving talks, lectures and tastings and generally immersing ourselves almost entirely in wine.

Frank Margan, Val Sowada, a photographer and I toured all the wineries, taking pictures and gathering information. We made friendships that exist today and had a great time doing so. The ancient Holden I owned somehow took us over 6500 kilometres, and developed alarming tendencies around corners as the boot became full of the legendary hospitality of the wine companies. On a couple of occasions we had to unload and ask friends to forward our spoils home ahead of us.

On this tour the celebrated 'Rape of Renmark' took place. We were collecting information from the various riverland wineries when someone mentioned that the local Wine and Food Society held tremendous dinners, using the cellar of the Renmark Hotel, the community hotel of the district. This had been established by the previous manager who was a table wine enthusiast. We went to the hotel and found a cellarful of aged vintages dating back to the late forties from great wine men like Maurice O'Shea, Colin Preece and Roger Warren. We enquired whether any of the wines were available for sale.

'Certainly. The customers in the dining room won't buy them because the labels are dirty,' was the reply. The wines were not expensive, and we would be 'doing the local people a favour' by reducing the stock. And the Wine and Food Society? Blow them, they just pleased themselves anyway.

So we bought the lot, at cost. Decimal currency had just been implemented, and I shall never forget the thrill of learning that the 52 Mildara was 31 cents a bottle, whereas the 53 was a bit more; we

A group of winos gathered outside the cellar at Greenwich. Rudy Komon, Murray Tyrrell, Keith Dunstan and Douglas Lamb are visible—so is my bum.

would have to pay 34 cents. Apparently we weren't very popular with the Society members.

There was a lot of very good, mature bottled red around then, and it was easy to promote. Cellars were established in all the major cities, in private homes as well as restaurants. Frank Margan and I wrote a book, which went to restaurateurs and retailers, showing all the various methods of storage at fairs, shows and symposiums. We also arranged prizes for the best wine list.

As stocks of red wines became depleted, I put forward a blueprint for white wine promotion, which eventually became the basis for the development of those sales in Australia. I must confess that at the time I had no idea how profound would be the effect of the 'bag-in-the-box' on bottled wine sales. When Penfolds brought out the first of such containers, the plastic bag being inside a simulated barrel made of tin, I was among its strongest advocates and was extremely disappointed when it failed because of technical problems. Little did I comprehend just how successful later 'bags' would be.

In time, the Wine Board refused to continue to support red wine promotion because we were selling all we could make (though they were aware that hundreds of hectares were being planted all over the place) and because continued promotion 'would result in a flood of imported wine'. If only those people were around today, to see the sorry state of red wine sales and the success of well-promoted overseas wines.

On another occasion I advocated a rosé promotion, using all agencies and the weight of individual advertising to push the rosé 'story'. We worked hard at this blueprint and had all sorts of discussions, but it was knocked back after less than an hour's meeting with the Board 'because not everyone makes a rosé'.

With Len Drayton in the Hunter, 1966.

These frustrations, no doubt shared by promoters everywhere, finally resulted in my leaving the Wine Bureau after two and a half years that were on the whole, fulfilling and happy. There were compensations: enduring friendships, the apparently endless hospitality and good nature of top people in the industry and the feeling of accomplishment we all shared.

During the mid-1970s, Don McWilliam gave a press party at Yendo, near Griffith. Forty members of the wine press attended, and enjoyed McWilliams hospitality. Don said, 'It's lovely to have you here today. If I'd given this party ten years ago Len would have been the only guest.' The revolution had happened in just ten years.

There were other interesting developments. A fellow called Martin de Berry popped in one day. 'I want to convert one of those grotty old wine saloons to an up-market place where young people can listen to good music, eat simple food and enjoy wine by the glass. Do you think this is a good idea?'

I did, and gave him every encouragement with Martin's, which led the winebar boom of the late 1960s and the 1970s. I've often thought that the industry should have erected a statue of Martin, especially the Cinzano company, for he revived interest in vermouth.

Typical of the good humour among wine people is a story about Eric Purbrick, who has owned Chateau Tahbilk in central Victoria for about 50 years. A Cambridge graduate, he was a barrister and an accountant before taking over the property. Princes and Prime Ministers are his frequent guests, and they dress for dinner *every* night. Eric is a man of style.

I visited Chateau Tahbilk in the 1960s during vintage, to collect information for an article. Everyone was busy, and Eric was shovelling stalks from the de-stalking machine that separates the grapes from the rest of the bunch. Some people arrived and became rather annoyed when no one appeared to look after them. Soon there were angry mutterings, particularly from a short, fat, red-faced publican: 'I buy their bloody wine all the time and there's no bastard around to look after us.'

Ever eager, I sprang to the fore. Could I help them? I knew enough to talk of the old cellar and the New Cellar which was built in 1875 with the low dome, part of which had to be propped up. I talked of old wood and new wines, and all seemed to be going well until we arrived at the de-stalking machine. There was Eric, in faded denims, his skin burnt brown as teak, shovelling away.

'Ah yes,' I said, 'another interesting aspect of the traditions of Tahbilk are the Italian families who were originally settled here to look after the mulberry trees. Their descendants still work here today. Here's one of them. Of course, we don't pay them, just fill them up with spaghetti and off they go like thrashing machines.'

Eric plodded on without a flicker of amusement on his face, but the publican became highly embarrassed. 'Eh,' he said, 'don't speak so loudly. He'll hear you.'

'Oh don't worry,' I replied. 'They don't speak a word of English. We'd never let that happen. They'd want Saturdays off as well as Sundays.'

We moved on. Just then, a huge forkful of stalks went flying past my ear as Eric miscalculated his aim. 'Eh,' said the publican, 'are you sure they don't understand English?'

At a Wine Board and Promotions Committee meeting in Hobart, I once fought for a pay increase for my bureau staff. I seem to remember that the State managers were getting $84 a week, and I thought they were worth at least $100. After discussing this for hours, I finally won over the Board, only to be told, 'Well, Len, *you* got all *you* wanted. We don't expect to hear from you for a couple of years.'

On the flight home the penny finally dropped; *I* hadn't received an increase, and in fact was getting only about $10 a week more than my managers. I was sitting with the same Ken Reid who, three years before, had asked me to join the Board. I asked him whether the Board's comment meant that I wouldn't get a rise for a year or more. He confirmed my suspicion. 'Well then,' I said, after a short silence, 'I think I'd better move on.'

'I don't blame you in the least,' was the reply. And that was that.

During this time, there were some problems with the catering for

'A fellow called Martin de Berry popped in one day. "I want to convert one of those grotty old wine saloons to an up-market place where young people can listen to good music, eat simple food and enjoy wine by the glass. Do you think this is a good idea?"'

Grilled duck breasts (recipe page 170).

the traditional Christmas party which the local association gave each year for the press. 'Why don't we do it ourselves?' I asked, and, like most people who can't keep quiet, I got the job. The first course was easy: a huge mound of freshly opened oysters. For the main course I obtained dozens of small chickens. I browned them on the legs and breasts, flamed them in brandy, stuffed them with sprigs of thyme and shoved them in the large ovens of the kitchen we had borrowed. It's remarkably easy to cook a hundred small chooks, and the fragrance lives with me even now.

Such is my enthusiasm for chicken that I once accepted an invitation to talk at the Poultry Growers Association annual dinner. I understood that I would receive a presentation painting for this gesture.

I worked hard at my speech, and made my audience roar with laughter. Everything went marvellously until the end of the speech, when I said that they could do something for me. Recently, I told them, I had cooked a batch of chickens that tasted of fish. Investigation revealed that this was because they had been fed a diet of fish meal. 'Please, Mr and Mrs Poultry-raiser,' I said, 'put the flavour back in chicken.'

To say that I sat down to muted applause would be stretching the truth. It terminated abruptly as soon as my backside hit the seat. The Association sent me the painting later; a large part of it was dominated by a toilet block.

Chicken really is one of my favourite meats because it is so adaptable. Chicken broth is one of the great clear soups, and I also like breast of chicken in strips in flambés and stir-fried food, large chickens for casseroles and stews and a big cockerel, farm fed, for roasting.

Again with Frank Margan, this time at the Steingarten vineyard in the Barossa Hills (note rocks and 'basket' pruning) in 1966. Mark Tummel of Orlando stands between us.

Chicken with cucumbers

2kg chicken
1 carrot
1 onion
2 large tomatoes
500g cucumbers
salt and fresh black peppercorns

300g clarified butter
pinch powdered thyme
1 bay leaf
1 cup cream
paprika
Serves 4

Rare beef as it is served in the Tasting Room.

Slice the carrot and onion thinly. Peel, seed and chop 1 tomato. Peel the cucumbers, cut into quarters and remove the seeds. Round off the corners to form large nut-like forms. Place the cucumbers into boiling salted water for 3 minutes. Remove, drain and season with salt and pepper. Slice the second tomato. Preheat the oven to 180°C/350°F.

Place the onion, carrot and chopped chicken giblets into a well-buttered ovenproof dish. Cook gently for 5 minutes. Brush the chicken with 125g of melted butter and place on the bed of vegetables. Place in the oven for 45 minutes, turning the chicken from time to time and basting it. Sprinkle with a pinch of salt. After 15 minutes add the thyme, bay leaf and tomato.

Place 180g butter into a saucepan and when hot add ½ cup of cream and the cucumbers and cook gently with the lid on over a low heat. When soft season with salt and paprika.

When the chicken is cooked place on a warmed serving dish. Pour ½ cup of cream into the dish in which the chicken was cooked, bring to the boil and then simmer for 2 minutes. Strain and pour over the chicken. Place the cucumber around the chicken and decorate the breast with tomato slices which have been slightly warmed in butter.

Roast chicken with a julienne of vegetables

whole chicken
4 sticks celery
2 onions
2 spring onions
3 carrots

green beans
chicken stock (cubes may be used but
    are not so tasty)
Serves 4

While the chicken is roasting, prepare a julienne of vegetables. Slice longways and very thin the celery, onions, spring onions, carrots and runner beans. When the chicken is cooked place the julienne of vegetables in a large saucepan containing 2cm of boiling chicken stock. Cover and cook for 5 minutes—or less if you prefer vegetables to be crunchy. Drain and keep warm. Pour the chicken stock into the roasting pan with the juices of the chicken and boil down. Carve the chicken into pieces. On a large platter, arrange the chicken pieces and the julienne of vegetables, then pour the juice over both.

Chicken Hazel Phillips

This was a Graham Kerr television dish in honour of dear Hazel. It has quite a strong taste and I have enjoyed a good red with it.

1.2kg chicken	*50g tin anchovies (flat fillets)*
1 garlic clove	*30g butter*
2 large tomatoes	*salt and black pepper*
60g onion	*2 teaspoons capers*
125g green capsicum	*parsley, to garnish*
90g mozzarella cheese	*Serves 2*

'It's remarkably easy to cook a hundred small chooks, and the fragrance lives with me even now.'

Cut the chicken in half, discarding the wings and backbone. Peel the garlic clove. Seed, skin and chop the tomatoes. Slice the onion finely. Cut the capsium into strips. Cut the cheese into thin slices. Soak the anchovies in a little milk; drain and cut lengthwise.

Heat the butter in a frying pan. Add the chicken and, when it is golden, add the garlic, capsicum and tomatoes. Season with salt and black pepper. Cover and simmer for 20 minutes. Remove the lid and place several slices of cheese and a few strips of anchovy on each chicken half. Cover and leave until the cheese melts, coating the chicken. Place on a heated serving dish. Reduce the vegetable pulp and juices and pour over the chicken. Sprinkle with capers and parsley.

Chicken Calvados Albert

Served at a dinner given by the celebrated gourmet, Tony Albert. Once he was walking down the street clutching a Michelin guide when he was stopped by a couple of evangelists. One opened his Bible and pointed to a passage in it, asking, 'Have you fought the good fight?' Tony immediately opened the Michelin guide and pointed to a page. 'No,' he replied, 'but I've dined at Le Tour d'Argent.'

2 small chickens cut in half	*Calvados*
lemon juice	*for the sauce:*
1 medium-sized onion	*veal stock*
salt and pepper	*1 glass Madeira*
fresh thyme	*½ glass Calvados*
butter	*1 truffle*
olive oil	*Serves 4*

Rub the chicken halves with lemon juice and a little olive oil. Add a little salt, ground pepper and fresh thyme. Place a few dollops of butter on top of each chicken. Then place a little olive oil and butter in a baking dish. Place a quarter of an onion on each dollop of butter on the halves of chicken and put them into the baking dish. Cover the dish with foil and cook for about 30 minutes at 190°C/

375°F. Remove the foil. Put back into the oven at 225°C/425°F until the chickens are brown, basting continuously.

To make the sauce add a glass of Madeira and a half glass of Calvados to a basic veal stock. Reduce the stock until it thickens into a medium glaze. Thinly slice a truffle and add to the sauce.

Shortly before serving, pour Calvados over the chicken halves and flame them. Remove the chickens from the dish. Pour the sauce over the chickens and serve with a French salad and small, new parboiled potatoes lightly fried in butter.

Feathered fare

An authentic old Australian recipe, from a 19th-century cookbook. You could use any other kind of bird.

1 mallee hen	*250g small pork sausages*
6 rashers bacon	*250g peeled mushrooms*
flour	*¼ cup stock*
salt and pepper	*¼ cup white wine*
paprika	Serves 4

Pluck and clean the mallee hen. Remove the rind from the bacon. Chop and lightly fry the bacon. Turn the bacon and fat into a casserole. Rub the bird with flour seasoned with salt and pepper and paprika. Place on the bed of bacon. Arrange pricked sausages and sliced mushrooms around. If preferred, stuff the bird with sausage meat or liver forcemeat, and omit the sausages. Cover and cook in a slow oven for 1½ hours. Uncover, add the stock and wine. Cover and cook for 10 minutes more.

'Chicken broth is one of the great clear soups, and I also like breast of chicken in strips in flambés and stir-fried food, large chickens for casseroles and stews and a big cockerel, farm fed, for roasting.'

Poulet sauté à la doria

1.5kg chicken	*30g butter*
1 medium cucumber	*1 tablespoon veal stock*
salt and pepper to season	*½ teaspoon lemon juice*
1 sprig parsley	*60g butter*
1 tablespoon olive oil	Serves 6

Disjoint the chicken. Seed the cucumber and cut into pieces the size of garlic cloves. Season the chicken with salt and pepper. Preheat the oven to 180°C/350°F. Finely chop the parsley. Place the oil and the butter in a frying pan and sauté the chicken pieces until well browned. Add the cucumber and season with salt and pepper. Cook a few minutes longer. Place the chicken and cucumber in a casserole and cook in the oven for 30 minutes. Drain the fat from the frying pan, and deglaze with the veal stock and lemon juice. Place the fresh butter in a pan and brown, add the minced parsley and then add to the gravy. Pour the gravy over the chicken and cucumbers and serve.

Chicken with ginger

1 medium-sized chicken
salt and pepper to taste
butter and vegetable oil for frying
1 tablespoon flour
1 teaspoon crushed ginger

1½ cups white wine
2 cups water
1½ cups coconut milk or sour cream
Serves 4–6

'This recipe is from Rosie Sinclair, who as Rosemary Fenton, was Miss Australia. She married Ian Sinclair, the politician and grazier. In fact, they did some of their "courting" in the Tasting Room. Ah, the sheer romance of it.'

Cut the chicken into serving pieces. Sprinkle with salt and pepper, and shallow fry it in a cast iron casserole with a mixture of butter and oil. Sprinkle the pieces with flour and add the crushed ginger, wine and water. Bring gently to the boil, then simmer for 30 minutes, covered. Remove the chicken pieces and strain the liquid. Put all back in the same casserole, check the seasoning and, just before serving, add the coconut milk or sour cream. Serve very hot (but be careful not to let the coconut milk boil) with boiled rice.

Chicken Pontalba

1kg boned chicken leg, thigh and
  breast
1½ cups béarnaise sauce
60g white onions
30g shallots
3 garlic cloves
30g mushrooms
125g ham
2 small potatoes
1 tablespoon parsley
125g butter

½ cup white wine
paprika to garnish
for the béarnaise sauce:
500g butter
4 egg yolks
juice of 1 lemon
salt and pepper
2 tablespoons capers
2 tablespoons chopped parsley
1 tablespoon tarragon vinegar
Serves 3

First prepare the sauce. Melt the butter. In the top of a double boiler beat the egg yolks and the lemon juice. Cook very slowly over a low heat. Don't allow the water in the bottom pan to come to the boil. Add the melted butter slowly to the egg mixture stirring constantly. Season with salt and pepper and add the capers, parsley and vinegar. Thinly slice the onion. Finely chop the shallots and garlic. Finely slice the mushrooms. Cut the ham into small dice. Dice the potatoes and deep fry until light brown; drain. Finely chop the parsley. Flour the chicken pieces. In a large pan melt half the butter and sauté the onion, shallots and garlic until tender. Add the mushrooms, ham and potatoes and continue to cook for 5 minutes. Add the wine and parsley and heat through. Remove the ham and vegetables from the heat and keep warm. Fry the chicken pieces in the remaining butter until golden brown. To serve, arrange the chicken pieces on a bed of the ham and vegetables and cover with béarnaise sauce. Surround with toast triangles and sprinkle lightly with paprika.

Chicken Cynthia à la Champagne

2 chickens, each weighing 1kg
flour to coat
salt to season
60g mushrooms
60g butter
1 orange
1 tablespoon oil

1 tablespoon Curaçao
¾ cup dry Champagne
1 cup chicken consommé
½ cup cream
150g sultana grapes
Serves 4

Disjoint the chickens—use only the breasts and thighs. Flour and salt the chicken pieces. Finely slice the mushrooms and sauté in 30g of butter. Peel the orange and cut into segments. Preheat the oven to 180°C/350°F. Place 30g of butter and the oil in a frying pan and sauté the chicken pieces for 10 minutes on each side. Remove to a baking dish and continue cooking in the oven for 20 minutes. Remove the fat from the baking dish and add the curaçao and champagne. Cover with the consommé and let the chicken simmer on top of the stove until tender—about 20 minutes. Add the mushrooms and then the cream. Heat through. Serve in a chafing dish. Garnish with orange wedges and grapes.

Typing an article for the *Bulletin* in 1966 outside the Angaston Hotel in the Barossa Valley; it was about Peter 'Mudflat' Lehmann. The sturdy Holden took us to most major wineries in Australia.

Cantonese style fried crispy chicken

1.2kg chicken
4 green spring onions
60g grated fresh ginger
1 teaspoon aniseed
1½ tablespoons Mui Kwai Lo
   Chinese wine or sherry
1½ teaspoons brown sugar

2 tablespoons malt vinegar
1 tablespoon white vinegar
1 tablespoon cornflour
¼ teaspoon Chinese Five Spice
   powder
salt and pepper
Serves 4

Make a soup by placing the chicken, spring onions, grated ginger, aniseed and Chinese wine or sherry into enough water to cover. Bring to the boil and cook for 15 minutes. Remove the chicken.

Rub the chicken with a mixture of the brown sugar, both types of vinegar, cornflour, spice, salt and pepper. Repeat this process for 10 minutes. Hang the chicken in a draughty place for 3 hours until it has dried. Tie the forelegs with string.

Prepare a deep frying pan. When the oil is very hot, hold the chicken by the string in one hand and pour the hot oil into the inside of the chicken with a large spoon held in the other hand. Continue this process for 15 minutes. Apply the same method to the outside of the chicken for another 15 minutes. When the chicken is brown it is ready to serve.

Sunday chicken legs

A great Sunday stand-by.

2–3 chicken legs each person	2 teaspoons ginger, chopped (or powder)
oil	
150ml brandy	black pepper, crushed
2 onions, finely chopped	sweet sherry
8 spring onions, finely chopped	soy sauce
100g broccoli stalks, finely chopped	black sauce, just a touch
150g celery, finely chopped	Tabasco
1 green capsicum, finely chopped	one or two drops honey
2 cloves garlic, crushed	chicken stock (cubes will do)
1 chilli, finely chopped (or a little dried grated chilli)	

Seal and brown the chicken legs in hot vegetable oil in a very big frying pan, flaming with brandy. Remove the legs and sauté the vegetables in the residue. Add the garlic, chilli, ginger and black pepper. After tossing this around for a few minutes, add some sweet sherry, soy sauce, black sauce, tabasco and honey. Stir well, cook until almost tender, add the chicken stock, place the legs back in the pan and cover. Cook until the legs are done—this should take about 10 minutes. Serve with Chinese egg noodles, rice or spaghetti.

Quick chicken legs with bean sprouts

'Another of those Sunday evening dishes, when masses of kids and friends are around. If you get help with the vegetable preparation while you're doing the legs, this dish takes just over 30 minutes from start to finish.'

2kg chicken drumsticks	1 large onion
oil	2 carrots
soy sauce	2 stalk celery
Chinese Five Spice powder	100g broccoli
1 clove garlic, crushed	1 cup chicken stock
sugar	150g mushrooms
for the rice and vegetable accompaniment:	100g bean sprouts
1½ cups rice	Serves 8–10

Place the drumsticks in a frying pan with a little oil and brown thoroughly. Add plenty of soy sauce, some Chinese Five Spice powder, garlic and sugar. Simmer gently until cooked, then turn in the reducing sauce until thoroughly coated. Keep hot.

Cook the rice and also keep hot. Scrape the onion, carrots, celery and broccoli stalks, slice and cook in a little oil. When hot and becoming tender, add the stock (cubes are all right) and steam for a minute or two. Add the sliced mushrooms and broccoli tops. Cook for a couple of minutes. Do not overcook any vegetable. Add the bean sprouts. Since they can tangle, take out half-cooked pieces, put in a layer of sprouts, then one of pieces, then sprouts and so on. Heat a few minutes only, until the sprouts are hot, and serve, with the chicken legs and rice.

Chicken à la Evans

Another of those leftover dishes which was devised as we went along from what was available in the refrigerator. Simple to do, yet quite delicious.

1kg chicken pieces, frozen can be used
10g butter
3 onions, peeled and sliced
75ml brandy
2 carrots, sliced
2 stalks celery, sliced
1 capsicum, deseeded and sliced
½ bottle white wine
2 cups apple juice

salt and pepper
garlic powder to taste
English mustard to taste
1 tablespoon cornflour
2 tablespoons water
12 whole button mushrooms
parsley, chopped
250g apples peeled and diced
Serves 6

Using a large, heavy pan, sauté the onions in butter. Add the chicken pieces, brown and flame in brandy. Top with the carrots, celery, capsicum, white wine and apple juice. Season with salt, pepper, garlic powder and English mustard. Simmer for about ½ hour or so until the chicken is cooked through. Mix the cornflour with water and add to the chicken with the mushrooms, parsley and apple pieces. Simmer until all is tender. Serve with rice.

Chicken flambé

One of the standards of Rothbury.

chicken breasts, skinned and finely sliced
butter
onions, chopped
celery, very finely chopped
capsicums, very finely chopped
brandy

chicken booster
salt and pepper
chilli powder
soy sauce
Hoi Sin sauce
puréed tomato
parsley

In a large frying pan melt some butter, allowing it to get fairly hot. Add the onions and sauté for a little while. Add the celery and capsicums. Add the chicken breasts. Toss the pieces around quickly and then flame in a little brandy. Quickly add chicken booster (in powder form), salt, pepper, chilli powder to taste, soy sauce, Hoi Sin sauce, or any other flavour you may like. Add cooked puréed tomato, chopped fresh parsley and serve. Take care to cook the chicken quickly as it toughens the longer it is cooked.

Petto di pollo fantasia

A recipe from my good friend Beppi Polese.

6 chicken breasts with wings, boned and halved	125g mushrooms
juice of 1 lemon	2 cloves garlic
salt and pepper	2 tablespoons chopped parsley
½ cup flour	7 tablespoons grated Parmesan cheese
10 tablespoons butter	2 eggs, beaten
	Serves 6

Remove the wing tips and wash the chicken breasts in water and lemon juice. Dry them with paper towels. Beat them with a meat pounder, leaving the little wing bone bare. Season the chicken breasts with salt and pepper, then dredge lightly with flour. Melt 5 tablespoons of butter in a large skillet and when it is golden, brown the chicken breasts lightly on both sides. Reduce the heat and simmer for about 20 minutes.

Remove the breasts from the skillet and place on a chopping board. Cut a neat hole, about 2.75cm in diameter, from the centre of each breast. Grind the meat taken from the hole with the mushrooms, garlic and parsley and mix with the Parmesan cheese and salt and pepper. Bind the mixture with the beaten eggs. Make six round croquettes with this mixture and put one in the empty space in each chicken breast. Melt the remaining butter in the skillet and sauté the stuffed chicken breasts until they are a little browner. Arrange the breasts on a heated oval serving dish and pour the juices in which they were cooked over them.

Tasting at Seaview Wines in the 1960s, when I was Director of the Wine Bureau.

Walnut chicken in Peking sauce

From the Imperial Peking Harbourside, Sydney.

¼kg chicken fillet, skinned and cut into small pieces	4 soup spoons ground bean sauce
2 tablespoons cornflour	4 teaspoons sugar
¼ teaspoon salt	few dashes Chinese rice wine or dry sherry
1 tablespoon peanut oil	¼ teaspoon red colouring powder (if preferred)
1 egg yolk	Serves 4
2 tablespoons sesame oil	
20 walnuts	

Place the chicken pieces in a large bowl. Add the cornflour, salt, peanut oil and egg yolk. Season and mix well. Let stand for 20 minutes. Place a little sesame oil in a wok or saucepan and heat to a moderate temperature (the oil must not be too hot). Add the walnuts to the saucepan and swirl in the oil for 2 to 3 minutes. Remove the walnuts and place in a drainer for later use. Place the chicken pieces in the same saucepan and oil as used for cooking the walnuts, and cook for 2 to 3 minutes. Remove the chicken to a dish. In a clean saucepan place a little oil, the ground bean sauce with water, the sugar and the Chinese rice wine. Cook for 1 minute then add the chicken pieces, walnuts and red food colouring. Cook for ½ minute, add the sesame oil and serve.

Chicken in savoury sauce

One of my favourite light, flavoursome dishes, most likely to be cooked when on one of those perennial diets.

2kg skinned chicken pieces
1 cup chicken stock
1 cup sliced carrots
2 medium tomatoes, peeled
½ medium red capsicum, seeded and
  cubed
½ cup sliced mushrooms

1 cup sliced onion
juice of 1 lemon
¼ teaspoon salt
dash each pepper and nutmeg
2 cups cooked rice
Serves 4

Steam the chicken pieces until tender. Discard the bones and cube the meat. In a saucepan combine the stock, carrots, tomatoes, red capsicum, mushrooms and onion, and cook until the vegetables are tender. Season with lemon juice, salt, pepper and nutmeg. Pour into a blender and process until smooth. Return to the saucepan, add the chicken meat and heat gently. Serve on a platter surrounded by rice. Divide evenly.

Chicken jambalaya

1kg boned chicken pieces
butter
oil
2 onions, sliced
1 celery stalk, chopped
2 bacon rashers, chopped
ginger to taste
3 tablespoons brandy
salt and pepper

chicken stock cube
2 capsicums, 1 red, 1 green
shallot greens, good quantity
parsley
chives
soy sauce
Hoi Sin sauce
chilli sauce
Serves 6

'Not really a true jambalaya, but an adaptation we used at Rothbury when flambé cooking for over 600 people with four of us in action.'

Into a large pan put butter and oil, and heat. Add the sliced onions, chopped celery and bacon rashers. Cook until nearly soft. Add the shaved or chopped ginger, plus pieces of boned chicken. The pan and fat must be very hot. Stir and flambé with brandy. Add salt, pepper, chicken stock cube, finely chopped capsicums, shallot greens, parsley and chives. Cook, keeping as dry as possible and frequently turning ingredients over. Add the magic mixture to taste. This is a blend of soy, Hoi Sin and chilli sauces. Just sprinkle lightly for a delicate influence, or liberally if you want the dish hot and tangy. Could be served with rice.

Coq au vin Bourguignonne

1 large good quality chicken
50g butter
2 rashers bacon or salt pork
²/₃ cup brandy (in Burgundy they use
    the local Marc)
1 tablespoon flour
12 cultivated mushrooms about 2cm
    across
12 pickling onions
for the marinade:
2 carrots
2 onions

1 stick celery
2 whites of leek
2 large mushrooms
2 cloves crushed garlic
crushed bay leaf
thyme
parsley
salt and pepper
1 bottle good soft red wine
vinegar
olive oil
Serves 6

'There are endless varia-
tions of this famous
chicken-in-wine dish,
including some sloppy
overcooked versions which
pay but scant homage to
the background of the
dish. In fact, overcooking
the chicken is one of the
problems and should be
avoided. In Burgundy the
chicken is often marinated
overnight, and I prefer
this method.'

Chop up quite fine the marinade mixture. Add the herbs, seasoning, the wine, a dash of vinegar and olive oil. Chop up the chicken into reasonably sized pieces and cover with the marinade. Leave overnight. Heat some butter in a large covered pan or casserole; add the chopped bacon or pork. Sauté. Remove the chicken pieces from the marinade and brown on all sides. Add the brandy and flame. Add the marinade, cover and simmer until the chicken is tender, but not overcooked. Remove the chicken and keep warm. Strain the liquid and discard the vegetables. Replace the liquid in the pan, add flour and butter kneaded together and reduce and thicken the liquid. The cultivated mushrooms and onions may be cooked in this liquid or sautéed separately. Bring together the chicken pieces, mushrooms and onions, coat with the thick reduced sauce and serve.

Coq au vin blanc

1 large good quality chicken
olive oil
1 rasher bacon, rind removed
1 onion, chopped very fine
1 carrot, chopped very fine
1 stick celery, chopped very fine
1 crushed clove garlic
thyme
crushed bay leaf
parsley

salt and pepper
²/₃ cup brandy
250g sliced leek whites
1 bottle dry white wine
vinegar
¼ cup flour
30g butter
12 cultivated mushrooms
Serves 6

Heat a little oil, add the chopped bacon and chicken chopped into pieces. Brown on all sides. Add the chopped vegetables, garlic, herbs and seasoning. Sauté. Add the brandy and flame. Add the sliced leek whites, white wine, a little vinegar and seasoning. Cover pan or casserole and simmer until tender. Remove the chicken pieces and keep warm. Add kneaded flour and butter to liquid and simmer until mixture thickens and reduces. Add the mushrooms or sauté separately. Correct the seasoning. Bring together the chicken and mushrooms in the reduced sauce and serve.

———————— ❧ ————————

Curried chicken from the Gulf of Arabia

1.5kg chicken, cut into eight pieces
2 teaspoons salt
½ teaspoon nutmeg
1 teaspoon cumin
½ teaspoon paprika
½ teaspoon ground cardamom
½ teaspoon black pepper
1 teaspoon turmeric
3 tablespoons ghee
2 large onions, finely chopped
2 cloves garlic, crushed
1 teaspoon grated fresh ginger
1 teaspoon chilli powder
cinnamon stick
2 large tomatoes, blanched, peeled, chopped
2 loomi (dried limes) or thinly pared rind of 1 lemon
1 teaspoon salt
1¼ cups water
Serves 4–5

'This recipe came from a Syrian, Arto de Haroutunian. I've never been a great curry fan—something to do with the wine I suppose—yet this is an easy dish to do, once all the ingredients are organised, and it's very tasty.'

Mix together the salt, nutmeg, cumin, paprika, cardamom, black pepper and turmeric, and rub half of this mixture over the chicken pieces. In a large pan heat the ghee, add the chicken pieces and fry until browned all over. Remove from the pan. Add the onions to the pan, fry until soft, then add the garlic, ginger, reserved spices, chilli powder and cinnamon stick. Fry for another 5 minutes, stirring all the time. Place the tomatoes, loomi or lemon peel, salt and water in the pan and bring to the boil. Return the chicken pieces to the pan, cover and cook on a low heat for 1 hour or until chicken is tender.

———————— ❧ ————————

Chicken pie

4 cups cooked chicken, cut into chunks
100g butter
½ cup flour
2 cups chicken stock
1 cup cream
½ teaspoon freshly ground pepper
salt
12 small white onions, cooked
¾ cup of peas, cooked
shortcrust pastry to fit 23cm pie dish
Serves 6

Preheat oven to moderately hot (220°C/425°F). Melt the butter in a saucepan, stir in the flour and cook, stirring for two minutes. Slowly add the stock, cream, pepper and salt to taste. Cook for five minutes, until thickened and smooth. Put the chicken pieces in a deep pie plate or casserole, cover with the sauce, and stir in the small onions and peas. Place the prepared pie crust over the casserole, allowing enough overhang so that the edges can be crimped. Cut vents in the crust to allow the steam to escape. Bake for 20–30 minutes, or until the crust is nicely browned.

Chicken in carrot crust

This is yet another way to cook any piece of meat in a crust, so that all the juices remain inside. I've cooked pigeons, guinea fowl and pheasant in various dough mixes, and in the bush in North Queensland we used to rub the muddy clay from the billabongs into the feathers of the wild duck and then throw them onto the ashes of the fire, even without gutting them. When the birds were baked, the crust would be broken and torn off with the skin. The meat was delicious.

1 large chicken
salt and freshly ground black pepper
bay leaf
rosemary sprig
2 chicken livers
2kg carrots
1kg flour
¾ cup coarse sea salt
Serves 4–6

'The meat was delicious. We used to rub the muddy clay from the billabongs into the feathers of the wild duck and then throw them onto the ashes of the fire, even without gutting them.'

Preheat the oven to 250°C/475°F. Dry the inside and outside of the chicken. Season the inside only with salt, freshly ground black pepper, the bay leaf, rosemary, and chicken livers. Truss the chicken, tucking in the wings and securing the legs. Lightly oil a shallow baking dish.

Grate half the carrots. Cook the remaining carrots until soft, then purée. In a large mixing bowl combine the flour, sea salt and grated carrot. Add the puréed carrot gradually and knead the mixture until it becomes a homogenous paste (all the purée may not be needed). Lightly flour a pastry board and press out the dough with floured hands. Place the chicken breast side down and smooth the paste over the back, sealing any cracks with a palette knife. Carefully lift the chicken onto the baking tray back down and continue to sculpt the paste over the breast until the chicken is completely sealed in a carrot crust. Place in the oven for 15 minutes. Lower to 150°C/300°F and cook for 1 hour 15 minutes. Bring to the table and cut the crust open.

Galantine of duck, Chinese style

A great standard for accomplished cooks.

1 duck, weighing about 2kg
200g finely chopped onion
1kg finely minced veal (very cold)
200g Chinese barbecue pork cut into 1cm dice (chilled)
3 Chinese sausages cut into 1cm pieces (chilled)
1½ teaspoons Chinese Five Spice powder
½ teaspoon ground ginger
¼ teaspoon garlic powder
2 eggs
¼ glass dry sherry
salt and pepper
200g duck livers
oil
Chinese colouring powder
have ready string and one piece of muslin cloth or tea towel
Serves 6–8

IS THAT THE 1921 CLOS DE LA ROCHE, OR THE 1929 CHATEAU HAUT BRION?

THAT'S A VERY VERY *HARD* QUESTION. BUT THEN..

LIFE WASN'T MEANT TO BE EASY...

The original of the Nicholson cartoon of Malcolm Fraser at a Single Bottle Club dinner. Note the cigar with wine, something that would never happen!

Fry the onions in a little oil until cooked but not coloured. Set aside and allow to get cold.

With a sharp fork, prick the duck all over the breast, piercing the skin and the fat below it. Roll the duck over and cut the flesh down the back from the neck to the tail and scrape all the meat off the backbone. Remove all the bones from the duck, being careful not to make holes in the skin.

Put all the bones and giblets and any vegetable parings into a large saucepan of water and put on the boil for stock.

Combine the mince, onions, pork, sausage, Five Spice powder, ginger, garlic powder, eggs, sherry, salt and pepper and mix until all comes together, taking care that the mixture remains cold.

Lay the duck skin-side down on the muslin and cut some of the meat from the fleshy parts and put over parts of the skin that are bare of flesh. You should now have a fairly even distribution of flesh over the skin. Put half of the mince mixture down the middle of the duck. Place the duck livers on the mince and cover them with the remaining mince. Roll the duck over the mince and then roll as tightly as possible into the muslin. Tie the ends with string and then tie tightly in three parts (along the galantine). Place the galantine in the boiling stock and gently simmer for approximately two hours after the stock comes back to the boil.

Remove the galantine from the stove and allow to cool in the stock. When cool enough to handle, but still warm, remove from the stock, cut the string and unwrap the muslin. Rewrap and retie as tightly as possible in the previous manner. Put back into the stock and allow to cool. When cold put the galantine in the fridge and chill, preferably still in the stock, for 24 hours. Remove the galantine from the muslin and wipe dry. Heat a little oil in a large pan, and add a little red colouring powder. Fry the galantine until it is red all over. Put it back in the fridge to set. Slice and serve cold with Chinese ginger pickles, Chinese mushrooms and tree fungus with sesame seed dressing.

Grilled duck breasts

4 complete duck breasts
oil
20g butter
3 medium-sized parsnips
cream

1 tablespoon red wine
brown veal stock
20g green peppercorns
Serves 4

Cook the breasts whole in oil and butter in a heavy frying pan. Do not overcook. In the meantime boil the parsnips and blend when cooked with a little cream. Remove the duck breasts, slice into long strips, arrange on a dish and keep hot. Into the pan pour the wine, some veal stock and the peppercorns. Reduce over a fierce heat. Pour this over the slices of breast, add the parsnips at one end and serve.

Polynesian coconut duckling

2.5kg duckling
2 coconuts
2 cups shredded coconut
2 small pineapples
1 small pawpaw, peeled
2 garlic cloves
2 onions
50g fresh ginger root
¼ cup flour
185g butter

1 cup water
1 tablespoon curry powder
chutney, to accompany
1 teaspoon salt
for the coconut milk and cream:
2 cups coconut flesh or desiccated
   coconut
2 cups water
Serves 4

'Fresh coconuts are best for obtaining coconut cream. Many people ruin this kind of recipe by thinking that the coconut milk or cream is the fluid inside the coconut.'

Crack open the coconuts. To make the coconut milk and cream, boil the water and pour over the coconut in a bowl. Cover tightly and allow to infuse for 30 minutes. Strain through muslin. Allow to stand for 1 hour and remove the cream. Toast the shredded coconut. Cut the duckling into 4. Trim off excess fat. Halve the pineapples lengthwise and remove the meat, leaving the shells 12mm thick. Dice the flesh. Slice the pawpaw. Peel and finely chop the garlic, onion and root ginger. Sift flour. Preheat oven to 180°C/350°F.

In a large pan heat 125g of butter and sauté the duckling until lightly browned on both sides. Add the water, cover and simmer for 1 hour until tender. In another saucepan melt the remaining butter and then add the garlic, onions and root ginger and sauté until the onions are tender and golden. Add the curry powder and salt and cook, stirring, for 1 minute. Stir in the flour and add 1½ cups of coconut milk to form the sauce. Add ½ cup coconut cream and heat, but do not allow to boil or the coconut cream will curdle.

Place a layer of pawpaw in each pineapple shell and top with a layer of diced pineapple. Cover with 2 tablespoons of curry sauce and heat in the oven for 15 minutes. Place a piece of duck in each pineapple shell and cover with curry sauce. To serve, sprinkle with toasted coconut and serve with a small dish of chutney.

Confit of duck

From Anders Ousback, my protégé, friend and colleague.

3 ducks
1kg butcher's salt

6 litres duck or goose fat
Serves 6

Cut the ducks in half; remove the necks and wings. Pack the halved ducks in coarse salt and refrigerate for 16 hours. Remove the ducks and wash them under cold water.

Pat dry; lay in a pot, and cover with duck or goose fat. Bring to the boil and reduce the flame to near minimum, so that the oil just trembles. Cook for about 3 hours. Allow to cool.

Lift the duck halves, one by one, from the oil and cut the breast from the thigh. Gently slide the bones from the meat and lay the breasts and thighs on a baking tray. Put the breasts (and thighs if you are big eaters) into a 180°C/350°F oven for 30–40 minutes till the skin firms up. At the last minute grill to crispen.

This all sounds a bit messy, but the advantage—quite apart from the flavour—is in the pre-preparation. Once cooled the confit will keep in the fat until eaten, because the salting and slow cooking preserves the duck.

If you can be bothered, roast the duck neck and wings to a good colour with a veal shank (cut as for osso bucco) and make a stock with sautéed vegetables and aromatics. Strain, allow to stand in the fridge and remove the fat. Reduce the stock on the side of the stove, skimming occasionally, till a glaze is obtained. Finish with old sherry, red wine vinegar or port. An alternative is a vinaigrette of walnut oil, chopped shallot and parsley, old vinegar, salt and pepper.

The confit goes splendidly with sautéed potatoes, sautéed baby turnips, green beans or hot potato salad.

Wild duck flambé belle terrasse

1 wild duck
60g butter
¼ cup Cognac
½ cup cream
⅓ cup sour cream

2 chicken stock cubes
½ teaspoon paprika
¼ teaspoon Tabasco
salt to season
Serves 2

Preheat the oven to 230°C/450°F. Reserve the duck liver and mash. Place the duck on a grid in a roasting pan and roast for 20 minutes or until done, basting from time to time with butter. When cooked, cut off the 2 breast fillets and pour the pan juices into a frying pan. Add the Cognac and set alight. Add the cream mixed with the sour cream and the chicken stock cubes together with the mashed duck liver and cook until the sauce is hot, stirring from time to time. Do not boil. Season with paprika, Tabasco and salt. Arrange the duck breasts on a hot serving dish and pour the sauce over them.

Pavé de dindonneau farci à la mangue

Stuffed supreme of turkey with macadamia nuts.

Hermann and Faye Schneider run the famous Two Faces Restaurant in South Yarra, Melbourne, as well as Roesti in Hardware Street in the city. Twenty years or so ago, Two Faces had been recommended to me as a top place. I went there and was delighted, so much so I returned the next two days. On the third visit, a cautious Hermann Schneider introduced himself and wanted to talk wine. From this simple beginning a friendship was forged, I like to think, that has been a strong influence on the retention of quality in wine and food in the face of all the compromises that are being made today. Hermann is acknowledged as one of our greatest food professionals. He is a perfectionist and I am given to understand that the shy, almost retiring side of his character that we see has its counterpart when aroused by professional sloppiness back or front of house. I've had many, many meals at Two Faces, including some of the best banquets I've experienced in Australia. And, again, one is always totally impressed by the attention to detail, the balance of food with wine, the utter professionalism of the whole. Two Faces has won many awards plus all sorts of honours from overseas. The rather drab basement which is its home does not equal the two and three star restaurants of France in appearance, but the food does, and to Hermann and Faye that is enough. Incidentally, they have also a magnificent wine list, long the joy of him and the despair of her.

1 buffet (breast) of turkey weighing
 2–2.5kg
1 egg white
1¼ cups pure cream
1 cup finely ground raw macadamia
 nuts

salt and pepper
bouquet garni
3 mangoes
½ cup sweet wine
Serves 6

Bone and skin the turkey breast, cut from each side 3 supremes and retain the trimmings for the stuffing. Carefully insert a sharp knife into each supreme to make a pocket. Put the denerved trimmings in a food processor with the egg white, pass this through a sieve and place on ice. Blend in ¾ cup of cream and macadamia nuts and season. Fill each supreme gently with this stuffing by inserting a steel nozzled piping bag. Close each supreme with a small skewer.

Make a stock from the turkey bones and the bouquet garni; reduce to about ¾ cup of syrup concentrate. Peel the mangoes and cut into 6 cheeks. Purée the rest of the mango flesh in a vitamizer. Make a sauce by gently reducing the mango pulp with the sweet wine and the reduced stock. Add the rest of the cream. Season. In a skillet gently pan fry the supremes in butter and finish in the oven for 5–6 minutes. Garnish with the warmed mango slices and coat with the sauce.

Pheasant braised in port

2 pheasants
salt and pepper
185g clarified butter

1 cup cream
½ cup port
Serves 4

Season the pheasants with salt and pepper and cook in the hot butter
in a deep uncovered pan on top of the stove. After about 20 minutes
add the cream and half the port and place a lid on the pan. Simmer
for 10–15 minutes or until the pheasants are almost cooked. Add the
remainder of the port, basting the birds, and replace the cover for 5
minutes longer. Place the pheasants on a hot serving dish and pour
over the sauce.

Pheasant with chicken liver sauce

A very good dish with a strong sauce to overcome the dryness of the
meat, which is usual with penned, commercially raised birds.

pheasant
2 cups good red wine
strong game stock, or reduce a tin of
    game consommé
large tablespoon redcurrant jelly

large glass brandy
Dijon mustard to taste
squeeze of lemon juice
2–3 chicken livers
Serves 2–3

Roast the bird for up to an hour until done (but not overdone). Remove it from the oven, cut it into pieces for serving and put it back
into the oven which has been turned off. Reduce the red wine and
game stock together to ⅓ of their original quantity. Add the redcurrant jelly, brandy, mustard, a bit at a time, whisking constantly.
Reduce until a smooth, thick consistency is achieved. Add a squeeze
of lemon juice. Slice the chicken livers as finely as possible. Add the
slices to the sauce and they will cook instantly. Add the sauce to the
bird pieces and heat through for 3 to 5 minutes. Serve with plain new
boiled potatoes.

The menu of the Single Bottle
Club dinner held at The
Lodge. The only failure was
the 1891 d'Yquem.

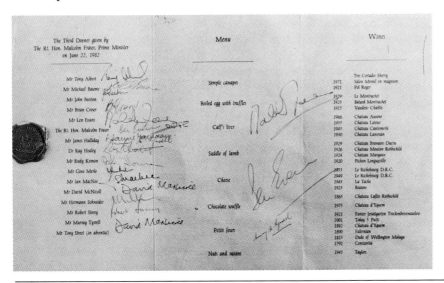

Guinea fowl with grapes

This is a standard of Hermann Schneider of Two Faces, Melbourne.

1 guinea fowl, or chicken	white wine
oil	cream
bacon	paprika
mirepoix (finely diced and seasoned celery, carrots and shallots)	grapes, peeled and seeded
	Serves 1–2

Pot roast a guinea fowl (or chicken) in a little oil in which some chopped bacon and a mirepoix have been sautéed. When cooked, deglaze with white wine. Remove the bird and keep warm. Strain the residue and take the fat off. Reduce. Add the cream and a touch of paprika. Heat gently. Add the pieces of fowl taken off the bone (except the wings). Add the grapes. When hot, serve.

Quails Corino

quail (chicken pieces may be used)	3 onions
butter	apples
pepper	chicken stock
brandy	fresh grapes
bacon	

'An on-the-spur-of-the-moment dish devised when Carlo and Franca Corino came to have lunch with us when staying with Bob and Wendy Roberts at Mudgee. Carlo is the very able wine maker with Montrose Wines.'

Split the quail up the back and remove the back bone and rib cage, spreading them flat. Put them into a pan for five minutes in a little butter, add pepper, and then flame in brandy. When done, place in a baking dish with all the pan juices. Into a saucepan place some diced bacon and three finely shredded onions and stir until nearly cooked. Then add diced, peeled and cored apples, plenty of them, plus a little chicken stock. When the apples are cooked, add a couple of handfuls of fresh grapes. One should peel and de-seed these but I don't bother. Pour the contents of the saucepan over the quail and put in a hot oven for 15 minutes. Adjust the timing for larger poultry pieces.

Pigeon and peas

6 large or 12 ordinary pigeons	2 cups chicken stock
100g fatty bacon	1 bottle soft red wine
200g butter	glass of port
½ cup brandy	300g fresh small peas, shelled
½ cup flour	Serves 12

Remove the livers and giblets from the pigeons and chop finely. Dice the bacon. Melt the butter in a large heavy saucepan and brown the pigeons thoroughly. Flame with brandy. Remove. Add the giblets and bacon to the butter and cook. Add the flour and cook for a minute or so. Add the stock, red wine and port and simmer for ten minutes. Add the pigeons and peas and cook until tender.

Saddle of venison Erzherzog Johann

1 saddle venison	salt, to season
16 fat bacon rashers	black peppercorns, to season
30g lard	stock, to moisten
juniper berries, to season	Serves 8–10

Trim and skin the saddle. Rub with pepper, salt and crushed juniper berries. Make incisions with pointed knife and insert 6 chopped bacon strips. Place remaining bacon strips over meat. Grease a baking dish with lard. Preheat oven to 185°C/375°F.

Place meat into the baking dish, add a little stock and roast for 1 hour, basting from time to time. Remove bacon strips from outside of meat to brown. Serve accompanied by potato croquets and cranberry jelly.

'There's a great deal more venison around these days. It's full of flavour and rather gamey. I preferred the meat we used to cook in New Zealand in the early 1950s when I was chopping trees down there. We would hang the meat for up to three weeks and simply roast it. Perhaps I was hungrier then.'

Rabbit pie

I love rabbit. Good rabbit meat is expensive now, and someone has even suggested that chicken is sometimes substituted for it! This is a delicious dish.

1 rabbit	2 tablespoons flour
4 onions	salt and fresh black pepper
250g shoulder bacon	1 sprig rosemary
3 eggs	1 sprig thyme
12 small sausages, highly spiced	500g puff pastry
1 cup dry white wine	Serves 4
200g clarified butter	

Cut rabbit into serving pieces. Finely chop the onions. Dice the bacon into 1cm cubes. Hard-boil 3 eggs and cut each into 6 pieces. Brown the sausages. Warm the wine.

Place the butter into a heavy pan and when hot add the onions and bacon and cook until golden brown. Flour the rabbit pieces and season with salt and pepper. Place them into the pan with the onions and brown. Add the wine, the rosemary and thyme and season with salt and pepper. Cover and allow to simmer for 1 hour or until the rabbit is tender. Preheat the oven to 220°C/425°F. Roll out the pastry to fit over a pie-dish. Pour the rabbit stew into a pie dish and add the eggs and sausages.

Lay the puff pastry over the pie dish, seal the dough to the rim of the dish by dampening with cold water and pressing together. Cut a small hole in the crust and insert a chimney of heavy paper rolled like a cigarette. Brush with egg yolk mixed with a little cold water. Bake in the oven for 20 minutes and serve.

CHAPTER SEVEN

Meat dishes: the Beef Room

T HERE IS A PROVERB or saying to the effect that anyone can be taught to cook, but the people who can roast have to have it born in them.

Of course, this came from the days when the roasting of large animals took a large part of the cook's time. Roast oxen, pig and lamb were done whole or in haunches, on the spit, and it took a very careful eye to judge how well they were cooked. For my eldest daughter's 21st birthday party I roasted each of one of the above, and we started 12 hours before the event.

Even when using an oven it is difficult to gauge correctly just how much of the meat has been cooked. I like any beef and lamb cooked to the point where all the blood has been converted to juice, with the lamb being cooked a little longer than the beef. When cut, the beef should be light red and the lamb pink. It is essential to let a roast of meat 'stand' for up to half an hour after it has been roasted, and therefore the meat should be removed from the oven *before* it's quite cooked to the degree you want. This standing allows the meat to set, and makes it much juicier and tastier.

It's quite suprising, but I've met all kinds of proficient cooks who can serve delicious entrées, vegetables dishes and puddings, yet cannot roast a joint of meat properly. I've seen them use thermometers and thermostat ovens and other gadgets and still miss out. Perhaps it's a matter of feel.

My favourite cut of beef is rump from an old beast that has been gently ranged. I get the oven very hot before putting the roast in, then keep it at the highest temperature for up to half an hour if the meat is a sizable piece, before turning the heat right down to then roast it for a longer period than is generally stated. (Generally I can tell by the look of the rump how much cooking is required.) Then I turn the heat off and leave the meat in the oven to set.

I like leg of lamb as well as the saddle, and I hate to see lamb well done. We used to have a great deal of trouble persuading butchers 'to muck up their chops and cutlets' to bone the saddle from the inside as one piece so that it could be stuffed, but now that's commonplace. I like leg of pork and especially pork neck, which is sometimes difficult to find because Australian butchers cut through it.

September 1980. The Petrus Dinner on my 50th Birthday. I enjoyed several lunches and dinners but this was probably the most formidable; 20 vintages of the great Chateau Petrus. Standing left to right: Doug Crittenden of Melbourne, Primo Caon of Adelaide, Don McWilliam, Ian Macnee, Peter Fox, Ray Healy, John Beeston, John Massingham, Ray Kidd, Victor Kelly, James Halliday, all of Sydney, Brian Croser of Petaluma, Tony Bilson, Rudy Komon and Graham Gregory. Seated left to right: Judy Crittenden, Murray Tyrrell from the Hunter, Jenny Fox, myself and Trish, Peter Meier, Bob Roberts from Mudgee and Max Lake. Front, left to right: John Rourke, Chris Hayes and Patric Juillet.

I find fillet of beef easy to cook, and have described the method on page 180. At Bulletin Place we use neither the rump nor fillet, but the sirloin strip, since it is a good cut of beef and is virtually prepackaged by the beast itself in a system of portion control. This decision was made when we started the Beef Room in the early 1970s, and we've never varied the cut.

The Tasting Room was a great success at the time, but it was also personally very demanding. I had to be there every day to bang the gavel and make a speech and describe the wines and to keep things moving along. Great fun but very demanding. We had discussed opening another floor of Bulletin Place, and it was clear I couldn't be in two places at once. So we designed a restaurant that did not need a 'personality' other than the pleasantness of the staff; relied upon its own atmosphere and empathy to create its own personality; and gave great value for money. By allowing the customers to do much themselves, the staff costs, and therefore the prices, were kept down. It also provided part of the atmosphere of the place, making it rather like a 'club'.

Again, we stripped the heavily painted walls to find lovely old bricks underneath. Bars, counters and dressers were all made from bits and pieces of old pulpits, prayer rails, tailors' cutting tables, sideboards, desks and bank counters. The tables came from old Singer sewing machines, bought from the Salvation Army for $2 each.

Around the walls I stuck various signs, placards and photographs which appealed to my imagination or sense of humour or sense of the ridiculous. Early ones included 'Monsieur Paul Bibron de Paris, Professor of Dancing and Calisthenics'; 'THIS LAND IS AURIFEROUS AND SUBJECT TO MINING CONDITIONS' (wondering how many bush walkers would know what auriferous meant); and a pub sign of a hermaphrodite kangaroo, which caused much amusement.

The kitchen was simple: a stove, a large baking oven and wash up and preparation areas. We charged about $5 a head when the Beef Room opened. The customer arrived, paid, and then had a drink or two at the bar, included in the price. When customers were seated, the waitress took the order: sirloin of beef—rare, medium or well done, thick or thin—salad or vegetables. It was as simple as that. On the sideboard, and also included in the price, there were many different kinds of bread, fruit, coffee and a 20-kilogram slab of cheddar cheese which stayed there until whittled away. The customers served themselves with all these as they wanted them. At the end of the meal, a glass or two of port was included. The only 'extra' was the table wine, chosen by the customer and paid for on the spot.

Today the 'extras' include an optional entrée and an optional dessert. There is a choice of meats, beef being one of them, and the customer now pays on completion of the meal. Otherwise, nothing has changed.

The Australiana collection in the Beef Room has expanded mightily over the years. Sometimes I think the room is over-capitalised, but I don't suppose I would have it any other way.

'Some of the finest food I've enjoyed at Bulletin Place has been in the Beef Room at the special dinners: the Bulletin/ Quelltaler Awards, *the* Epicurean Award, *the* Sydney Wine and Food Society *and the various great wine dinners.'*

In the evenings, the Beef Room is reserved for functions, because evening trade in the city is pretty quiet and our style suits such functions as parties and dinners, many of which are all inclusive. The Beef Room can cater for a simple dinner for 50 people or a special dinner for 30 people at $150 a head, which features a range of great Bordeaux or Burgundy wines.

I've often enjoyed the beef in the Beef Room, especially as an antidote to the more delicate food downstairs in the Tasting Room. Many friends who were first customers of the Tasting Room also use the Beef Room, but basically each eating place has its own supporters.

Some of the finest food I've enjoyed at Bulletin Place has been in the Beef Room at the special dinners: the *Bulletin*/Quelltaler Awards, the Epicurean Award, the Sydney Wine and Food Society and the various great wine dinners.

On a famous occasion at a Hennessy Award dinner I heard the shortest speech ever. We had some marvellous wines with very good food in the company of Colin Campbell, the Export Director of Hennessy Cognac. At the end of the dinner we were served five different Cognacs, and these had to be assessed in order of age, with each Cognac being identified in age terms.

At the end of this contest I called for a vote of thanks. Sitting next to me was Rudy Komon, grand old man of wine and food, and opposite, David McNicoll, the famed *Bulletin* columnist.

'And now, to give the vote of thanks to Hennessy,' I said, 'is a gentleman who needs little introduction.' I looked fondly at Rudy, who was in on the joke. 'This man is so distinguished that rooms stand when he enters, so vulnerable that old ladies help him across the street, so wise that even owls pay their respects. I give you the oldest and most infirm of us here today—David McNicoll.' David thought I was sending up Rudy and had no idea he would be called upon to speak. So he stood, said 'Evans, you're a—!' and sat down again, to sustained and ecstatic applause.

Oh, the pain of it; two smashing ladies and work to do. Suzanne and James Halliday and Di 'Bubbles' Fisher mingle in the background.

Steak au poivre ma façon

500g sirloin
¼ cup Cognac
salt to taste
roughly ground white peppercorns to
    season
45g butter
1 teaspoon rosemary leaves

1 teaspoon sage
3 x 3cm squares jellied veal stock
⅓ cup cream
1 teaspoon Dijon mustard
1 teaspoon mild mustard
crushed black peppercorns to season
Serves 2

Remove gristle from the meat and cut into 2 thick steaks. Place Cognac over the heat. Beat the steaks to flatten them a little and then season with rock salt and press the roughly ground white peppercorns into each side. Heat the butter in a frying pan, and when very hot add the rosemary and sage and then steaks and brown them on each side. Pour over the heated Cognac and set alight.

Remove the steaks from the pan, place on a heated serving dish and keep warm. In the pan on the heat add the veal jelly and melt. Add the cream and stir the pan to deglaze. Add the mustards to the sauce and the crushed black peppercorns and bring to the boil. Pour the sauce over the steak and serve.

Herbed barbecued steak

'My alternative to charred barbecue steak. If we are going outdoors, I prepare the mixture beforehand, coat the steaks with it, then put them in a strong plastic bag and add more herb mixture.'

steak
basil
oregano
thyme
rosemary

parsley
olive oil
pepper
garlic

Chop fresh basil, oregano, thyme, rosemary and parsley and mix with olive oil, pepper and crushed garlic. Coat steaks before grilling.

Fillets of beef Brennan

4 thin medallions of beef fillet
1 large tomato
¼ teaspoon salt
dash fresh black pepper
60g butter
30g mushrooms

1 tablespoon plain flour
¼ cup red wine
½ cup mushroom juice
¼ teaspoon Worcestershire sauce
Serves 4

Finely slice the mushrooms. Cut the tomato into slices. Season the fillets with salt and black pepper. Preheat the grill. Place the butter in a saucepan and add the mushrooms; sauté for a few minutes. Add the flour and cook slowly until slightly browned. Add the wine, mushroom juice, Worcestershire sauce, salt and pepper. Grill the fillets to taste. Grill the tomato. Place a tomato slice on each fillet and cover with the mushroom sauce.

Fillet of beef with garden vegetables

This is my way of cooking beef fillet, which suits us very well.

1 beef fillet, trimmed
150g baby carrots
150g baby turnips (if none
   available, trim large ones)
150g Brussels sprouts
150g peas

150g green beans, sliced lengthwise
150g fresh cauliflower flowerets
150g small onions
150g celery, cut into 5cm lengths and
   stalks cut lengthwise in three

Heat a large skillet, brush with oil and roll the fillet onto it, carefully browning each side quite heavily. In the meantime, preheat the oven to maximum heat. When the fillet is browned, transfer it to a baking dish and place in the oven. Leave for five minutes only. Switch off the oven. Let the meat rest in the oven for half and hour. If the fillet is quite small (from a small beast) these times may be shortened. The fillet should emerge, crusted on the outside, pink and juicy throughout with no 'blue' (uncooked) meat. Slice diagonally and present on a long serving platter.

While the meat cooks, blanch the vegetables in boiling water until almost tender, and then finish them in foaming butter. If possible, they should be done separately, or at least, blanched well in advance and sautéed in butter in different segments of the pan. Arrange vegetables in clumps around the meat and serve. Potatoes and a light gravy should be the only accompaniments.

Tournedos Bordeaux style

6 tournedos steaks
for the sauce:
60g shallots or spring onions, very
   finely chopped
60g butter
½ bottle good Bordeaux red (other
   red wine will do, but use a good
   one)
thyme

1¼ cups meat glaze
100g sliced champignons (optional)
lemon juice
salt
pepper
6 large pieces of bone marrow, or
   more of smaller pieces, cut about
   2cm thick
Serves 6

'A tournedos is a slightly larger piece of beef fillet than a fillet mignon. It should be nicely rounded and about 2.5cm thick. It can be tied. Please avoid putting a bacon strip around it as it does nothing for the meat.'

Make the sauce by sautéing shallots in a little butter in a saucepan then adding the wine and thyme. Reduce over a fierce heat. Add half the meat glaze. Add the champignons if desired and cook until tender. Add some lemon juice and the rest of the glaze.

Put butter in a large frying pan, heat to foaming, cook tournedos on both sides to required degree. In the meantime poach the marrow in the sauce. Arrange tournedos on individual serving plates, put a piece of poached marrow on top, smother with the sauce and serve.

Tournedos South American style

6 tournedos	oil
1¼ cups tomato purée	butter
Tabasco	salt
6 half red capsicums, trimmed thin	pepper
6 large mushrooms	Serves 6

Reduce tomato purée to almost a paste. Add a dash of Tabasco. Grill the capsicums until quite soft. Pan-fry the mushrooms in butter and oil. Season and pan-fry the tournedos to the required degree in oil and butter. On each plate, centre a blob of tomato purée. Cover with the mushrooms. Stand the tournedos on the mushrooms, spread the top with purée, and then cover with grilled capsicum.

Pot au feu

'One of the great standards, of which there are almost endless variations. I often use beef brisket instead of rump, cooking it longer. It's a cheaper cut, which isn't really the point. Simply, it seems more suitable for this dish.'

8 medium-size onions	1 veal knuckle
4 carrots in chunks	1kg marrow bones
4 leeks	2 chickens
3 stalks celery in 5cm pieces	750g rump steak
1kg oxtail	2 egg yolks
1kg shin beef	French mustard to taste
500ml round steak	

In water place half the vegetables (onions, carrots, leeks, celery), plus pieces of oxtail, bones of shin beef, cut-up round steak, a veal knuckle, and marrow bones. Bring to the boil and skim. Bring to the boil and skim again. Simmer for 5 hours. When the stock has thickened, cool, de-fat, remove the shin beef and oxtail and put to one side. Remove the other bits and throw away. Correct the seasoning of the stock. Add remaining vegetables and quartered chicken, or chickens, the shin beef and oxtail, and the rump steak. Cook for half an hour to an hour. Remove and slice the rump, which will not be fully cooked. Place on a large platter with all the other meat and vegetables, and keep hot. Strain off some liquid and serve this as a soup. Take more liquid, thicken with egg yolks, add French mustard and pour this sauce over the meat on the platter.

Corned silverside with dumplings

2kg corned silverside	for the dumplings:
malt vinegar	1 cup plain flour
2 teaspoons brown sugar	pinch baking powder
bay leaf	40g fresh beef suet
cloves	salt and pepper
peppercorns	milk
750g small white onions, peeled	Serves 4
750g carrots, thickly cut across	

Put corned silverside in a large saucepan in cold water so that it is covered, adding vinegar, sugar, bay leaf, cloves and peppercorns. Bring to the boil, skim, and simmer for two hours, occasionally skimming. Then add whole onions and pieces of carrot and cook until tender. Remove the meat, carrots and onions from the liquid and keep hot. Strain the liquid and return it to the saucepan on heat. Add the dumplings and simmer for 15–20 minutes until they are cooked. (They rise to the surface.) Slice the beef very finely across the grain, and serve with carrots, onions and dumplings. To make the dumplings, sift the flour, salt and baking powder together, then work in the pieces of suet with the fingers. Add enough milk to bind the mixture together into balls about 3cm across.

'This is one of my childhood memory dishes of which I'm still passionately fond. It is essential to serve a sauce boat of the liquid, at least if I'm there, for the juiciness of this on the plate is mandatory as far as I'm concerned. Equally, very hot English mustard should be served.'

Braised geed

This Israeli dish is said to be an aphrodisiac.

500g penis (of ram or bull)	*cumin*
1 chopped onion	*saffron*
coriander	*salt*
garlic	*oil*
1 chopped tomato	Serves 4
black pepper	

Scald the penis and clean it. Boil for 10 minutes, then remove from the pot and slice. Brown the onion, coriander and garlic together in oil. Add the penis slices and fry. Mix chopped tomato, pepper, cumin, saffron and salt. Cover the penis slices with this mixture. Cover the pan and cook over a low flame for 2 hours, adding a little water to prevent burning. Season and serve hot.

Tasting a great range of Hennessy Cognacs in the Beef Room in the mid-1970s. Sir William Tyree, previous winner of the Hennessy Gold award, sniffs on.

Veal cutlets cordon bleu

A very quick dish, which is a particular favourite of the kids.

4 x 90g veal cutlets	*plain flour to coat*
2 thin slices Swiss cheese	*breadcrumbs to coat*
2 thin slices ham	*1 tablespoon butter*
1 egg	Serves 2
salt and pepper to season	

Beat the egg. Beat the veal cutlets to flatten them. Place flour and breadcrumbs on 2 dishes. Place a slice of ham and then a slice of cheese on each veal cutlet. Cover entirely with another veal cutlet. Season and coat first in flour then beaten egg and breadcrumbs. Place butter in a frying pan and when hot add the cutlets and sauté till crisp on each side.

Nodini di vitello al Gorgonzola

Veal cutlets with Gorgonzola cheese

From Beppi Polese of Beppi's. Aldo Zuzza, was headwaiter there for many years until he opened the highly successful D'Arcy's.

6 veal cutlets

5 tablespoons olive oil

salt and pepper

5 tablespoons butter

125g Gorgonzola cheese

for the green sauce:

450g parsley

4 anchovies in brine

½ lemon

1 green capsicum

1 clove garlic

¼ onion

60g capers, drained and chopped

½ cup olive oil

salt

Serves 6

To make the sauce, wash parsley well. Scrape the salt from the anchovies, wash them with lemon juice and remove any bones. Scorch the capsicum over a gas flame and peel. Cut the pepper, wash out the seeds, rinse and cut into strips. Put the parsley, anchovies, strips of pepper, garlic, onions and capers into a vegetable grinder or food processor to produce a very finely chopped mixture. Dilute the mixture with olive oil and lemon juice. Taste the sauce for saltiness. Place in a sauce dish.

Soak the veal cutlets in the oil. Drain them and put them on a very hot grilling rack until brown on both sides. As they are turned, shake some salt and pepper over them. Cream the butter and cheese together with a fork. Shape this mixture into rounds. Place a round on each cutlet as it is taken from the griller. Aarrange the cutlets on a warm serving dish and serve. Accompany with green sauce.

Tasting the fruits of investment. My two preoccupations —Petaluma and Rothbury.

———————— ❦ ————————

Veal fillets Diana

An ideal quick lunch for two.

2 x 150g veal fillets

40g butter

20g carrots cut lengthwise into fine
    julienne strips

20g celery cut lengthwise into fine
    julienne strips

lemon juice

30g bean sprouts

20g onions, very finely chopped

salt

pepper

Serves 2

Flatten the veal to almost paper thinness. In a medium-sized frying pan, heat half the butter. Add the julienne strips of carrots and celery and sauté. Season. Add a squeeze of lemon juice and the bean sprouts, heat and set aside, keeping warm. Wipe the pan and re-heat, add the rest of the butter, then the onions and quickly sauté. Add the veal fillets and cook very quickly. You might only be able to cook one at a time, but it doesn't matter, since these steaks cook almost straight away. Put half the vegetable mix on each steak and serve.

Involtini Villa d'Este

Stuffed veal rolls

veal escalopes sliced thinly (2–3 per *parsley*
person, depending on size) *110g butter*
prosciutto or cooked ham, 1 slice per *1 cup dry white wine*
escalope *1 cup cream*
slices of mozzarella or similar Serves 6
melting cheese, 1 per escalope

Have the veal cut paper thin and pound well. On each slice of veal spread lengthwise a little prosciutto, some cheese and some parsley. Roll each slice individually and fasten with a toothpick. Put the rolls in a large frying pan with butter, and cook, stirring them until well browned all around. Pour in the wine and keep on high heat until the wine has nearly all evaporated. Lower the heat, cover and cook until cheese has melted into the butter and wine, forming a sauce. Just before serving, remove the toothpicks and add the cream.

Lunch in the Beef Room, Bulletin Place.

Medallions of veal or lamb with cream of chive sauce

1.5kg loin of veal or lamb, cut into *½ cup brandy*
16 x 85g medallions *2 cups cream*
½ cup + 2 tablespoons clarified *salt to taste*
butter *⅛ teaspoon white pepper*
4 cups raw mushroom stems, wiped *¼ cup dry white wine*
clean and sliced *2 tablespoons fresh chives, minced*
3 bay leaves Serves 8
2 teaspoons Worcestershire sauce

Heat a large sauté pan and add 5 tablespoons of the butter, stir in the mushroom stems and bay leaves, cook over medium high heat, stirring until the mushrooms darken a little. Add the Worcestershire sauce. Warm the brandy, ignite and pour over the mushrooms, shaking the pan constantly until the flames are extinguished. Add the cream, gently boiling and stirring often, until the cream has reduced and thickened. Strain the cream and discard the mushroom stems (they are used only to infuse the sauce with flavour). Add salt and pepper to the cream. Set aside.

Heat another large sauté pan or skillet, add the remaining butter. When the butter is hot, add the meat and quickly sear and cook (about 2 minutes on each side) just until done. Transfer the meat to a warm plate. Over high heat add ¼ cup wine to the skillet and deglaze the pan, stirring and scraping the bits from the bottom. Add the cream to the pan juices, heat thoroughly, add the chives. Stir. Add the medallions of veal to heat through. Serve.

Piccata of veal al limone

1kg veal scallopini (about 16 slices)
6 tablespoons clarified butter
1/4 cup lemon juice
1 tablespoon Worcestershire sauce
1 cup demi-glace or 2 cups strong beef bouillon
180g cold butter
salt to taste
Serves 8

Heat the butter over high heat and add the veal, quickly sear each side (about 20 seconds in all). Transfer the veal to a warm plate. Turn the heat to medium high and add the lemon juice, Worcestershire sauce, demi-glace or bouillon. Stir and cook 1 minute. Start adding the cold butter in bits, swirling the skillet constantly to keep the sauce moving. As soon as the butter incorporates with the sauce, add more. The secret of this sauce is to quickly blend the butter into the sauce without allowing the butter to get overly heated. You accomplish this by rotating the skillet rapidly over heat and then removing the skillet from the heat as soon as the last bit of butter disappears. Pour the sauce over the scallopini and serve.

Emince de veau Zurichoise

1kg veal
4 shallots
125g champignons
1/2 cup oil
60g butter
1 cup dry white wine
1 1/2 cups cream
1 1/2 cups brown sauce
salt to season
fresh black peppercorns to season
paprika to season
Serves 6

Slice the veal into small pieces (1cm). Chop shallots finely. Slice champignons finely. Place the oil in a pan and when it is hot add the veal and sauté until brown (about 3 minutes). Remove from the pan and place on a hot plate. Place the butter in the pan in which the veal has been cooked and when it has melted add the shallots and champignons. Add the wine and then the cream and bring the sauce to the boil and simmer 3–5 minutes. Add the brown sauce and season with salt, black pepper and paprika. Cook for a further 5 minutes and serve.

Scallopini of veal

625g veal loin
olive oil
clarified butter
for the sauce moutarde:
1/2 onion
60g butter
90g mushroom stems
1/4 cup dry sherry
bay leaf
pinch of rosemary
salt
white pepper
2 cups cream
60g Dijon mustard
1 tablespoon demi-glace
Serves 6

Slice veal thinly in approximately 60g medallions. Veal should be flattened with the flat side of a meat cleaver. A very thin medallion is preferred. Sauté veal slices in equal parts of hot olive oil and clarified butter. There should be three slices per portion, and each slice is sautéed for no more than 30–40 seconds on each side. Remove sautéed veal slices and keep warm.

To prepare the sauce moutarde sauté finely chopped onion in 60g of butter. Add mushroom stems and continue to sauté lightly. Add sherry and simmer. Simmering is finished at the point when the sherry has been nearly entirely reduced. Add the bay leaf, rosemary, salt and white pepper. Add the cream and continue simmering. Reduce. Add mustard and demi-glace and once again bring to simmering point. Remove from heat. Strain the sauce and correct seasoning. Pour sauce over veal slices and serve.

Lamb with egg and lemon sauce

From a Tess Mallos recipe, *arni fricasse*. Tess has done tremendous work as a consultant to the Australian Meat and Livestock Corporation.

Bobby Patterson, who ran Bulletin Place so well for most of the 1970s.

1 small leg of lamb, boned	*1 teaspoon chopped fresh dill*
1 large onion, chopped	*salt and pepper*
1 clove garlic, crushed	*6 large stalks celery*
butter	*1 tablespoon cornflour*
1 cup lamb stock, made from bones,	*3 eggs*
* or water*	*juice of 1 lemon*
chopped parsley	Serves 6

Trim and cut the boned lamb into large cubes. Gently fry the onion and garlic in butter until transparent. Add lamb and stir over heat until meat colour changes—do not brown. Add stock or water, parsley and dill. Season with salt and pepper, cover and simmer for 45 minutes. Wash the celery and cut into 5cm lengths. Blanch for three minutes and drain. Add to the lamb and cook for a further 15 minutes or until meat is tender. Thicken the liquid in the pan with a tablespoon of cornflour mixed with cold water (this acts as a stabiliser for the next step). Beat the eggs till frothy and gradually beat in the lemon juice. To this slowly beat in 1 cup of the thickened liquid from the pan. Pour egg and lemon sauce into the pan and gently tilt back and forth over heat to blend sauce with the pan contents and to cook the egg. Adjust seasoning and add more lemon juice if you like. Transfer to a warm serving dish and sprinkle on more chopped dill or parsley.

The celery may be replaced with leeks, cooked globe artichoke hearts, very young blanched broad beans, cos lettuce or endive. Pour boiling water over the lettuce or endive before adding during last 10 minutes of cooking.

Admiral Hardy's old English lamb

This comes from the *Piddle Valley Cookbook*, the royalities of which were used to restore the village church in Piddlehinton, in Dorset. We had great fun in the Indulgence column of the *Weekend Australian* when we discovered that Piddle wine was being made; and that there was a Great Piddle and a Lesser Piddle, even a Middle Piddle.

1 leg lamb
1.15kg potatoes
15g cooking fat
1 large orange
2 tablespoons clear honey

1 tablespoon plain flour
2 cups vegetable stock
sprigs of mint
pepper and salt
Serves 6

Preparing pork loin with dates (recipe page 193).

Preheat the oven to 180°C/350°F. Peel potatoes and parboil for 5 minutes. Melt the cooking fat in roasting tin and add parboiled potatoes. Scrub the orange and grate the rind. Place rind, honey and ½ level teaspoon of salt in a basin and mix together. Remove pith from orange with a sharp knife and cut flesh across in 6 slices. Score fat of meat in a diamond pattern. Put in a roasting pan with potatoes and spread with the orange and honey glaze. Cook in the centre of the oven for 2 hours, basting meat and potatoes occasionally. Lift the lamb and potatoes onto a warm serving dish and keep hot.

Strain most of the fat from the roasting tin, stir in the flour and vegetable stock and bring to the boil. Taste and season and pour into a warm gravy boat. Arrange slices of orange, slightly overlapping, with sprigs of mint along the meat. Arrange potatoes around the meat. Serve with green vegetables.

Roasted herbed saddle of lamb

2–2.5kg saddle of lamb, boned
1 teaspoon salt
¼ teaspoon freshly ground black pepper
3 tablespoons finely chopped breadcrumbs
1½ tablespoons finely chopped shallots

1–1½ tablespoons finely chopped parsley
½ teaspoon chopped garlic
butter
Serves 8–10

Score fat on top of the saddle. Rub salt and pepper over it and place lamb in lidded, heavy frying pan. Turn the roast until all sides have been sealed and browned. Meanwhile, mix the breadcrumbs, shallots, parsley and garlic in bowl. Melt a little butter. Remove lamb from the oven and pat the breadcrumb mixture on top of the saddle. Dribble butter over top. Continue to roast the lamb in the frying pan for another 45 minutes or until tender.

Transfer the saddle to a large, heated serving dish. Serve with red currant jelly or cumberland sauce.

Roast saddle of lamb, stuffed and served with snow peas

A recipe from two of my greatest friends, David and Margaret Levin of the Capital Hotel in London. I read about their hotel in 1972, a year after it had been opened, and I've stayed there ever since when in town. What makes the hotel is the quality of the restaurant (a one-star Michelin, rare for the United Kingdom) and the superb staff. Robert, the concierge, sets the standard, with infallible memory and resources, and this permeates throughout.

1 large saddle of lamb
125g mange touts per person
for the stuffing:
250g veal trimmings
250g mange touts (blanched)
1 egg
125g mushroom duxelles

for the sauce:
½ glass Madeira
½ glass white wine
2½ cups veal stock, reduced
125g butter
Serves 12–14

Pork loin with dates. (recipe page 193).

Bone and skin the saddle, taking care to remove as much excess fat as possible, without puncturing the fat. Mince the veal trimmings and mange touts, add egg and duxelles and a few breadcrumbs to bind. Season and stuff the saddle. Take care to keep the fat underneath trimmed so the two sides just meet. Roast in a fairly hot oven 230°C/425°F, taking care to keep the meat pink. Once cooked, take out and let stand. Make the sauce in the roasting pan. Remove the excess fat, add the Madiera and white wine, and reduce. Add veal stock and reduce again. Cube the butter and add slowly. Strain. Check seasoning.

Cook mange touts and arrange on a serving dish. Serve lamb on top. Serve sauce separately.

Rack of lamb bouquetière

2 x 750g rack of lamb, trimmed
salt and fresh black pepper to season
1 onion, sliced
1 teaspoon thyme

1 bay leaf
1 cup white wine
1 cup glace de viande
Serves 4

Season the lamb with salt and pepper. Preheat oven to 220°C/425°F. Roast the lamb for 30 minutes. Add onion, thyme and bay leaf to the meat and roast 5 minutes longer. Remove meat from the oven, discard onion, bay leaf and fat. Deglaze the pan with white wine, add glace de viande and allow to simmer 5 minutes. Strain the sauce.

Place the rack on a serving dish and glaze with a little of the sauce. Serve the rest of the sauce separately. Garnish with artichoke bottoms stuffed with peas and baby carrots, potatoes and tomatoes alternately around the meat. Add a bouquet of watercress.

Lamb with green peppercorns

500g lamb loin, 12cm x 3cm	salt
30g butter	pepper
dash vegetable oil	malt vinegar
½ cup brown veal glaze	Serves 3
20g green peppercorns	

'This very simple dish is highly effective. Everything is in the obtaining from the butcher of the trimmed long loin of lamb. Butchers don't like selling the individual loin because 'it mucks up the chops'. But do prevail because its worth it.'

Heat the butter with a dash of oil in a frying pan and cook the lamb fairly quickly, turning on all sides. It must be underdone. Remove and keep warm, allowing the loin to set. To the pan residues, add the glaze and the peppercorns and season. Add just a drop or two of vinegar. Work together until hot.

Cut loin lengthwise quite thinly, arrange the long pieces on each plate next to each other slightly overlapping, and then pour the glaze crosswise over the strips at the centre of them. I like this simple dish with a purée of parsnips.

Lamb chops Souvarov

4 x 250g double lamb chops	1 teaspoon shallots, chopped
500g puff pastry	1 teaspoon chives, chopped
for the stuffing:	salt to season
4 large mushrooms	black pepper to season
30g butter	egg yolk for glazing
185g chicken livers	Serves 4
1 tablespoon dry sherry	

Roll out pastry to 1cm thickness. Cut enough to cover the lamb chops. Cut out some half-moons of pastry for garnishing. Finely chop the mushrooms. Preheat the griller and the oven to 180°C/ 350°F. Place butter in frying pan, add chicken livers and mushrooms and sauté lightly. Add sherry, shallots and chives and then season with salt and pepper. Allow to cool. Work into a paste with a wooden spoon. Grill lamb chops 3 minutes each side and then place a little of the stuffing on each one. Place the chops on the prepared puff pastry and seal. Decorate and brush with egg yolk. Place the chops on a greased baking tray and bake in 180°C/350°F oven for 25 minutes, then raise heat to 200°C/400°F and bake a further 15 minutes.

Serve with tarragon-flavoured brown sauce.

Noisettes of lamb with Madeira

2kg trimmed loin of lamb	⅔ cup Madeira, preferably
30g butter	Portuguese
1 tablespoon oil	⅔ cup cream
¾ cup brown veal glaze	Serves 6
¾ cup meat glaze	

Make sure the loin is trimmed free from fat, bone and muscle fascia. Cut across into noisettes just over 1cm thick. Heat a mixture of butter and oil in a large frying pan and cook noisettes for 2–3 minutes each side, leaving the insides still pink. In the meantime, combine the two glazes in a small saucepan, heat, and reduce to a thick consistency. Add Madeira and correct the seasoning. Add cream and heat to below boiling.

Arrange each serve of noisettes and cover with sauce. Serve with mashed potatoes and long-sliced green beans. One can also pan-fry the whole loin in butter, then slice it lengthwise when still pink. I prefer the noisettes.

Truffled noisettes of lamb with potatoes Lyonnaise

A recipe from Fanny's in Melbourne.

2–3 noisettes, 3cm thick
20g truffles
2 soup-spoons parsley
100g new potatoes
20g onions

1 egg yolk
1 small soup-spoon meat glaze
oil, butter, salt, pepper
Serves 1

Heaven knows why I'm playing golf in my office.

Finely chop truffles and parsley with a sharp knife. Slice potatoes 2mm thick on a mandolin. Finely slice onion into rings. Lightly beat the egg yolk in a bowl. Mix the chopped parsley with three-quarters of the truffle; keep 5g for finishing the sauce. Salt and pepper each noisette then dip in the egg yolk and roll firmly in the parsley and truffle mixture. Heat a dash of oil in a non-stick frying pan and place in the noisettes. Cook 3 minutes each side. Add butter and allow to cook off the heat for a few minutes. The potatoes Lyonnaise are sautéed at the same time in a frying pan and cooked for about 3 minutes. Add the onion rings. To the butter in which the meat is cooking add the remaining truffles and a spoonful of meat glaze. Bring to the boil and season with salt and pepper.

On a dinner plate place the potatoes in the middle, the lamb around the potatoes, and pour the juice around the potatoes.

Pork loin with dates

2kg pork loin (boned and well
trimmed of fat, remove crackling
and cook separately)

250g fresh dates
Serves 6

Place dates on the loin, roll and tie tightly with string. Cook for 1¼–1½ hours at 200°C/400°F. Score the crackling and rub salt into the skin. Cook in the oven on 230°C/450°F until crisp.

To serve, slice the pork and garnish each plate with a sprig of watercress. Serve with red cabbage and small jacket potatoes.

Smoked pork with juniper berries

The smoked pork for this dish came from Schultzes, the butchers in Angaston in the Barossa Valley. The dish I devised as I went along. It really did turn out well.

1kg smoked loin of pork, skin on
2 carrots, chopped
2 onions, chopped
30g butter
6 crushed juniper berries
cabbage
¾ cup chicken stock

sherry vinegar
garlic
black peppercorns
salt
carraway seeds
Serves 6

Sauté in butter the carrots and onions in the bottom of a casserole dish, add a little water and then sit the loin on top, fat side up. Score the hide with a razor blade and sprinkle crushed juniper berries on top. Bake for an hour and a half at medium temperature. When cooked cut the crackling off and slice the meat very thinly. Reduce the remaining fluid and add to the sliced loin.

Slice the cabbage as finely as possible. In a large pot mix the chicken stock with some sherry vinegar, crushed garlic, black peppercorns and a pinch of salt. Place cabbage in this mixture and sprinkle with carraway seeds. Cover and cook quickly for a few minutes once it has come to the boil.

'Beverley Sutherland Smith is a top food operator. This recipe, an ideal "quickie", is from her book A Taste in Time, and I've used it with good effect. Beverley is a dedicated professional, and writes charmingly on her favourite subject.'

Pork chops with mustard and chive sauce

4 large or 8 small pork chops
2 tablespoons flour
salt and pepper
1 tablespoon oil
45g butter
for the sauce:
¾ cup cream

1 teaspoon freshly chopped spring onion or onion
3 teaspoons mustard
2 tablespoons finely chopped chives
1 tablespoon dry white wine
salt and white pepper
Serves 4

Trim the rind and excess fat from the chops. Place flour and salt and pepper on greaseproof paper. Put oil and butter on to heat. Dust the chops with the flour and cook over high heat, turning once when golden. Turn down the heat and cook 20–25 minutes or until tender, turning several times.

To make the sauce (this can be prepared in advance and reheated), place cream and remaining ingredients in saucepan. Cook over high heat, stirring for the first minute until mixture is reduced and coats the back of a spoon. If not using immediately, put to one side. Otherwise, drain the chops and spoon sauce over them.

Jarret de porc aux lentils

Hock of pork with lentils

I enjoyed this dish when dining at La Bagatelle in Darlinghurst, run by Jean Luc Lundy. He was good enough to pass on the recipe.

8 hocks of pork (ask your butcher to cut the foot end off the bone so the round base will sit on the serving dish)
4 medium-sized carrots
3 onions
2 bouquet garni
salt and pepper to season
500g lentils
3 teaspoons mustard
2/3 cup cream
Serves 8

Small dice the carrots and onions, then place in saucepan of water together with one bouquet garni, the hocks and salt and pepper. Cook for 1½ hours. When cooked remove the hocks. Meanwhile, wash the lentils well and place in separate saucepan of water with bouquet garni, one diced onion and 1 teaspoon salt. When lentils are cooked add the mustard and cream, mix well. Return the hocks to the lentils and simmer until heated through.

Serve on a dish with the round base of the hock sitting upright on the lentils.

Home-style spare ribs

Yet another of those caught-short dishes for a mob of kids after a day in the country or on the beach. You know, they wanted to stop at one of those fast food operations and you wouldn't. And then on arriving home there seemed to be nothing in the fridge, until you found the pack of frozen spare ribs.

1 pack frozen pork spare ribs
4 cloves garlic, crushed
honey to taste
salt and pepper
ginger powder to taste
chilli powder to taste
sesame oil
soy sauce
Hoi Sin sauce to taste

Max Lake, Murray Tyrrell, myself and Rudy Komon in the Beef Room; the lady needs no introduction.

Mix together garlic, honey, salt, pepper, ginger powder, a touch of chilli powder, sesame oil and soy sauce. Having run the spare ribs under a hot water tap to separate them, place them (still frozen) into a large baking dish with the sauce. Roast in a hot oven for 20 minutes, then turn down to a moderate temperature for a further hour or until the ribs are cooked. Turn every 15 minutes so that the ribs are totally coated with the sticky sauce. If the sauce looks like burning, add a drop of hot water. This will keep everything moist and help the ribs pick up more sauce. As a final touch, add a couple of spoonfuls of Hoi Sin sauce.

Peking spare ribs in golden sauce

1kg spare ribs
2 teaspoons Chinese Five Spice
  powder
1 large piece ginger, chopped
1 stick shallot, chopped
2 crushed cloves garlic
1 teacup Chinese vinegar
½ cup sugar

½ teaspoon salt
3 stars of anise
2 cinnamon sticks
1 piece shredded ginger
1 stick shredded shallot
¼ teaspoon pepper
¼ stick hot chilli
Serves 4

'A recipe from Alfred Lai, the owner of the Imperial Peking, Harbourside, Sydney. This restaurant has won many awards including the Bulletin *award for the best Chinese restaurant in Australia.'*

Rinse spare ribs lightly, cut into individual rib pieces and mix with the Five Spice powder, ginger, shallot and garlic. Let stand for 12 hours. Heat oil in a wok and fry spare ribs until golden colour. Add remaining ingredients and water, and cook gently until the spare ribs become soft. Take out ribs and reduce the remaining sauce until sticky. Pour onto ribs with sesame oil and serve.

Peter Morse and Michael McMahon, two of my 'boys' now both successful in the food and wine industry, at a function in the Beef Room.

Barbecued pork spare ribs

1kg barbecue pork spare ribs
4 tablespoons barbecue sauce
1 teaspoon soy sauce

3 tablespoons sugar
3 tablespoons May Kwai Lo or
  brandy

Rinse spare ribs lightly, cut into individual ribs and mix well with remaining ingredients. Let soak one hour, turning occasionally. Pre-heat oven to 230°C/450°F, place spare ribs in a shallow roasting pan. Bake 25 minutes until the outside of the meat is brown.

Pork and potato pie

500g pork or veal, finely cut
500g potatoes, peeled and par-boiled
90g butter
1½ cups chicken stock
½ cup cider
1 teaspoon crushed juniper berries or
  mixed herbs
salt and pepper

for the potato pastry:
⅓ cup plain flour
⅓ cup self-raising flour
½ teaspoon salt
75g butter
⅔ cup cold cooked, mashed potato
water
Serves 6

Fry the pork or veal in butter until cooked through. Veal will take about 10 minutes, pork a little longer. In a pie dish place the meat and potatoes, and add stock, cider, herbs and salt and pepper to taste. Place a pie funnel in centre of dish and cover with a pie crust. Brush with cream. Bake in a moderate oven 180°C/360°F for one hour.

To make the potato pastry, sift together the plain flour, the self-raising flour and the salt. Rub in the butter followed by the potato. Add enough water to make the ingredients cling together.

Vlado's sausages

Vlado Gregurek owns Vlado's, the greatest steak restaurant in Australia. He has won every award in the book, including the first three *Bulletin*/Quelltaler awards in the Best Steak category, polling more votes than any other restaurant in Australia in *all* categories. The love, care and attention he gives to his various cuts of meat is incredible. He cooks on a charcoal fire in front of everyone, and indeed it's worth the price alone to see him at work, orchestrating his performance to the finest degree. Prior to the main course, there are a succession of meat and offal titbits, as well as salad and the celebrated grilled capsicum, served cold in a dressing. His sausages are superb, quite the best I've ever enjoyed. Since it's difficult to write about a grilled steak, I asked Vlado for his sausage recipe. I give it in full, to show you his attention to detail. (Vlado uses a water pressure machine to make the sausages. These machines are readily available.)

'The love, care and attention Vlado gives to his various cuts of meat is incredible. He cooks on a charcoal fire in front of everyone, and indeed it's worth the price alone to see him at work, orchestrating his performance to the finest degree.'

for the sausages:

pork (Only female, 6–8 months is best, shoulder of pork without hand and a well-fed, pinkish colour. First bone out the meat, then remove skin and ensure that no gristle or sinews are left.)

prime ox beef (First cut off rump steak and round part of rump or topside—no dark meat. Thoroughly remove all fat and sinews—pure meat. Fresh or aged up to 10 days.)

for the dressing:

garlic (Use only fresh, peeled and minced through a fine mesh and then thoroughly crushed by knife to ensure that no small pieces are left. At the same time salt must be added so garlic is completely absorbed by salt.)

salt, according to quantity of meat

noble, fine, sweet red paprika (usually Hungarian)

fine white pepper

The proportion of pork and beef depends upon the richness of the pork. With good quality not over-rich pork, the quantity of the mixture is 70 per cent pork to 30 per cent clean lean beef. Otherwise, 65 per cent pork to 35 per cent clean lean beef if the pork is very fatty. Mince the beef once by itself on a fine mesh. Mix with the pork, which has been cut in small squares. Mix well and mince once again through a wider mesh. Mix again for a short time making sure the pork and beef are well mixed. Add the dressing and mix thoroughly again.

To prepare the dressing, mix all the ingredients thoroughly in a separate round bowl. Do not over-use any of these ingredients. To make the dressing less sharp, add a little sugar. Spread on the meat mixture. Mix thoroughly, making sure that the dressing is evenly distributed through the meat. Work the mixture until it has the same, even colour. The mixture should be kept in a cool room at 0–2°C for 24 hours before using to allow dressing to be completely absorbed by meat. It can be kept from three to four days at this temperature. Medium-sized hog casing is recommended.

CHAPTER EIGHT

Stews and casseroles: outdoors

THOUGH THE INTRODUCTION to this chapter hasn't got much to do with my wine and food career, it may interest those who don't know what a ring barker and sucker basher is.

When I arrived in Sydney in 1955, it was cold and wet. Work was difficult to find, and I don't think there was any dole to speak of. Certainly I never got any. With my mate, an ex-Marine commando I had worked with in New Zealand in the Forestry Service, I took a room in a cheap boarding house in Kensington, which we shared with another new arrival. I don't think I have ever been so miserable, before or since, and that includes being bombed out three times in the war, being lost for days, without cover, in dense fog and snow high in the mountains in New Zealand, and being absolutely flat broke in Darwin and Brisbane.

We got work as car body welders at General Motors in Pagewood, putting together the rear ends of Holdens, eight an hour, eight hours a day, day after day. I had never counted time before, and I don't think I have done so since, but those days were hideous, a never ending bleakness. Since then, anyone in a repetitive process job has my total sympathy, and I've always done my best to provide some change and stimulation for anyone who works with me.

After three months the ex-commando and I had saved about £50 each, so it was up to Queensland where, we had been told, there was much work!

Not so much, as it turned out, and we finished up in Goodiwindi clearing scrub—chopping down most trees, but ring barking the larger ones and bashing the suckers from those which had been ring barked before. Repetitive work, but at least it was in the open and I was seeing Australia. The job finished when the camp boss, drunk, hit one of the Aboriginal workers with a shovel. I took the shovel from him, and with a full body turn and keeping the left arm straight, gave him some back. He seemed to resent this, which led to further unpleasantry. Happily, I was fitter in those days. I was also brighter, I think, and took notice when he warned us off. 'If you're not out of town by tomorrow, me and my mates will get you.' So it was the milk train in the early hours, and my career as a ring barker and sucker basher was at an end.

With my mother in Singapore, 1955. I had come straight from the dingo fence at Boulia in northwest Queensland and was asked to go to a fancy dress ball that night. So I went as myself.

'I don't think I have ever been so miserable, before or since, and that includes being bombed out three times in the war, being lost for days, without cover, in dense fog and snow high in the mountains in New Zealand, and being absolutely flat broke in Darwin and Brisbane.'

There was no work in Brisbane. Every day we went to the employment office to receive the same reply. Our money was sufficient to pay for bed and breakfast for a month, the rest to find. I was quite happy in the library, but my friend found it suffocating. We used to visit the Botanical Gardens every day. After one particularly long stretch of inertia mixed with frustration, I suggested we go to the gardens to look at the monkeys. Quite seriously, he revealed that he was not at his pitch of futility. 'No,' he said, 'I feel okay. Let's save that 'til later.'

We would go into the cafés and restaurants, owned mostly by Greeks and Italians, to offer our services in return for a feed; grease traps, stove strip-downs, anything in return for the major meal of the day. We usually met with one of three responses: nick off; yes, here's a job, and you'll get a good plate of steak and eggs for it; you look like good people, so have what you want and pay us when you can. Happily, we let none of the last two classes down.

Eventually, we landed a part-time job at Cadbury, shifting half-hundredweight boxes of chocolates. Somehow, a box would always fall to the ground in the hectic early morning rush, though there were often arguments about which flavour would get dropped accidentally. For anyone who wonders, Cadbury's Fruit and Nut makes an excellent lunch.

Then a strange advertisement appeared in the *Courier-Mail*: 'Inexperienced fencers wanted for Boulia.' I had been taught to use both rapier and épée, but why were they needed there? It transpired that workers were needed to build a new dingo fence that would finish up being the longest wall in the world. Why 'inexperienced'? The contract fencer just happened to be, at that time, fed up with all the 'gun' fencers who told him how to build the fence. Of the contingent that resulted from that once-off advertisement, only the two of us stayed.

We were given the name of the contractor and the rough location of where he would be. So we went to the railway ticket office to find that a third-class fare would cost seven pounds. Seven pounds! How far away was Boulia? Three and a half days. Later, travelling the interminable route, I asked a fellow passenger if I would be working in the Outback. 'Boulia,' he shouted. 'Bloody Boulia. You go through three bloody Outbacks to get there!'

At the railhead at Dajarra, I was surprised that we weren't met. Some days later, after thumbing a ride with a semitrailer, followed by a trek in a Land Rover, followed by a lift in a post van, we were given horses and told to follow a fence line for a day. Sure enough, there was the fencing camp.

In the camp we lived off corned beef, damper, jam, porridge and 'hot' steak—freshly killed meat, good for as long as it stayed fresh. Vegetables were very scarce and fruit was almost unobtainable. Soon the backs of hands, arms and legs were covered with Barcoo rot, a sort of weeping fungus on the skin that developed from any scratch or cut. The flies were appalling, jamming eyes, ears and mouth in their search for moisture, and soon we learned to use the bobbing

'Eventually, we landed a part-time job at Cadbury, shifting half-hundredweight boxes of chocolates. Somehow, a box would always fall to the ground in the hectic early morning rush, though there were often arguments about which flavour would get dropped accidentally.'

corks around our hat brims to maximum advantage. (I loved the *Punch* cover that shows a group of Outback Aussies with the caption 'Who's the poofter with the Champagne corks?')

New boys at the camp received a fairly rough, if good-natured time, and we were cheerfully derided for 'pegging' our belongings— lifting them off the ground by hanging them on stakes, following the bush practice of New Zealand. Days later, there was a freak storm and a flash flood. As we watched from our high bush beds, a stream half a metre deep and hundreds of metres across swept all before it, except our boots, clothes and belongings.

The flood immobilised everything. The rains continued and soon we were very short of food. For three days six of us lived off a carton of tins of raspberry jam. Then a couple of us decided to look for a beast. I shall never forget that day. We were up before dawn for a cup of tea, and then off, using cut poles to ford the creek, which had become a torrent. We had a 12-kilometre walk in thick mud up to the knees before we found a steer. Fortunately, he was as slow as we were, and one shot brought him down. After skinning and gutting and then cutting off the haunch, my mate and I each loaded about 30 kilos of meat into sugar bags that had been made into packs. I can still feel the rope burns on my shoulder bones. On the return trip, we could see the camp fire from a long way off, and this kept us going. When crossing a creek, my mate lost his footing, lost his pack of meat and nearly lost his life. I have never laughed so much in my life. We finally reached the camp site after nightfall.

For all the mosquitoes, flies, bad food and bore water that tasted like stale coconut milk, I loved the job. Or, to be honest, loved the adventure. 'Adventure,' someone once said, 'is discomfort viewed at a distance.' Certainly we endured extreme discomfort, but there was a great satisfaction in building that fence over territory that, some said, white man had rarely seen.

The fence was comprised of panels 34 metres long set between large strainers, with ten long steel posts and 11 short wooden posts in between holding up five wires. On these wires were hung two rolls of expanded wire, dog-size on top and rabbit below. The rabbit wire went 46 centimetres into the ground and there was a barbed wire tied at the bottom to put off the dingoes. Actually, I've never seen a dingo burrow much, but they will enlarge a hole started by a fox or wombat. The fence stood two metres above the ground. When we came to a creek, we had to build a floodgate that would rise to let flood water pass under, and then fall back into place. The one road was the main bull train road to Brisbane, and we spent days inserting huge strainers about 70 centimetres across, over two metres into the ground, to hold the great gates. I wonder sometimes if they are still there. I'd like to hang a plaque on them. Years later I surprised David Bright on his property in the Monaro by hanging a pair of big gates across his road. Then he changed his mind and the direction of the fence line, and the gates have been open ever since. It's a very sad thing, an unused gate.

'For all the mosquitoes, flies, bad food and bore water that tasted like stale coconut milk, I loved the job.'

All the workers were paid for each post erected, panel tied, wire strained and so on. We got two shillings for sighting and driving each steel. I suggested that two people should do it instead of one, since it would be much quicker to sight the fence. The contractor quickly pointed out that we'd have to share the two bob. We understood, but thought that as a pair we would drive more than double a normal days' work. Very soon we were doing three and four days' output each day and the contractor reduced the price to one shilling and sixpence a steel. At least we made him some money.

Even in winter and spring, the days were very hot, and we prayed for a breath of wind. The flies came at you constantly and the corks bobbed incessantly. As soon as the sun went down the mosquitoes arrived in huge squadrons. But the sunsets were glorious. The sky filled with almost unimaginable colours—purples, red, prussian blues—fires, flames and flicks of the most intense hues. The bird life was remarkable; there were thousands of parrots, cockatoos, galahs and budgerigars. Emus, 'roos and bush turkeys were prolific, and, if one stood still when troops of 'roos approached, they would come quite close. And there was the companionship. We worked seven days a week from dawn to dusk. Returning to camp we would cook what food there was and then yarn for an hour or two before bed. I think it was then that my love affair with Australia began.

We were a lean, mangy crew. Never more than a dozen and often as few as four, the bunch included social misfits, misanthropes, restless ex-military men and professionals, wanderers like me, plus the genuine bushman who had never been anywhere else, didn't want to go anywhere else, had never done anything else except bush work and had no inclination to change. Yet among them were some of the kindest, most down-to-earth and well-read people I have ever met among the world's toilers. The Barcoo rot rarely seemed to affect these bushmen—I suppose their blood had simply adapted to the lack of fruit and vegetables—and they seemed to need far less water than we softies. Incidentally, when I returned to Brisbane, after several months, quite flush with funds, my rot cleared up completely after three days of eating vegetables and fruit. But it took ten days of long soaking before there was no thick red rim of dirt left around the bath.

One day, we were crossing a particularly barren rock outcrop. There was no topsoil and ramming in the rack would have been useless anyway, since we had to blow post holes out with dynamite. Consequently, posts had to be cemented in. The only sand available was in a river bed about 160 kilometres away. I was persuaded to go along to help because we would go through Boulia, and I would be able to buy eggs and chips at the local café, a rare treat indeed. We left in the afternoon, arrived at the creek bed, started shovelling the very dry sand on to the lorry, only to find that it disappeared through the cracks in the boards of the flat top. There was no tarpaulin available, no plastic, hence no sand. No matter, back to Boulia for a feed. We arrived there five minutes late and the café was shut. No

'We worked seven days a week from dawn to dusk. Returning to camp we would cook what food there was and then yarn for an hour or two before bed. I think it was then that my love affair with Australia began.'

amount of pleading opened it. It was the proprietor's beer time, and that was that. Back at camp after midnight and we were absolutely starving. Happily, by some gigantic fluke, someone had brought some vegetables in and they had made a stew in a camp oven under the ashes of the fire. Somehow we sensed the aroma, and there was no thought for the men who were obviously looking forward to a good stew the next day. In retrospect, that after–midnight stew must be one of the greatest meals I've ever eaten.

I love stews, casseroles, daubes, navarins, ragouts, cassoulets, and the like, particularly when the weather is cold and the belly is empty. They can be prepared well in advance and often get better with a little keeping. Here are some of my favourites.

A cartoon by Tony Rafferty done at a fund-raising charity event.

Beef, onions and beer

This dish is a rough country special, best served with baby new potatoes.

1kg beef	vegetable oil
salt	350g onions, sliced thickly
pepper	1 bottle beer
¼ cup flour	Serves 4–5
60g butter	

Mix salt, pepper and flour. Cube the beef and flour it in a bag. Heat butter in heavy casserole with a little oil. Sauté the onions and remove. Brown beef on all sides. Add beer and onions and correct the seasoning. Cover and cook in a moderate oven for 1½–2 hours.

———————— ❧ ————————

Beef stew with walnuts

750g round steak	30ml brandy
¼ cup self-raising flour	1 cup red wine
salt	2 cups meat stock
pepper	crushed bay leaf
pinch thyme	150g chopped celery
45g butter	15 walnuts, shelled
250g small onions, peeled	

Cube the steak. Put flour, salt, pepper and thyme in a bag. Put in the steak and agitate to coat thoroughly. Heat the butter in a heavy saucepan. Add the onions and sauté gently for a couple of minutes. Brown on all sides. Flame in brandy. Add red wine and stock, and casserole in a moderate oven for two hours. Correct seasoning. Add chopped celery and chopped walnuts and simmer until celery is tender.

———————— ❧ ————————

'A dish which doesn't take too long too long to do and which is a "safe" dinner party main course.'

Emince de fillet de boeuf Bourguignonne

1.5kg beef fillet (250g per person)	¾ cup red wine
18 small onions	⅓ cup glacé de viande
12 mushrooms	black peppercorns to season
50g clarified butter	salt to season
½ lemon	chopped parsley
1 teaspoon sugar	50g fresh butter
2 teaspoons shallots	Serves 6

Parboil onions for 20 minutes. Wash mushrooms and cut into quarters. Sauté in butter and squeeze over lemon juice. Season and cover for 2 minutes then uncover and cook until tender. Add butter to another pan and sauté onions till golden, sprinkle with a little sugar and let the onions glaze. Add onions to mushrooms. Slice fillet steak 1cm thick. Finely chop shallots.

Season meat and place in a frying pan with a little clarified butter to seal on each side. Remove the meat to a warmed dish and add the shallots. Deglaze the pan with the red wine. Reduce to one-third. Add the glacé de viande to the pan and season with pepper and salt. Add mushrooms and onions so that they heat in the sauce and then add meat. Place the fresh butter in the sauce and the chopped parsley and mix gently until the butter is dissolved.

Serve accompanied by boiled potatoes with parsley.

Beefgulyas Vienna style

From Zuden Drei Husaren, a Viennese restaurant that used to be owned by Herr Fodermayr, a golfing chum of mine. I use shin beef as the stewing meat for this simple and traditional dish, since the gristle holds it together so well and tastes so good.

1kg beef (stewing)	*1½ tablespoons tomato paste*
1kg onions	*1 teaspoon salt*
½ cup oil or lard	*1 teaspoon vinegar*
1½ tablespoons paprika	*1 pinch marjoram*
2 tablespoons water	Serves 4

Slice the onions. Cut the meat into 5cm pieces. Fry the onions in hot oil till golden brown. Add the paprika and stir well. Add the meat, cover and let it simmer for 5 minutes. Add the water and tomato paste, salt, vinegar and marjoram. Cover the saucepan and simmer on the most gentle heat for 2–3 hours, adding more water only if it becomes necessary.

Serve accompanied by boiled potatoes, noodles or dumplings.

Kidney stew with onions and mushrooms

1kg beef kidney	*1¼ cups brown veal stock*
¼ cup flour	*2 rashers bacon, finely diced*
salt	*250g large field mushrooms*
pepper	*½ cup chopped parsley*
2 large onions, sliced	Serves 6
marjoram	

'This delicious stew is quite rich. Serve it with mashed potatoes.'

Clean the kidneys, remove centres cut into small pieces. Dredge with flour, salt and pepper. Put into a casserole with chopped onions, pinch of marjoram, stock, and finely chopped bacon which has been sautéed in its own fat. Cook in a moderate oven for one hour. Add the mushrooms, which have been coarsely chopped. Cook for another hour. Correct seasoning, sprinkle with parsley and serve.

Summer lamb stew (recipe
page 210).

Steak and kidney pudding

This is one of the great traditional dishes, easy to do, yet with a fine flavour. It's the favourite dish of Michael Parkinson, and the only time I'm allowed to have it is when he and his wife Mary come to dinner.

for the steak and kidney:	1 medium onion, finely chopped
1½kg chuck steak cut into medium-sized cubes, gristle removed	meat stock
½kg veal kidney, cut into small pieces	water
	for the suet pastry:
flour	3 cups self-raising flour
salt and pepper	180g fresh suet
nutmeg	salt
	Serves 8

Grate the suet, and rub it into the flour carefully between thumbs and forefingers. Add salt. Moisten with enough water to make into a soft dough. Roll out, dusting with flour. Use ⅔ of the pastry to line a large, well greased pudding basin, retaining ⅓ for the top.

Put some flour, salt, pepper and a pinch of nutmeg into a bag. Add the pieces of beef and veal kidney, hold the top of the bag and move the pieces around inside. Remove from bag. The pieces should be lightly coated. Mix with the chopped onion and put inside the lined basin. Cover with meat stock and water. Put the rolled piece of suet pastry over the top, pinching the edges together. Cover with a cloth and tie firmly.

Stand the pudding basin in a pot filled with enough water to be halfway up the sides of the basin. Cover, and bring to the boil. Boil for 4–5 hours, occasionally topping up the water.

Remove, take off the cloth, invert the basin over a serving dish and put it in the middle of the dining table with a flourish! Ideal with mashed potatoes and Brussels sprouts.

Liver stew

500g calf liver, cut into thin strips	2 cups tomato puree
1 cup sliced carrots	1 pinch oregano
1 cup cut green beans	1 bay leaf
120g onion, diced	crushed garlic
1 medium green capsicum, diced	salt and pepper
½ cup sliced celery	Serves 4
1 cup beef stock	

In a large saucepan combine carrots, beans, onion, capsicum, celery and stock. Cook, stirring often, for 10 minutes. Add tomato purée, oregano and bay leaf. Simmer for 50 minutes, stirring occasionally. Remove the bay leaf. Season the liver with salt, pepper and garlic. Cook until done to taste. Stir into vegetable mixture and serve hot.

Braised oxtail

4kg oxtail cut across into sections
   relating to the bones
1 cup flour
salt and pepper
100g bacon fat
1 carrot, chopped finely
1 stick celery, chopped finely

1 large onion, chopped finely
1 turnip, chopped finely
bay leaf
thyme
parsley
1 litre meat stock
1 cup tawny port

Place half the pieces of oxtail in a large paper or plastic bag together with flour, salt, pepper. Agitate until all is coated, remove and shake off excess flour. Melt the fat in a heavy frying pan and brown the oxtail pieces. Put in a heavy bottomed pot. Put all chopped vegetables into the remaining fat and cook for 10 minutes until tender and browned. Add to oxtail. Add bay leaf, thyme, parsley, stock and port. Bring to the boil, then simmer for 3–4 hours. Let cool. Remove oxtail pieces and throw away. Put the liquid in the fridge overnight to de-fat. Remove fat in the morning, and bring the liquid to simmer while cooking the remaining oxtail as previously. Repeat 3–4 hour simmering, let cool and de-fat overnight.

Heat and serve with plain boiled potatoes.

'For this dish, buy twice as much oxtail as you need, discard half of it after making what normal people think is the finished dish, and take a couple of days to do the dish, cooking at least twice. This allows you to put it in the fridge so that you can de-fat without doing the endless skimming normally required. The rest is so easy to do.'

Emince de fillet de boeuf Bourguignonne (recipe page 204).

Braciuole ripiene

1kg veal steak
for the stuffing:
2 garlic cloves, chopped
1 teaspoon parsley
60g Parmesan cheese
2 slices bread
¼ cup milk
60g lean ham
1 medium-sized onion

1 medium-sized carrot
1 stalk celery
1 egg yolk
pinch nutmeg
salt, fresh black pepper, to season
60g clarifed butter
2 tablespoons veal stock
Serves 4

Cut veal steak into thin 15cm by 4cm slices and flatten. Finely chop the parsley. Grate the Parmesan cheese. Soak the bread in milk and squeeze dry. Chop the ham into small dice. Finely chop the onion, carrot and celery. Mix ham, garlic, parsley, Parmesan cheese, bread and egg yolk together and season with nutmeg and salt and pepper. Spread a little of the stuffing on each slice of veal. Roll the veal around the filling and secure with string. In a large pan melt the butter, and when hot brown the veal rolls. Add the chopped onion, carrot and celery. Cover the pan and allow to cook gently for 20 minutes, adding the stock towards the end of the cooking time.

Osso buco alla Milanese

A great Italian standby.

2 shins veal, sawed into easy to
　handle pieces
3 medium onions, finely chopped
2 carrots, finely chopped
2 sticks celery, finely chopped
50g butter
1 clove garlic, finely chopped
2 strips lemon peel
½ cup vegetable oil
¾ cup plain flour
1 cup dry white wine

1½ cups chicken or beef stock
300g tinned Italian tomatoes,
　coarsely chopped with their juice
¼ teaspoon dried thyme
6 leaves fresh basil
2 bay leaves
2 or 3 sprigs of parsley
freshly ground black pepper
salt
Serves 6

Preheat the oven to 180°C/350°F. Choose a heavy casserole dish with a tight-fitting lid that is just large enough to contain the veal pieces in a single layer. Put in the onion, carrot, celery and butter and cook over medium heat for 8–10 minutes until the vegetables soften. Add the chopped garlic and lemon peel at the end. Remove from the heat.

Heat the oil in a frying pan over medium-high heat. Turn the pieces of veal in the flour, shaking off any excess. When the oil is quite hot, brown the veal on all sides. (Brown the veal as soon as it has been dipped in flour, otherwise the flour may dampen and the meat will not brown properly.) Stand the pieces of veal side by side on top of the vegetables in the casserole. Tip the frying pan and draw off nearly all the fat with a spoon. Add the wine and boil briskly for about 3 minutes, scraping up and loosening any residue stuck to the pan. Pour over the pieces of veal in the casserole. In the same frying pan, bring the broth to a simmer and pour into the casserole. Add the chopped tomatoes with their juice, thyme, basil, bay leaves, parsley, pepper and salt. The stock should come up to the top of the veal pieces. If it does not, add more.

Bring the contents of the casserole to a simmer on top of the stove. Cover tightly and place in the lower third of the preheated oven. Cook for about two hours, carefully turning and basting the veal pieces every 20 minutes. When done they should be very tender when pricked with a fork, and their sauce should be dense and creamy.

———————— ❧ ————————

Summer lamb stew

1kg loin of lamb, boned
60g butter
2 lettuces
500g green peas, shelled or frozen
6 spring onions
1¼ cups brown veal stock

salt and pepper
1 teaspoon sugar
20 champignons
1 cucumber, fair-sized
Serves 6

Heat a little butter in a pan. Cube the meat and brown in butter. Slice the lettuces finely and toss with the meat, then add peas, chopped spring onions, stock, salt, pepper and sugar. Remove to a casserole, and cook in a moderate oven for an hour. Add champignons and cucumber, which has been peeled and diced. Simmer for another ¼ hour. Serve with rice.

Irish stew

This is my wife's recipe for one of my favourite simple winter stews, which I regard as a great antidote to all the rich food I enjoy all over the world. Oh, hold on, what's that? Ah yes, she sometimes adds a cupful of pre-soaked haricot beans.

2kg best end of neck or hogget chump chops
2 cups white poultry stock
1 cup white wine
salt and pepper
750g large onions, chopped roughly

1kg large potatoes, peeled and cut across in thick pieces.
250g celery, chopped roughly
250g carrots sliced thickly
cornflour
½ cup chopped parsley
Serves 8

Trim chops, place in a pan with stock, wine, salt and pepper. Bring to the boil and simmer for 30 minutes. Cool and de-fat. Add all the vegetables. Simmer for the time it takes to cook the vegetables, and the meat is tender. Thicken slightly with cornflour, add parsley, and check seasoning.

Practising at RAF Cosford in 1949. Note the Oxford bags from school days.

Lamb casserole with pickling onions

1kg shoulder of lamb, boned
500g pickling onions
40g butter
vegetable oil
200g turnips
150g celery
150g carrots

1¼ cups brown veal stock
½ cup white wine
2 tablespoons tomato paste
salt
pepper
bouquet garni
Serves 4–6

Coarsely chop the lamb. Peel the onions but leave the base intact to prevent disintegration. Heat the butter with a little vegetable oil and brown the lamb on all sides. Remove. Gently sauté onions. Remove. Add the other vegetables, very finely sliced, and sweat them gently. Put in the casserole, add the lamb, stock, wine and paste, salt, pepper and bouquet garni. Cook in a moderate oven for 45 minutes or until lamb is tender. Add onions ten minutes before cooking is finished. Remove bouquet garni and serve.

Pork fillet d'Annelise

1kg pork fillet, trimmed and cut into medallions
1½ tablespoons vegetable oil
60g butter
3 cloves garlic, finely chopped
small bunch spring onions, finely chopped
2 stalks celery
3 capsicums (red, green, yellow) cut into juliennes about 3cm
1½ tablespoons brandy
¼ cup plain flour
2 teaspoons prepared English mustard
3 teaspoons tomato paste
3 teaspoons chopped fresh basil
3 teaspoons chopped fresh parsley
dry white wine
⅔ cup cream
salt and pepper
Serves 6

Take half oil and half butter and stir-fry the garlic, shallots, celery and capsicums until soft (Chinese wok is recommended). Add seasoning. Drain and set aside. Using the remaining butter and oil brown pork medallions, add brandy and flambé. Add flour to pork and, stirring continuously, cook for 2 minutes. Add mustard, tomato paste, basil, parsley and sufficient wine to make a covering sauce. Simmer gently for 20 minutes. Finally stir in the cream and add cooked vegetables.

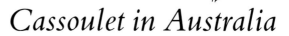

Cassoulet in Australia

A great winter dish, ideal for Sunday lunch. The variations of cassoulet are endless in France, changing from region to region. But the basis remains white haricot beans. Over the years I've cooked many of these variations. This dish is a wonderful companion when there's plenty of good wine tasting to be done. During one Barossa Vintage Festival, Michael Hill Smith decided to serve it for the Yalumba Museum Tasting. Only trouble was that the beans fermented overnight (the air at vintage time being full of yeast cells) and we didn't like the new blue bits. So we bought every tin of white beans in South Australia, and somehow faked it. No one seemed to mind.

1kg dried white haricot beans, soaked overnight
½kg good garlic sausage
½kg pork sparerib, bone removed
1kg leg of lamb meat
4 duck breasts, skin on
½kg salt pork, rind on
bouquet garni
2 large onions, with cloves stuck in
4 cloves garlic, crushed
salt
pepper
breadcrumbs
Serves 8–10

Cut the rind from the pork ribs and salt pork (bacon can be used if not available) and dice into little squares. Add the rind to the drained and soaked beans, in a large, heavy casserole. Add the salt pork diced. Add the garlic, onions and bouquet. Fill up the casserole with water and simmer gently for 2 hours. While this is happening, roast

the pork and lamb and pan-fry the sausage and duck breasts. Do not cook fully. Cut the pork and lamb into forking pieces, slice the sausage and duck breast across into like pieces.

Drain the beans, retaining the juice and discarding the onions and bouquet. Into a large oval fireproof casserole with quite deep sides, put a layer of the beans which still includes the little squares of rind and salt pork. On this place the pieces of the four meats. Put another layer of the beans on top and dust with breadcrumbs. Enough of the bean liquid should be added to keep the whole moist during the next 2 hours. Place the casserole in a low oven and cook for two hours or so until the liquid is absorbed. If it gets too dry add a little more. Finally, the top should be crusty with the inside still moist and succulent.

Barbara's cassoulet

Publisher Barbara Beckett once made this cassoulet for 20 people at a dinner at Brokenwood Winery in the Hunter Valley. Most of the people were sleeping overnight to help prune vines the next day. Not much sleep was had—as one person stopped farting another would start up—so be warned.

1kg white haricot beans
½kg belly of pork including skin
½kg bratwurst sausage
1kg lamb or mutton
confit d'oie or some goose, turkey or
   duck
1 cup goose fat
2 onions, diced

4 cloves garlic
2 large tomatoes, diced
bouquet garni
pepper and salt
3 cups fresh breadcrumbs
Serves 6–8

'A lovely soup can be made from leftover cassoulet. Just put it through a blender and add the leftover stock to reach the required consistency.'

Soak the beans overnight. Take the skin off the pork belly and make a stock by boiling the skin for several hours with 1 teaspoon of salt.

Next day put the beans in a large pot, along with onions, garlic, tomatoes, bouquet garni, pepper and salt and pork stock. Boil until beans are almost cooked. Save all the stock. Take out bouquet garni. At the same time roast the pork, sausage, lamb and poultry (if not already cooked) in the goose fat.

Put all the meats, cut into bite-size pieces, in the bottom of a deep earthenware pot. Cover with the beans and goose fat. Pour stock over the beans to within 4cm of the top of the beans. Spread a layer of breadcrumbs on top and put the pot into a slow open (160°C/ 300°F). Every hour stir the brown crust into the beans and add another layer of breadcrumbs. The breadcrumbs gradually soak up the surplus liquid and give the dish the right texture. Keep the remainder of the beanstock to add more liquid if necessary or for reheating the next day. The last crust should remain intact for serving. The whole process takes 4–5 hours.

Aussie buco

6 lamb shanks
1kg tomatoes
3 onions

salt and pepper
thyme
Serves 6

Skin, seed and liquidise the tomatoes. Brown the lamb shanks in heavy pan. Chop the onions. Put shanks, onions and liquid tomatoes in a casserole with salt and pepper and a touch of thyme. Bake in a moderate oven for 1½–2 hours. Serve with rice or boiled potatoes.

Rabbit in white wine

1 rabbit
2 tablespoons oil
30g butter
250g small onions
125g button mushrooms
125g bacon pieces
¼ cup flour
1 cup chicken stock
½ cup white wine
½ cup cream

for the marinade:
1 cup white wine
2 tablespoons olive oil
1 onion, thinly sliced
½ teaspoon dried thyme
1 bay leaf, crushed
2 tablespoons parsley, finely
 chopped
salt and pepper
Serves 4

Joint the rabbit and marinate for a few hours in the mixture. Then heat the oil and butter and sauté the onions, mushrooms and bacon pieces. Remove from the pan. Add the dried rabbit pieces, sauté until brown and put in a casserole. Stir flour into the fat in the pan and pour in chicken stock and white wine, stirring constantly. Add the onion, mushrooms, bacon and the marinade and simmer. Pour over the rabbit in the casserole and simmer for 1–1½ hours. Add cream.

Old rabbit stew

1kg rabbit pieces
¼ cup flour
vegetable oil
1 large onion, sliced
1¼ cups brown poultry stock
1¼ cups red wine
1 tablespoon anchovy sauce

2 pinches marjoram
1 tablespoon tomato paste
teaspoon sugar
150g sliced mushrooms
salt and pepper
Serves 4

Soak the rabbit pieces in cold water for ½ hour. Drain, dry and dust with flour. Heat a little oil. Seal the rabbit pieces and lightly brown. Place in a casserole. Add sliced onion, stock, wine, anchovy sauce, marjoram, tomato paste and sugar. Cook in moderate oven for an hour. Add mushrooms, correct seasoning, and cook for another hour or until rabbit is very tender.

Stew Sauternais

500g veal
500g beef
500g lamb
500g pork
1kg fresh chestnuts
500g chipolatas
120g butter

vegetable oil
1¼ cups Sauternes (or sweet wine)
1¼ cups brown veal stock
bouquet garni
salt
pepper
Serves 8–10

Boil the chestnuts for a little while. Cool and peel, taking care to remove the white pith. Brown and cook the sausages gently in a little butter and oil. Set aside. Brown all the other meat, diced, in a heavy casserole. Add Sauternes and stock, and bouquet garni. Correct seasoning. Cook in a moderate oven for an hour and a half. Add chestnuts and simmer for 15 minutes. Add sausages, heat and serve.

Duck ragout

2 ducks, oil glands removed
1 large onion
100g carrots
1 stalk celery
salt

pepper
400g parsnips
red wine vinegar
Serves 6–7

Simmer the ducks covered in water with chopped onion, carrots and celery, salt and pepper. Cook the ducks until tender. Remove. Strain the stock. Take the meat off the ducks and replace the carcasses in strained stock. Simmer and reduce by half. Remove the carcasses and strain again. Cut duck meat into longish chunks. Grate parsnips into fine shreds. Add duck and parsnips to the reduced stock, adjust seasoning, and sharpen with red wine vinegar. Reheat and serve.

Chilli con carne

500g dried kidney beans
1kg lean chuck steak
1 tablespoon olive oil
1 teaspoon chilli powder
1 teaspoon cayenne pepper
1 teaspoon cumin seed

1 tablespoon soya sauce
1 large brown onion, roughly
    chopped
150g tomato paste
salt
Serves 8

Soak the beans overnight. Drain. Cube the beef. Heat the oil in a large saucepan. Add chilli, cayenne, cumin and soya. Sauté onions with these spices until the onions are soft and spices have turned dark brown. Add beef and seal meat on all sides. Cover with water, add tomato paste. Bring to the boil. Add beans and simmer for 1½–2 hours until the meat breaks apart and beans are soft.

CHAPTER NINE

Vegetables and salads: France and California

I T HAPPENED AT LUNCH, as it so often does. 'Kit' (Christopher) Stevens, Master of Wine, famed wit, cricket lover and sleeper at dining tables, and Peter Fox and I were enjoying each other's company. Peter and I had started the Evans Wine Company, and had bought vineyards at Fordwich in the Hunter Valley, and in Clare and Coonawarra in South Australia. 'I'd love to have a go in France,' I said. 'I'm quite sure we can make wines better than most of them. It would be fascinating to find out.'

Kit is an international wine broker, representing different people in various markets. He operates from Cognac, for no special reason I've ever been able to discern, and travels the world as a sort of oenological Flying Dutchman. We soon had a phone call from him.

'Château Suduiraut, the most famous vineyard in Sauternes except for Yquem, is for sale. They want fifteen million francs. [About three million dollars at the time.] The Château is magnificent but needs repair. The gardens were designed by Le Notre who did those at Versailles. The vineyards need attention. But the wines are great and stocks are good.'

We became interested. Peter was soon off to London on his own business, and said he would have a look at the situation. He met Kit there, and his report to me was enthusiastic. 'The owners are getting old and want to retire, and they have three daughters who are married and live in different parts of France. It's difficult to get to know what's included in the price but it's a marvellous place. You'd better come over soon.'

Peter and I went together a couple of weeks later, and he told me of a much smaller place in Graves, owned by an Englishman, where he and Kit had stayed. It was Château Rahoul. From the first pictures I saw of it I liked it. I wondered if it would do; perhaps we were setting our sights too high with Suduiraut. However, more negotiations over the latter ensued. We had a thorough look at the place and the inventory; the owners had not quite made up their minds about what they wanted to leave in the place. We decided to return in a month or two.

When we did, making a total of five trips between us, it was to finalise the negotiations. The owners took us to a delightful luncheon

Château Rahoul.

at a Michelin-starred restaurant at Langon, just south of Sauternes. All the courses of the meal were accompanied by different vintages of Suduiraut in an attempt to prove that Sauternes may be enjoyed with anything. It almost came off. The fish was matched by a light wine of some age, the pâté by younger wine that was sweeter but not too luscious. Only the lamb course was unbalanced, served with a light vintage of the famous Château, rather acid, neither sweet nor dry, which did nothing for the meat. We went back to the Château to talk further.

The price mounted. If we wanted all the current stocks, bulk plus those in bottle, then the price would have to rise by some many million francs. Surely we didn't want the curtains? Of course, they were designed for the huge, high windows and doors. That would be extra. The light fittings? Extra. The tapestries and carpets? Now we were talking National Trust material. Extra, extra, extra.

I insisted that we must have the museum of old stock. 'But monsieur, you are demanding the life work of my father, his heritage to us,' protested the eldest daughter, who was representing her sisters. 'No I'm not,' I replied. 'He bought the Château in the thirties, and most of the museum is older than that. It was here before he arrived.' 'Touché,' cried the father, gleefully. I had the impression that sometimes he was happy to see someone disagree with his daughter. 'This is the list of our requirements,' I said. 'We will make you an offer by tomorrow night which will stay open until the end of the month. To whom do you wish me to make this offer?' And father, mother and eldest daughter said, in unison, 'Moi!'

In the gathering dusk, with a light drizzle falling, Peter and I stood outside the Château while the family decided who would take the offer. Neither of us spoke until a duck quacked with an almost mournful note. 'Ask them how much they want for the bloody duck,' said Peter. I knew how he felt. Whatever the offer, there would be something wrong with it or something to be excluded.

The offer was refused and in fact I don't think that the owners were ever serious about selling the Château. The eldest daughter runs it to this day, I believe, and although I've often driven around the property since to show it to people, I've never been inside again to taste.

We had the same problems some time later when we finally bought a much smaller place, Château Padouen, in Sauternes. From the beginning of that particular negotiation we insisted to the agent who was now running our operations there that there was to be no equivocation about this and that. We were buying lock, stock and barrel, literally and metaphorically. Everything was fine until the day that settlement was made and the money handed over. The owner promptly came and took away all the light bulbs!

Château Rahoul in Portets, on the old Route Nationale, had become our headquarters, thanks to the obliging hospitality of the owner, David Robson. The Château had been there since 1666, according to the date carved into part of one wall. It had been added

Château Padouen.

to frequently, and Robson had removed two towers added in the 19th century by an impressionable Victorian owner trying to make a grand affair out of what was really a *petit château*.

Robson, an Englishman, was a most meticulous man, and he had made a delightful home out of the place. The cellars were in first-class order, though the machinery and equipment was antiquated, and the vineyards had been bought by him in top order. I thought we would be able to make better wine with newer equipment and techniques, plus a greater use of new wood for maturation. Peter needed little persuasion for he found the place very comfortable and enjoyed it. By this time Kit had found a wine-maker, Peter Vinding-Diers, who had worked for some years at Château Loudenne, the celebrated entertainment spot owned by Gilbeys. Peter had learned his business in South Africa, but was actually a Dane who had been educated at Eton.

We bought Rahoul, and enjoyed it. Our first vintage was '78, for which we were joined by various Australian friends. Château Padouen, in Barsac (Sauternes), built as a hunting lodge in 1701 for the Dukes of Eperney at Cadillac, across the Garonne, was also bought at this time. (Rahoul cost about $600,000, Padouen $300,000.) Rahoul had a production potential of 5000 cases of red from cabernet sauvignon, cabernet franc and merlot, and 500 cases of white, mostly from semillon. Padouen had a potential of 2000 cases of wine, from the classic Sauternes mix of semillon, sauvignon blanc and muscadelle.)

1978 was a good year for red wine. The cabernet sauvignon was from young vines, and therefore slightly 'green', but most of the merlot, the main crop, was first class, and the '78 is still improving, seven years later.

The Australian input at Rahoul, other than labour, was not high, since we were fairly keen to see how Vinding-Diers operated. But Padouen was different.

Château Rahoul.

"'You've drunk all my champagne you bastards,'' I shouted. Rudy looked at me with a soft smile. "And what is it for?'' To which there was no reply.'

My great desire was to make a really top wine. I knew that the Yquem density of flavour and lusciousness would be impossible to achieve, but other Châteaux in Sauternes were no longer able to afford to support the rigorous multi-picking of the vineyards, grape by grape, which is the requirement of a classic Sauternes. I planned to do it by insisting on a large picking team, a number of which would be unpaid Australians. It took us only one vintage to realise that 'unpaid' is a fairly loose term. The consumption rate in wine and food terms of Australians is usually high; on holiday it is higher; on working holidays it is extremely high. The wine bill alone would have paid for dozens of extra pickers. But it was tremendous fun.

It wasn't only the pickers whose holiday consumption was high. Many of our friends used to visit when we were not there, and tie in a brief stay with their travels. We would send letters to confirm visits and then reserve certain rooms for our guests. One day, Peter rang from France. 'We've had some painter friends of yours staying for the three days you specified. It's Rudy Komon and Mr and Mrs Fred Williams. They're lovely people and they've included us in all their restaurant visits and things, but they want to stay longer. Is this all right?' I said that it was. 'The only trouble is,' he added, 'that they're drinking a fair bit of your Champagne.'

At each vintage we would drink Champagne, of course, and we had a special deal with a well-known house to supply us at basic export prices, the same as that for Australia, since I used to import a quantity from them every year. We usually got through about 20 dozen bottles, and I believe there were about eight dozen at the Château at the time.

Rudy and the Williams stayed for two weeks and managed to get through most of the Champagne, with the Vindings and others' help. When they returned to Australia, I saw them for lunch right away. 'You've drunk all my Champagne you bastards,' I shouted. Rudy looked at me with a soft smile. 'And what is it for?' To which there was no reply.

A month or so later, a large, rare gouache arrived from Fred, with a message: 'I hope this makes up for the Champagne.' What's more, he told me, it was of Lyn, his wife. It hangs opposite my desk in my office at Bulletin Place. Much later, after Fred had died, I told Lyn that I looked at her backside nearly every day. 'Nonsense,' she said, 'that wasn't of me ... wait a minute, you do!'

So in that first year at Château Rahoul, when the grapes were very ripe but not much infected with noble rot, *Botrytis cinerea*, which shrinks them and concentrates sugar and flavour, we went up and down the rows on five separate occasions, picking only the very ripe berries from the bunch, and going back when the balance was further ripened. This is back-breaking, tedious work, and now, every time I sip Château d'Yquem, I raise my glass in silent toast to those whose meticulous and extraordinary work makes it so exceptional.

The following year we devised a new method—or rather we revived a very old one. Four large white tables were made; the grapes

The Fred Williams gouache of his wife Lyn.

were picked; and only two sortings were made for each section of the vineyard. The 'botrytised' bunches were picked, as well as those partly affected. Then the baskets were emptied on the tables and we snipped the ripe berries from the concentrated, almost rotten ones. Each 'cutter' had a plastic garbage bin on either side. The ripe berries went into one to be made into normal, dry wine, and the rotten ones went into the other to be made into sweet wine. The measure of the success is easily understood. Baumé is the name of a method of measuring sugar in grapes. 10.5–13 degrees Baumé is the normal range of initial sugar required for dry wine. A good sweet wine needs a residual sugar, after fermentation, of a least 4 degrees Baumé. So 17 degrees Baumé is at least the required amount of initial sugar.

Often, Baumés of only 15–16 degrees are obtained in Sauternes, and sugar has to be added, which, naturally enough, is not the same thing. So, when we picked at 16 degrees Baumé in 1979, half the grapes went into dry wine and half to sweet. The sweet must (grape juice) had a Baumé of over 19 degrees, since the dry batch was down to under 13 degrees.

Word of our high Baumés soon got around, and a Monsieur Franc, the Government inspector, called in. He watched our antics in amazement. The rotten grapes, the heavily botrytised ones, represented the very best concentrated material, perfect for making a top sweet wine. It was as if every suitable grape had been picked by hand. Monsieur Franc checked these grapes again and again. Finally, he said, 'They are perfect. But it is easy to see why—you're cheating!'

Well, the cheating made some very good wine, quite exceptional for the lowly status of the little Padouen.

In 1979, Brian Croser arrived to give advice on red wine making, and virtually to teach Peter how to make dry white. Some additional land was purchased, and soon we were winning gold medals for our wine. 1980 was only a fair year, but 1981 was good.

Château Rahoul had been dubbed the United Nations by the locals, and they did not go out of their way to be friendly. But when we won our first gold medal they were very pleased we had bought this honour to Portets, and their pride in us grew as the medals continued to be awarded in various classifications.

In 1982, Rahoul was one of 67 Châteaux in the district of Graves to apply to the powers that be to be granted 'Grand Cru' (Great Growth) status. Sixty-six Châteaux were rejected. Our case was left open because the powers were very aware of and impressed by the increase in quality of the Rahoul wines, both red and white. However, they decided to defer a decision until the quality of further vintages had been determined. The Evans Wine Company lost Château Rahoul in late 1982, however in 1984, Grand Cru status was granted; a very rare happening in France. I was delighted, even though I was not part of the team that was awarded the honour. However, there's no doubt that the path we set out on and the support we gave Peter Vinding-Diers led to this success.

'Monsieur Franc checked these grapes again and again. Finally, he said, "They are perfect. But it is easy to see why— you're cheating!" Well, the cheating made some very good wine, quite exceptional for the lowly status of the little Padouen.'

The French connection taught me two things. First, as I expected, we could improve wine qualities by our better attention to care and technique. I don't say this would happen everywhere, for there are some fine modern wine makers in France, but it would apply in the majority of cases. Secondly, we have a tremendous amount to learn about viticulture. The French understand and respect their land; they know what they can get from it, what it will do, how far it will go. They seem to care for each vine individually. They know that great wine comes from great vineyards, and that it *cannot* come from ordinary land. In my egotism I had fondly supposed that if we could get together a good team at Rahoul and support it with top equipment and new wood every year, we could make great wine. The French knew better, and that was why the place was not expensive. They understand the worth of each plot of land, and price it accordingly.

So next time, and I predict there will be a next time, we shall look for a more famous Château that has become run down, but one which has made great wine in the past. Then we shall see what we can do. Still, *la place de Grand Cru ce n'est pas mal, eh?*

In 1979 the Evans Wine Company was also looking to the United States. We planned to form a triangle of wine production: Australia, France and the United States. Wine makers could be moved around; each location could be an export centre for the other wines; we would use rebates and currency rates; and we could use the best techniques, equipment and ideas of each area.

Bob Mondavi assisted with our search, and after a couple of false starts we found an ideal location on the old Silverado Trail in the Napa Valley in California, the premium wine area in the premium wine producing State. The ranch was owned by Don and Virginia

'The French connection taught me two things. First, as I expected, we could improve wine qualities by our better attention to care and technique. . . Secondly, we have a tremendous amount to learn about viticulture. The French understand and respect their land; they know what they can get from it, what it will do, how far it will go. They seem to care for each vine individually. They know that great wine comes from great vineyards, and that it cannot *come from ordinary land.'*

Château de la Jaubertie with the Rymans, Murray Tyrrell and Bill and Sonia McMahon.

Weaver, who had decided to move into St Helena in the Napa because Don had had a stroke and could no longer keep up with the beautiful garden that they had developed. At first they were suspicious of us, since once before someone had 'bought' the place and then decided he couldn't find the money. It took me three minutes to make up my mind, and Peter agreed readily.

The ranch was over 12 hectares, right on the intersection of the Rutherford Road and Silverado Trail; seven hectares planted with cabernet sauvignon, were set into the hills. A modern ranch house with a lovely garden, a creek, a natural forest of trees around it, and a mature olive plantation in front of it completed the property.

We soon found a top architect, who got to work on Brian's and my plans. I think I was more proud of this project than any I have undertaken. Brian Croser designed the basis of a functional yet attractive winery that opened onto an area of creek, lake, small wood, garden and olive grove. Across from the winery were selling and administration buildings, which I planned, the whole bounded by a three-metre wall.

Croquet at Château Rahoul.
Brian Croser is on the right.

Following the crash of Adelaide Holdings, after the death of Peter Fox, we were obliged to sell. I don't even know who bought the place, but if ever I find myself in the financial position to do so, I will go back, and hoist the Australian flag right there one day.

In France, Château Rahoul was sold to a Danish wine merchant who had visited it on a bus tour, and Château Padouen went to the Club Savoie, a wine buying group. There was an interesting conclusion to our sad withdrawl from the operation.

The dining room table at Château Rahoul was mine, a present from an English friend who had wanted to contribute. It wasn't a special table, but it was old and had a good patina and a sturdy feel to it. When the Château was sold, the agent who acted for the Australian interests omitted to exclude it from the inventory. Subsequently, I wrote to the new owner and asked for the table as my one tangible memento of the Château, though I stressed I understood his position legally. I met him a few months later, and he said I could have it, provided I replaced it with one of equal value. While I was thinking about this, a letter arrived. Since I had done such a good job with Château Rahoul, would I act as agent for it in Australia? If so, after selling the first 500 cases I could have the table for nothing.

I didn't reply to the letter and I haven't spoken to them since. But I remain delighted about the Grand Cru status.

Apart from all this talk of wine and holdings and ambitions, there was great joy in France. We had an endless stream of visitors, from the Billy McMahons and various ambassadors to unknown wine lovers who simply knocked on the door and said, 'We're here!' I don't think we ever turned anyone away, at least for a 'visit' to the cellars and lunch or something. Most got a bed, and many stayed for days. In vintage we made them work, although one famous lady proved the exception, showing a skill to avoid work which amazed me. But most people were quite dedicated in their support and they

Potatoes Roberts (recipe page 234).

Machine sheds and the elm park at Château Rahoul.

seemed to derive great enjoyment from helping.

I enjoyed certain aspects of French living very much. I enjoyed the equality between people, even the formality—the hand shaking in the morning and at night, the attention to the courtesy of the moment. We all loved the markets.

In Bordeaux, throughout the week, the markets started very early in the morning, and when we had a large house party we would shop there. Invariably, everyone rose at 3.30 for 4.00 am to have a cup of coffee before setting off. The Bordeaux market sells wonderful seafood, and we would have a marvellous time making our purchases before repairing to the market café for breakfast. Once, as we ate our croissants and *jambons au croûte* with *café au lait* we saw a worker having his early morning nourishment—a plate of very large oysters, a huge bowl of cheese soup, a baguette and a bottle of red wine. Without fuss, without hurry, he demolished the lot.

The Marché Couvert opened later and stayed open until noon. These were retail stalls that carried the best of everything—seafood, vegetables, fruit, cheese, a bewildering range of small goods and game. This was the market we visited when we wanted the best.

There were also local markets, held in rotation from Monday to Saturday, in a neighbouring town or village—Portets one day, Langoiran the next, Cadillac the next. These did not have the range or complexity of the Bordeaux markets, but the produce was fresh and often there were some outstanding individual items. The seafood at Archachon on Cap Ferret, the nearest Atlantic town to Bordeaux, was extraordinarily fine, especially the huge range of crustacea. This was the basis of the seafood stew I would create occasionally for a group of visitors.

After shopping at the markets we would often repair to a little village inn or restaurant for lunch. There were some delightful places and though the food was pleasant, without being remarkable, the prices were unbelievable: soup, entrée, steak and chips, cheese and dessert for just $3.50 as recently as 1981, and I doubt that the rise and fall of the French franc has had much effect. Sometimes we would spend twice as much on wine as on food, thus we soon became firm favourites in the district.

Apart from the hard work of vintage, and the entertaining and the wandering around the back roads of the district, we were left with one other impression. In the summer of 1981, Peter and Jenny Fox, and Trish and I decided to spend part of June and July at Rahoul, instead of the usual May (other than vintage) when we did the blending of the various barrels of the different varieties. It was a magical summer in France, and for the first time in years we lost track of time.

I have lived a fairly stressful life, but it has been of my choosing. During the past 20 years I've worked for others in fairly frantic circumstances, or for myself under conditions that have always been difficult, financially and otherwise. Fortunately, I have some minor, income earning talents, and it would be safe to say that our family

company would not have continued to survive had there not been this income. Time has always been precious. I am well organised, in work terms, even to managing to grab a few days here and there for fishing or whatever. Even then, there was always work to be done, an article to be written, a deadline on a consultancy to be met.

For three golden weeks in the summer of 1981, nothing mattered a damn. We got up when we wanted to, which was often quite early. Meals were haphazard, and were taken only on the demand of someone. Hours were spent by the pool, remarkable for one who burns to lobster red in five minutes. One day I was asked the time. I had been reading in the afternoon sun and occasionally swimming and daydreaming. 'Oh,' I said, 'I suppose it could be 4.30.' Someone suggested it was later, possibly 5.30. I went to find a clock, and reported that it was five to nine. I shall always be grateful for those weeks.

Broccoli mousseline (recipe page 229).

I was taught a great deal about French attitudes by Peter Vinding-Diers when, one day, I was cooking *bouef en daube*. To this dish, in which a big piece of beef is cooked in a meat broth with wine and various herb seasonings, I like to add large pieces of vegetables at some point in the cooking process, so that they simmer in the rich stock. In the larder we had everything I needed except carrots. There was a large vegetable garden behind the cellars, tended by the maître du chais, the cellar foreman who also happened to be our wine maker. 'That's our vegetable garden, isn't it?' I asked Peter. He nodded. 'I need some carrots, I'll go and get some.' Peter smiled. 'If you don't mind, you can't do that, as the patron. I can ask him, or you can go and talk to Ervé, and tell him what you're doing.'

So I went to see Ervé. 'Bonsoir, patron.' 'Bonsoir, Ervé.' I told him I was cooking that evening.

'Ah, you like cooking!'

'Yes, I do.'

'I don't like cooking much, so my wife does it all. It's interesting that you should cook. It's your life, I suppose.'

'Well, I certainly enjoy doing it when I'm relaxing. Tonight I'm cooking *bouef en daube*.'

'Ah, that is one of my favourites. I like the smells from the slow cooking.'

'Yes, then halfway through I add the vegetables—onions, potatoes, celery hearts, carrots. Except that I haven't any carrots.'

'Ah, but we have some splendid carrots in the garden of the Château.'

'That's marvellous. I'll get some.'

'No, no, you cannot patron. Let me get them. I know just where the best ones are. They will be good for your *daube*.'

I returned to the kitchen and not long after, Ervé arrived with some excellent washed and cut carrots. Next day, after greeting me, his first words were, 'Patron tell me about the *bouef en daube*. How were the carrots?'

Artichokes alla romana

8 good-sized artichokes (each 250g)
1 cup parsley
6 large cloves garlic, peeled
5 tablespoons anchovy fillets (oil
    included)
½ cup lemon juice

½ cup white wine
3 cups olive oil
3 cups water
salt to taste
Serves 8

Hold the artichoke on its side and with a sharp knife trim the leaves away as close to the bottom as possible, turning the artichoke as you work. Cut the leaves off the top just above the artichoke bottom. Using a teaspoon, scoop out the choke and discard. Trim the remaining greenish leaves and pieces away, leaving the bottom. Pare any tough outside fibres from the stem. Grind the parsley, garlic and anchovy fillets together. Stir in the lemon juice, wine, olive oil, water and salt to taste. Mix and blend well.

Preheat the oven to 190°C/375°F. Put the artichokes in an ovenproof casserole or pan. Try to place the artichoke bottoms in one layer, close together. Be sure the stems are covered with marinade. Pour the marinade over the artichoke bottoms, place on top of the stove and over high heat bring to the boil. Cover and transfer to the oven. Cook covered, turning and basting the bottoms every 15 minutes, for 45 minutes to 1 hour, or until the stems are tender. Make these at least a day in advance of serving so the flavours mellow. Serve at room temperature or slightly warmed.

Fresh asparagus with chives

A lovely dish, especially useful as a light entrée.

bunch fresh asparagus
80g butter
1 tablespoon vegetable oil

1 cup chopped chives
salt and black pepper
Serves 3

Cut off asparagus heads, diagonally below the heads, then continue to cut stalks diagonally into oval pieces about 5mm thick. Heat butter and oil in a pan until foaming. Add asparagus pieces and cook until *al dente* (tender but still crisp). Throw in chives, a little salt and plenty of freshly ground black pepper.

Baked avocado

'A Peter Howard recipe for avocado. He is one of the teachers at the excellent Ryde College of Catering Studies and Hotel Administration, in New South Wales.'

3 medium avocados, not too ripe
2 cups of pouring white sauce,
    chicken stock based
2 shallots, chopped
1 teaspoon chopped parsley
cream

salt and black pepper
nutmeg
breadcrumbs
butter
Serves 6

Halve the avocados lengthwise. Scoop out the halves. Be careful not to damage the skins. Dice the avocado flesh into small chunks. Place the diced avocado into a mixing bowl with the white sauce, shallots and parsley. Add enough cream to allow easy handling of the mixture. Combine the ingredients, season with salt and ground black pepper and nutmeg to your own taste. Refill the scooped-out shell with the avocado mixture. Place the halves in a baking dish, coat with breadcrumbs, top with small dollops of butter and bake in a moderate oven until the butter has melted and the breadcrumbs are lightly browned. This avocado dish can be done in individual oven-proof dishes if desired. It is ideal as an appetiser or entrée.

Red beans

3 cups red kidney beans
60g white onion
60g shallots
clove garlic
125g ham

60g butter
2½ cups water
1 teaspoon salt
½ teaspoon black peppercorns
Serves 6

A respite from sorting grapes at Château Padouen with Gino Merlo, Peter Vinding-Diers, our manager in France, James Halliday, myself and Peter Fox.

Soak the beans overnight in water to cover. Drain. Finely chop onions, shallots, garlic and ham. Melt the butter in a large saucepan and add the onion, shallots and garlic and sauté. Add the ham and continue cooking till golden. Add the drained kidney beans and remaining ingredients. Cook slowly over low heat 45 minutes to 1 hour, adding more water if necessary. Serve with hot fluffy rice.

Broccoli mousseline

A standard of my Tasting Room Chef, Carolyn Divjac. This is often served with a red sauce made from tomatoes or red capsicums.

500g broccoli flowerets, and small
    amount of stalks
salt and pepper
pinch nutmeg
2 eggs

2 egg whites
1¼ cups cream
melted butter
Serves 8

Blanch broccoli and stalks in boiling water for two minutes. Refresh under cold running water. Chop in food processor to obtain a coarse texture (don't purée). Turn the broccoli into a large bowl and add salt, pepper and nutmeg to taste. Lightly beat the eggs and egg whites together, and add to the broccoli, mixing well. Incorporate the cream. Using melted butter, coat eight small moulds thoroughly. Chill in the refrigerator for 10 minutes then pour in mousseline mixture. Place the moulds in a bain-marie and cover with aluminium foil. Place in 200°C/400°F oven and cook for 35–40 minutes.

Pickled Brussels sprouts

small Brussels sprouts   vinegar (variety of your choice)
brine

Soak the sprouts in brine overnight. Wash and place in a jar. Boil the vinegar. When cool, pour into the jar, covering the sprouts.

'This comes from a former British High Commissioner, Sir John Mason. He puts them in his martinis instead of an onion. I tried them without the gin and they were excellent. A splendid addition to mixed salad.'

———————✦———————

Roger Verge's stuffed cabbage

A recipe from Roger Verge of the Moulin des Mougins near Cannes in the south of France. Roger was guest of honour at the first Great Chefs of Australia dinner held at Rothbury. A charming man, we took him for a day on the harbour. We ate lots of seafood, drank lots of Hunter Valley semillon, the girls at Watson's Bay looked fantastic, coloured sails covered the harbour—it was a sparkling, dancing day. Roger just took it all in and kept shaking his head and saying, 'L'Australie, c'est formidable. C'est formidable.'

1kg loose-leafed cabbage
20g butter, chopped
2 tablespoons carrots, diced
1 tablespoon celeriac, diced
1 tablespoon chopped onion
100g cooked ham or cold roast pork
  diced

1 clove of garlic
1 small sprig of rosemary
1 cup stock made with chicken stock
  cube
salt and pepper

Serves 6

Bring 12 cups water to the boil with 3 tablespoons coarse salt. With a small sharp knife, cut out the stalk and wash the cabbage, in two or three rinses. Drain. Preheat the oven to 180°C/350°F. When the water comes to the boil, plunge the cabbage in and let it cook for 5 minutes, then refresh under cold running water. Spread a clean tea-towel on the table. Remove the outer leaves of the cabbage and cut away the tough central ribs. When you have six leaves, each the size of a small plate, lay them out on the cloth. If the leaves are too small, use two.

Melt the butter in a medium-sized saucepan. Add the diced carrots, celeriac and onions and allow to soften for 10 minutes, stirring occasionally with a wooden spatula. Add the diced ham or pork and the chopped garlic and cook for a further 5 minutes over low heat. Divide this mixture into six and put it on the cabbage leaves. Roll them up tightly into balls.

Put the sprig of rosemary in a small roasting tin and arrange the cabbage parcels, close together, on top. Pour in the chicken stock, which should come three-quarters of the way up the sides of the stuffed cabbage leaves. Cook in the oven for 30 minutes, basting every 10 minutes.

Red capsicum coulis

This is useful sauce, used quite often in the Tasting Room to accompany vegetable mousselines. Tomatoes may be used instead.

6 large red capsicums
2 tablespoons sherry
1 tablespoon white vinegar

salt and pepper
dash Tabasco
juice of ½ lemon

Carefully seed and core the capsicums. Place in a saucepan, cover with hot water and bring to the boil. Simmer rapidly for half an hour. Add more water if necessary to cover. Strain the capsicum and place in a food processor. Add other ingredients and blend until the mixture is a fine purée. Sieve carefully to remove any fibre.

'Capsicums sometimes have a slightly bitter after-taste. To counteract this, add a small amount of sugar.'

Cucumber salad

Rudy Komon and I both shared a regard for this simple salad. Others add cream and chopped dill.

2 cucumbers
salt
pepper
olive oil

malt vinegar
cream (optional)
chopped dill (optional)

Peel the cucumbers and cut them into thin slices, removing obvious pips. Put a layer in a dish and sprinkle a little salt on it. Repeat three or four times. Fit a plate inside the dish which rests on top of the cucumbers. Put a weight on the plate. Let stand for half an hour. Remove the plate and wash the slices free of salt (and also of any bitterness). The cucumber is now very tasty and crisp. Season with salt and plenty of black pepper, add some oil and vinegar.

Braised lettuce

fresh lettuces (one per person)
rasher of bacon
30g carrots
30g onions
30g leeks

60g butter
100ml chicken stock
salt
pepper

Remove outer leaves of the lettuces, cut around the stalk base and remove. If possible, use clean lettuces, otherwise rinse and shake dry. Chop bacon, carrots, onions and leeks into a very fine mixture. Heat the butter in a large saucepan, add the mixture and sauté quickly. Add lettuces, keep heat high, add chicken stock, salt and plenty of black pepper. Put the lid on the pan and cook until tender. Remove lettuces, keep them warm, reduce cooking liquid until only a little is left. Pour over the lettuces and serve.

Mushrooms with bean sprouts

I devised this dish from what was available and it turned out very well indeed (he said modestly). The flavours meld particularly well.

250g mushrooms
120g oyster mushrooms
2 cups bean sprouts
1 stalk celery
2 spring onions
parsley

1 strip bacon
pepper
2 powdered stock cubes
dash of Tabasco
dash of water

De-stem the mushrooms, slice the caps and finely chop the stalks. Leave oyster mushrooms whole. Chop the celery, spring onions and parsley. Dice the bacon. Place the bacon into a pan and gently sauté for a few minutes. Add the mushroom stalks, celery, spring onions, parsley, pepper and stock cubes. Simmer for five minutes, then add the mushroom slices and simmer for another 2 minutes or so. Add the oyster mushrooms, bean sprouts and a dash of Tabasco. Stir, then turn up the heat. When the pan is very hot add a dash of water. The resultant steam cooks the delicate mushrooms and the bean sprouts almost straight away.

Mushrooms Florentine with hollandaise sauce

We do this quite often, using large caps. Take care not to overcook the mushroom, which should be almost crisp in texture, contrasting with the richness of the sauce.

6 large, well-rounded mushrooms
   with stalks removed
250g spinach
soft butter

hollandaise sauce
salt
pepper
Serves 6

This variation features barely cooked spinach which had been drained well, finely chopped, patted dry, seasoned and packed into the bowl of the mushroom, which had been lightly brushed with soft butter. Pour hollandaise sauce over the top and bake until the mushroom is soft and the top lightly browned.

Stuffed mushrooms

8 good-sized mushroom caps
1 large onion
6 spring onions
mushroom stalks
1 stalk celery
120g butter

chopped parsley
extra herbs (basil, oregano,
   rosemary)
500g meat or fowl pâté
Serves 4

Finely chop the onions, spring onions, mushroom stalks and celery and simmer for a few minutes in plenty of butter. Take off the heat and add chopped parsley and other herbs if you have them—basil, a little oregano, a leaf or two of rosemary. Mix with the pâté, stuff the mushroom caps with the mixture and place on a buttered baking tray. Bake until mixture is piping hot, but don't overcook. The mushrooms should be hot but still crisp.

———————— ✿ ————————

Joan's mushroom cake

Joan Campbell, now food editor of *Vogue* is an old friend. Self-taught, she has a wonderfully down to earth attitude while producing top food. This is one of her recipes.

1kg baby mushrooms	*parsley for garnish*
6 shallots, finely chopped	*good pinch of nutmeg*
100g butter	*for the sauce:*
juice one small lemon	*45g butter*
salt and pepper	*¼ cup flour*
250g ham coarsely chopped	*¾ cup cream*
1 small clove garlic, crushed	*juice of sautéed mushrooms*
1 tablespoon chopped parsley	*1 tablespoon tomato paste*
1 cup soft breadcrumbs	*salt and pepper*
4 eggs	*little milk, if needed*
2 tablespoons sour cream	*15 small sautéed mushrooms*
2 tablespoons cream	Serves 6
5 tablespoons Cognac	

Preheat oven to 190°C/375°F. Trim the mushroom stems and wash quickly in a colander under running water. Chop the shallots and sauté in butter for a few minutes. Add mushrooms and cook rapidly with lemon juice, and salt and pepper for about 8 minutes. Strain the mushrooms and set aside the juice and 15 small mushrooms for the sauce. Put the mushrooms and ham into a food processor and chop coarsely. Mix with garlic, parsley, breadcrumbs, 4 egg yolks and 2 egg whites, cream, salt, pepper and Cognac and gently fold in the well-beaten whites of two eggs. Pour into a buttered mould and cook in a bain-marie for 45 minutes or until set. Stand for 5–10 minutes before turning out.

To make the sauce, melt butter in a saucepan, add flour and cook a few minutes. Add the cream, mushroom juice, tomato paste, salt, pepper and nutmeg. Bring to the boil and if necessary add a little milk, and the 15 whole mushrooms.

To serve, unmould the gâteau and pour over the sauce. Garnish with parsley. Ideal as an entrée or served as a luncheon main course with a tossed salad.

'These are easily prepared before a dinner, requiring a baking time of only ten minutes or so when your guests are having pre-dinner drinks or chats. I met the Qantas hostess who was part of the celebrated story regarding this dish. She was having a passionate affair with a Captain, and the stopover at the port of departure had been romantic, to say the least. Serving the first-class passengers with dinner she was asked, "Are the mushrooms stuffed?" She replied with a sigh, "No sir, just terribly tired."'

Parsnips and carrots in wine

'Use this parsnip dish as an accompaniment or as a meal by itself. Our family enjoys this quite often for a snack.'

1 cup long sliced parsnips
1 cup long sliced carrots
cold water
2 tablespoons butter
1 cup dry white wine

⅓ cup fresh lemon juice
1 teaspoon brown sugar
dash salt and pepper
2 tablespoons chopped fresh dill
Serves 4

In a pan place parsnips and carrots and cover with cold water. Bring to the boil and then simmer until the vegetables are tender, approximately 6–8 minutes. Drain and place aside. Melt the butter in another pan, add the vegetables, pour in the wine, and cook for 3–4 minutes over a medium heat. Reduce the heat and add the lemon juice, brown sugar, salt and pepper. Cook until the liquid is reduced by one third, this should take about 10 minutes. Place on a serving dish and garnish with dill.

Potatoes Roberts

12 good-sized potatoes
6 onions
green vegetables (spring onions tops, watercress, chives, parsley, lettuce, cabbage, broccoli, Chinese cabbage, celery tops)

2 cups veal or chicken stock
herb seasoning
3 tablespoons sherry or white wine
2 cups grated cheese

Peel and slice the potatoes. The slices should be round and very thin. Slice onions thinly. Gather plenty of greens and chop finely. Into a deep baking dish put a layer of onions, then a deep layer of greens, which should be firmly pressed down, then one of potatoes. Repeat about three times and keep pressing to fit in all ingredients. Try to cram in as much as possible. Then pour around veal or chicken stock. (Beef will do, though it's rather strong.) Add herb seasonings (basil is particularly good) and a little sherry or white wine. Bake for an hour or until the mixture is soft through. Add grated cheese on top for the last 10 minutes of baking.

Miniature spinach tarts

'Invented at Mudgee by me when staying with Wendy and Bob Roberts of Huntingdon Estate. I believe this is a genuine invention, and one of my few. (Most recipes are adaptions of other people's, which were variations of other people's.) This is a delicious dish, with a lovely fresh, light character.'

500g spinach
300g butter
2 onions, finely chopped
2 eggs
1¼ cups cream
¼ cup Parmesan cheese
salt and pepper

pinch of cayenne
for the rich short crust pastry:
1½ cups flour
90g butter
2 egg yolks
little water

Prepare pastry and line a 23cm flan ring. Chill. To prepare the filling, cook spinach for 3 minutes, drain and refresh under cold water.

Squeeze between two plates to extract all excess water, then chop. Melt butter in a saucepan, add onions and cook until soft, without browning. Add the spinach, making sure no moisture is left. Take off the heat and allow to cool. Beat the eggs and add the cream. Combine with spinach mixture, season to taste and pour into the flan case. Sprinkle with Parmesan cheese and cayenne. Put into a pre-heated oven 180°C/350°F for 30 minutes. Allow to cool. Using a biscuit cutter, cut out desired shapes and serve as finger food. Ideal as an appetiser or light entrée.

Tomatoes Florentine

2 large tomatoes
150g spinach (cooked and drained)
for the mornay sauce:
30g butter
1 tablespoon flour
1 cup milk
Serves 4

Cook the spinach, drain and then sauté in butter. Cut the tomatoes in half. Preheat the grill. To make sauce, melt the butter and then blend in the flour. Cook 2 minutes. Heat the milk and add to the roux, whisk until smooth and simmer 15 minutes. Place tomatoes under the griller until the tops are brown. Place a small mound of the spinach on each tomato half. Pour 1 teaspoonful of sauce over the spinach and place under the griller to glaze.

Rustle of veg

½ cup mushrooms, sliced thinly
50g green beans, cut diagonally into
    pieces
½ red capsicum and ¼ green
    capsicum, seeded and cut into
    strips 3cm wide, sliced diagonally
8 asparagus stalks, cut in diagonal
    pieces
1 medium zucchini, sliced thinly
6 sprigs parsley, chopped finely
80g butter
1 cup thickened cream
4 litres water
1kg fresh fettucine
small grating nutmeg
½ cup Parmesan cheese, grated
Serves 6–8

Using a heavy pan, sweat the vegetables in 40g of butter, then set aside. In another pan or flameproof dish put half the cream and the remaining 40g of butter and thicken over a medium heat. This should require no more than a minute. Bring the water to the boil, add two tablespoons of salt, then the fettucine. Drain, and add to the cream and butter mixture. On low heat toss the fettucine, coating it with the sauce. Add the vegetables, remaining cream, cheese, nutmeg, salt and pepper and toss. Serve with grated cheese.

'Rustle of veg is a standard from Oliver Shaul's Central Park Bar and Grill in Martin Place, Sydney. In 1967, when I resigned as Director of the Wine Bureau to become an independent, Oliver gave me one of my first consultancies, along with Millers Hotel and Qantas, and I helped establish the superb cellar of the Summit. Happily, I still get to taste some of these wines from time to time.'

Ernie's zucchini soufflé

500g small zucchini	1 tablespoon of salt
four tablespoons butter	dash of pepper
1 clove garlic, finely chopped	2 capsicums, finely chopped
3 spring onions, finely chopped	6 eggs
⅔ cup Sauternes	2 tablespoons grated Parmesan
juice of ½ lemon	cheese
⅛ teaspoon grated nutmeg	Serves 4

Butter a 4-cup baking or soufflé dish and chill it. Wash zucchini. Discard tops and a thin slice from bottom of each and cut into strips the thickness of a pencil and about 2.5cm long. In a large frying pan melt the butter. In it cook the garlic and spring onions for three minutes. Add the zucchini and cook for two minutes longer, tossing to coat each piece with butter. Add Sauternes, lemon juice, nutmeg, parsley, salt and pepper. Cook over high heat for 15 minutes, stirring occasionally, until most of the liquid has cooked away and the zucchini is tender but firm. Stir in the capsicums. Set aside to cool.

Preheat oven to hot. Separate six eggs. To the yolks add grated Parmesan cheese and heat until the egg yolks and cheese are blended and creamy. Stir in the zucchini mixture. Beat the egg whites until stiff and fold into the zucchini mixture with a wooden spoon. Pour into a prepared baking dish and bake in a hot oven for 25 minutes, or until set and fluffy. Wrap a clean napkin around the baking dish and serve the soufflé at once.

Green vegetable pâté

200g spinach	250g tongue (preferably lamb)
200g zucchini	250g liver (preferably lamb)
salt and pepper	fat or bacon fat strips
1 clove garlic, crushed	Serves 8
2 egg whites	

Mix the cooked spinach and zucchini in a blender to taste. Add salt and pepper, a squeeze of garlic and bind with the egg whites. Fill a pâté tin (or cake tin), by laying strips of gently sautéed tongue and liver alternately with the vegetable mixture. The tin should be lined with fat or bacon fat strips. Cook gently in the oven until firm. Allow to cool, then cut across in slices to serve.

Stir-fried vegetables

available vegetables (capsicum,	oil
beans, onions, shallots, celery,	chicken stock
broccoli, cauliflower, bean	
sprouts, mushrooms, carrots)	

At Eugenie les-Bains, Michel Guerard's restaurant, with the Rafia: Primo Caon and Gino Merlo protecting. Primo called this picture the *Capo di Tutti Capi*, which he translated as 'Big head'.

'This dish is becoming increasingly popular, although fried is not a good word, for I use very little oil and keep the mixture moving. The stock added to the very hot mixture quickly steams everything.'

Slice vegetables into fine, thin pieces. Heat a little oil in the bottom of a heavy pan or wok. Add the onions and cook for a little while as a flavour base. Add the rest in order of thickness. Keep stirring with a wooden spatula or spoon. After a couple of minutes, add a little chicken stock (a cube crushed in water will do). When the mixture is still crisp and undercooked, serve.

Balmain bug salad

2 Balmain bugs, cooked and cut in half

1 ripe tomato, skinned and seeded

12 small asparagus spears lightly cooked

4 loquats, peeled, seeded and quartered

for the vinaigrette:

2 teaspoons cider vinegar

1 tablespoon grape seed oil

salt and pepper

1 teaspoon chopped dill

1 teaspoon chopped shallot

Serves 1

Set 6 asparagus spears on the bottom of a plate. Toss remaining ingredients with cider vinaigrette, and set in the middle of the plate.

Grant Avenue salad

4–6 red lettuce leaves

2 cups iceberg lettuce, cut into small chunks

2 tomato slices

2 hard-boiled egg slices

1 cup cubed cooked turkey

4 fresh pea pods

1 cup bean sprouts

1/4 cup slivered carrots

1/4 cup slivered green onions

3 slices cucumber, 4mm thick, scored, halved

2 tablespoons water chestnuts, sliced thin

1 tuft Japanese (enoki) snow puff mushrooms (optional)

4 leaves fresh coriander

for the Grant Avenue dressing:

4 cups fresh mayonnaise

1½ tablespoons Dijon mustard

1½ tablespoons red wine vinegar

pinch powdered saffron

1 teaspoon curry powder

1 tablespoon honey

2 tablespoon lime juice

3/4 teaspoons Worcestershire sauce

3 or 4 drops Tabasco

1/4 cup chutney

Serves 1

'One of the standards of Fournou's Ovens, at the Stanford Court Hotel on Nob Hill in San Francisco. Americans are very good at salads and make a meal out of them. This one is ideal for such purposes.'

Line a 30cm serving platter with lettuce leaves and fill with a bed of iceberg lettuce. Arrange one tomato slice at each end and top with an egg slice. Spread turkey across the centre. Place pea pods in outer quarters of platter. Top the turkey with sprouts, then the carrot and onion. Scatter cucumber and water chestnuts around the platter and place tuft of mushrooms in the centre. Arrange coriander above each pea pod. Serve Grant Avenue dressing on the side. To make the dressing, blend together the mayonnaise, mustard, vinegar, saffron, curry powder, honey, lime juice, Worcestershire sauce and Tabasco. Stir in chutney. Refrigerate. (Makes about 5 cups.)

Vegetable terrine

This is actually from Château Rahoul. Each year an Australian acted as 'Châtelaine', running the social side of the operation, looking after visitors and ourselves, marketing, cooking and hopefully enjoying the odd glass here and there. Beth Slatyer of Canberra was the first, followed by Sarah Gough of Melbourne, who is now an important wine writer. Both lovely ladies and joys to work with. Afterwards, Margaret Lewis ran things with larger responsibilities, including the money side. Each has told me they wouldn't have missed the experience for the world. Beth is an accomplished cook, and this is one of her recipes.

4–5 carrots
250g green beans
250g shelled peas
½ cauliflower
bunch spinach
for the batter:
¾ cup sifted flour

1½ cups milk
4 eggs
3 tablespoons melted butter or oil
fresh herbs
salt and pepper
Serves 6–8

To make batter, add half the milk to the flour, whisk until smooth, then add the eggs and lastly the remaining milk with the butter or oil. Season generously with fresh herbs, salt and pepper.

Blanch each of the vegetables in boiling water. Line the bottom of a well-buttered terrine with the blanched spinach leaves, pour a thin layer of crêpe batter over and then place a layer of carrots followed by another layer of batter. Continue alternating a layer of vegetables with a layer of batter until the terrine is full. Cover with a layer of aluminium foil and cook in a water bath in a moderate oven for 1 hour. The water bath should be just simmering. Drain off any excess liquid, and let the terrine cool and refrigerate overnight. It is good served with a fresh tomato sauce.

Diet spring roll

'A recipe of my own devising. It's very tasty, full of goodness, yet very light. Any suitable vegetables may be used. Often used in our household when I'm on one of my interminable diets.'

100g carrots
100g onions
100g beans
100g capsicums
100g zucchinis
100g celery
100g shallots

1¼ cups chicken stock
salt and pepper
basil
parsley
cos lettuce leaves
Serves 4–6

Prepare a julienne of the vegetables. Poach shredded vegetables for minutes only in a covered stainless-steel container in chicken stock. Season to taste, adding freshly chopped basil and parsley. Drain the mixture and place some in between two freshly washed cos lettuce leaves. Fold the leaves over to make a lettuce sandwich, and eat like a spring roll. Ideal as a midday snack or a light dinner.

Blackstone salad

4 rings pineapple
1 orange
1 grapefruit
1 apple
1 green capsicum
1 red capsicum
6 dark cherries
lettuce

for the dressing:
½ cup French dressing made with
   lemon juice
1 tablespoon honey
½ teaspoon cinnamon
¼ teaspoon cloves
⅛ teaspoon ginger
Serves 4

Split pineapple rings in half. Cut orange, grapefruit and apple into sections. Cut capsicums into strips. Lay pineapple rings on a bed of lettuce. Fill in with alternating orange, grapefruit and apple sections. Garnish with strips of capsicum and top with a cherry. Spoon over a little dressing.

Forest Mere special salad

One of the special lunches from the celebrated 'dry-out' and health centre, Forest Mere in the United of Kingdom, once run by the parents of Graham Kerr.

1 cauliflower
125g cashew nuts
45g mild cheese
1 small leek
⅓ cup sultanas
fresh black pepper to season
salt to season

for the salad dressing:
½ cup wine vinegar
¼ cup olive oil
¼ teaspoon dry mustard
1 tablespoon sugar
Serves 6

An invitation to celebrate two great years and a very poor one (mine), at the famous Troisgros Restaurant.

Make salad dressing. Grate the cauliflower with cheese and nuts. Slice the leek finely. Place all ingredients in a salad bowl with sultanas and season with pepper and salt. Combine with a little salad dressing and serve chilled on a lettuce leaf.

Savoury wild rice

This recipe comes from Aspen, Colorado, where I ski sometimes. The wild rice is expensive, but really outstanding in flavour. It can be bought in Australia.

800g wild rice
100g spring onions, chopped
60g butter
1 can Campbells consommé

250g mushrooms, sliced
black pepper
Serves 6

Sauté the onions in butter, put in a casserole dish, add rice, consommé, mushrooms and pepper. Put top on, bake at 200°C/400°F for about 60 minutes or until the rice is cooked.

CHAPTER TEN

Caught short: more friends

I WAS ONCE IN TASMANIA doing some fund raising for charitable causes. Harry Secombe was appearing at the Wrest Point Hotel. An old mate, he offered to help and of course took over completely. The guests got two for the price of one and that's not even counting me.

We played golf the following morning. Harry, before his knighthood and his new slim persona, had a fairly wide swing, quite effective when you consider he couldn't see the ball with the shorter clubs. We had been drinking the night before. 'Bloody terrific wine that last night boyo,' he said. '—would like that.'

He mentioned a majestic name, which I will not drop because the person is not a friend of mine. I shall drop plenty of names in this chapter. However they will almost all be wine and food personalities, with some bearing on the evolution of this book, rather than just names.

That evening I rang John Avery of the celebrated wine merchants of that name in Bristol as he started his morning's work. Did he have a truck going to London that day? He did. Did he have any Rothbury 76 Hunter Semillon? He did. Would he deliver a case to—at—, compliments of H. Secombe and charge it to me. He would.

Next morning I waited until the eighth hole before I mentioned, quite casually, that—would now have a case of the wine that Harry had mentioned the day before. 'That's bloody fantastic,' he shouted 'How did you do that?'

I told him, explaining that there was a brotherhood of wine and food people scattered around the world who were strongly bound together. I said, 'These people are so bound together we call ourselves the Rafia.' At once Harry replied. 'You bloody traitor. I thought you were a member of the Taffya.'

But the Rafia does exist, if only in concept. Wine and food professionals, basically, are a gregarious lot, and they like sharing. I was once asked, 'Have you drunk or do you drink great wines by yourself?' The answer, simply, was 'No'. I cannot remember ever opening a top bottle of wine for myself alone. Frankly, I can scarcely remember opening *any* bottle just for myself.

The Single Bottle Club is, in my opinion, the greatest eating and

Michael Parkinson and Diana Fisher at lunch in the Hunter House.

drinking club I know, and many members of the Rafia are members of it. It evolved from a dinner I gave for Michael Broadbent, Master of Wine, the great palate and teacher who is head of Christies Wine Department. He visited Australia in 1977 and I gave a dinner, the menu of which is appears on page 116, which was also attended by the then Prime Minister, Malcolm Fraser, who happens to be a great wine buff. At the club dinners, which are held once or twice a year, everyone brings the greatest single bottle they have been able to find.

The Lafite was magnificent. It was given to me by Jean Troisgros, of the famous restaurant of that name in Roanne, when he visited as Guest of Honour at the Great Chefs Dinner held at Rothbury in 1980. We enjoyed the bottle at the dinner given by Malcolm Fraser at The Lodge in 1982. Days after the dinner, I read in a magazine that a bottle of the same wine had sold for $10,000. So I sent a clipping from the magazine to all the members with a note: 'And what do you intend to do next year?' One has to keep the Rafia aware of its dues.

The Rafia has been going on for years, though not in name. Wine and food people obviously have a freemasonry which is not only pertinent to Australia. But in Australia we've had the Wine and Food Society on Tuesdays, the Beefsteak and Burgundy Clubs, Bacchus, the Viticultural Club, the Monday Table, the First Thursday Club and the Friday Club. No one has ever done much with Wednesdays, it seems.

The Friday Club was a great introduction for me; I've discussed it in Chapter One. The then staff of the Chevron Hilton are still around. Indeed, Edward Tirado still works in the Hilton Bar, whatever it's called now, 25 years later. I gave him his first job as a cocktail barman in Australia, and it's the only one he's ever had. His many books on cocktails and the various positions he's held in their Guild reflect his cheerful durability, if nothing else. I think Eddie would agree that the originals of the hotel remember with great affection those early days, and it's surprising how many of them crop up occasionally. It's great fun to try a restaurant off your normal track and find an old mate serving, cooking or managing. In one recent week I met three old staff who are now in very good positions with top hotels.

And it's not only people one has worked with. I remember Dimitri Karageorge and Beppi Polese starting restaurants in the late 1950s and teaching us all so much about a better way of life. Wolfie Pizzem and Joe Malek started the Coachman in 1958, with the seats hanging out of their respective pants. The tremendous success of their Waterfront Restaurant in the Rocks Area of Sydney, and their others, are well known. Yet recently Wolfie said to me, almost wistfully, 'Do you remember the beginning of the Coachman. We didn't have a farthing to pay for anything.' On such premises great food and beverage empires were born.

I used to go to Melbourne a lot in the Wine Bureau days, and there forged, and tempered, many great friendships which are part of the brotherhood. I have the greatest respect for many of the top wine

Len and Trish serve Cassoulet in Australia (recipe page 212).

At the Convict Drinking Trough, our traditional halfway refreshment stop on the way to the Hunter, with a gorgeous armful of Maggie Tabberer.

and food people in Melbourne, but my greatest mates have been the Schneiders and the Dunstans, and others such as the Crittendens, the Sewards, Frank Doherty, the Gregureks, Sygie Jorgensen. Most of these people have one thing in common: a genuinely uncompromising attitude to the quality of the article they offer. (I'm aware that Keith Dunstan is a writer and not one of us, but he likes eating and drinking so much I had to include him. Besides, he put me in his book, *Ratbags*, so I accord him the same, dubious, honour.)

Dunstan, Doherty, Chris Daniels and I were once visiting Great Western when we ran into Spot Hurley, a squatter from Ballarat. He told us a story about the late Sir Frank Packer.

Spot had been a Squadron Leader during World War II, flying a Lancaster on night missions over Germany. He had an all-Australian crew, and on their first 72-hour pass to London, naturally enough they all went out together to do what they could. At some incredibly early hour, the grog went off. They were in the Savoy at the time, and with the resourcefulness one would expect of a Squadron Leader, and an Aussie one at that, Spot demanded to see the register. It transpired that a Mr Frank Packer from Sydney was staying at the hotel.

Spot rang him, explained the situation and the crew were invited to the press lord's suite. 'He had got everything,' said Spot. 'Beer, Scotch, gin, brandy, the lot. And it was all ours.' They were entertained right royally all night, given a good breakfast and sent happily, if erratically, on their way.

Some years later, in 1948, Spot was walking up the steps of the old Australia Hotel in Castlereagh Street. He felt a heavy hand thump his shoulder, and there was his wartime host. 'Goodday, Spot,' said Frank Packer. 'Your shout.'

Keith Dunstan was also present on a more infamous occasion, when he invited me to attend a dinner at the Melbourne Club. We sat with my great friend and mentor Eric Purbrick, of Chateau Tahbilk, and Doug Crittenden, who had the best licensed grocer's palate in Melbourne (now retired—Doug, not the palate).

The purpose of the dinner was to taste the new purchases of the wine-buying committee, to compare with like makes and varieties bought ten years before. Frankly, the food was ordinary, the new wines had little future, in my opinion, and the old wines did not justify their long keeping. Yet speaker after speaker raved on about them. Finally, I was introduced as a wine judge and asked to comment. I declined. I was pressed. I declined. The President admonished me, saying that they were not afraid of criticism. So I spoke.

I told them that I thought of the wines and suggested that wine buying was not a matter for a collection of doctors, solicitors, accountants and businessmen, but the province of the specialist, just as their professions were specialist. After all, I didn't go around teaching them how to heal, to interpret the law, to add or to make money. There was an uproar. Someone jumped to his feet to chastise me, upholding the honour and integrity of the committee (neither of

Entertaining my family and friends at Sunday lunch in my Hunter dining room.

'He felt a heavy hand thump his shoulder, and there was his wartime host. "Goodday, Spot," said Frank Packer. "Your shout."'

which virtue was in question), and demanding I be sacked, or tarred and feathered or something. It turned out he wasn't a member either but no matter. There were three amusing consequences.

The immediate one was that the dinner was adjourned. When we went into the lounge for coffee everyone, except the table I attended, went to one side of the room and steadfastly ignored us. Dunstan threatened to resign until he saw the humour of it.

Then, some years later I ran into the doctor who soon after the infamous dinner became the man in charge of the wine at the club. 'You did a great job for me,' he said. 'I never liked many of the old wines much and I was able to get rid of scads of them.'

Finally, many years later, I went back to the club for lunch. There was an old porter at the door with the long-suffering, resigned look of his kind. His face brightened perceptibly when he saw me. 'Good-day, Mr Evans,' he beamed. 'Go in and give 'em hell.'

In Adelaide I number among my friends Rama and Primo Caon. Primo, variously restaurateur, wine merchant, wine bar owner and now wholesaler, cares about things as much as anyone I know. And there are the Hardy's, lots of them, the Heskeths (Bob Hesketh, for his sins, became Chairman of the Wine Corporation) and the Schuberts. Max was honoured at Rothbury as the first recipient of our Wine Man Award, for services to the industry. His Grange Hermitage, which he evolved with the strong support of Jeffrey Penfold-Hyland, remains the single outstanding item of evolution among Australian red wine.

In McLaren Vale there was the late Bob Hagley, of Hardy's vintage port fame, and dear D'Arcy Osborne, one of the gentlest of all wine men. And in the Valley, Marg and Peter Lehmann, dear old 'Mud flat' himself. Peter, one of the greatest of all promoters and supporters of the Barossa Valley, has dispensed tremendous hospitality to all over the years, including serving huge quantities of artichoke soup, on one occasion, to the Australian Ballet. And of course there is the Hill Smith clan of Yalumba, but more of them in a little while.

In Perth I helped train John Hanley, who is now that State's top judge, and I worked with Bill Jamieson and Tony Devitt of the viticultural section of the Department of Agriculture. Jack Mann, a great old chap from Houghton's, was ever kind, talking of the three 'C's (Chablis, Christianity and Cricket) and of fancy labelling practices: 'They can adorn the outside. I'll adorn the bottles on the inside.'

The wine scene is vastly different in Western Australia now, with people like the Horgans, the Tates, the Panells and the Cullens changing the face of the industry.

In Brisbane I have particular friends who epitomise the success which may be achieved by hard-working people who make Australia their home. Mary and Gino Merlo own Milano, the number one restaurant in Brisbane. Gino started as a steward, then became a cane cutter in the north. He worked hard, saved his money and settled in Brisbane to start a small espresso bar. I met him not long after that, when he had started to serve a few pasta dishes. Now Milano is a

'Finally, many years later, I went back to the club for lunch. There was an old porter at the door with the long-suffering, resigned look of his kind. His face brightened perceptibly when he saw me. "Goodday, Mr Evans," he beamed. "Go in and give 'em hell."'

bustling medium to large Italian-style brasserie, packed both for lunch and dinner. It is remarkable for two things—the eagle eyes of the Merlos, ever attentive to their guests, and the best wine cellar in Australia. I helped put this together and can state unequivocally that not only was no expense spared, but that a great deal of thought was given by Gino to what were the best wines of Australia and the rest of the world. I don't think the cellar can be a truly economic proposition, but it gives him, and the likes of me, great pleasure. It was reported in a local Brisbane paper that a customer saw me using a special tasting glass. He asked a waiter why this was so, and was told that any customer ordering one of the top wines was served those glasses. Since the customer was drinking a 20-year old red at $45 a bottle, he wondered just how special the wine had to be. I happened to be enjoying a 1947 Château Rouget, available to all at $90 a bottle.

The Milano won the *Bulletin*/Quelltaler Restaurant Award for the best wine list in Australia for three consecutive years, and was then retired to the gastronomic hall of fame, membership of Prosper Montaigne, an age-old culinary order. I suspect that soon the Merlos will sell and, after a spell, move to other things.

Hotel men all over the world play a large part in the Rafia. I suspect they even have one of their own, a sort of loose linking based on understanding of service and quality, which is outside normal group channels. It's always nice to know which are the good Hiltons. More than once I've mentioned my old boss, Frank Christie. His boss in Australia was a great hotel man, Tony Carpenter, who opened the Sydney Hilton and acting as Australian Vice-President before moving to the United States to help run the Hilton International division there. Hans Sternik was manager of the Vienna Intercontinental when I met him, but soon became President of the chain. There's Julian Payne, manager of the London Ritz, and three chums, Martin Skane of Chewton Glen, Paul Henderson of Gidleigh Park (a Yank) and Douglas Barrington of Lygon Arms, who comes from Perth. All devoted hotel men, caring and ever helpful.

The two overseas hotel men who have made the greatest impression on me are friends themselves, though they live many thousands of kilometres apart. James Nassikas is the President of the Stanford Court Hotel in San Francisco, and one of its two shareholders and board members. I met him in the mid-1960s when he was running the Royal Orleans in New Orleans. A fidget, a worrier, a piano player with an often hidden sense of humour, he runs a great hotel. I know of none better in the States. The main restaurant of the hotel, Fournou's Ovens, is regularly among the best of the top eating places in the United States, and is often the only hotel restaurant listed. The rooms of the hotel are immensely comfortable, the service is great, the place is impeccably maintained. Of course, one has to put up with Nassikas.

Once I had a birthday dinner party at Ernie's, a restaurant that used to be a brothel in Montgomery Street, San Francisco. The Mondavis came down from the Napa for it, Roland and Victor Gotti, the

With the chef of Fournou's Ovens Restaurant in San Francisco. Jim Nassikas, the owner, is in the middle.

owners were there, plus Dan and Beryl Murphy, of Melbourne, who were staying at the hotel. Everything went well for a while, but there was a period of shocked attention when the multi-millionaire Nassikas suddenly got to his feet, stormed over to the other side of the room, and picked up a piece of paper someone had discarded. In somebody else's restaurant? *That's* dedication.

Mention of the Mondavis reminds me of my debt to Bob, for he, of all Americans, is probably their international Rafia representative. The Mondavis, with father Bob, sons Michael and Tim, and daughter Marcia, have made a great success of Robert Mondavi Wines, of Oakville in the Napa Valley. I find Americans three-layered. The first layer is easy to penetrate. At this strata they are affable, courteous, helpful, considerate. But one can go so far and no further. At the second level they are difficult to know. They do not like too many people to know them too well, and there seems to be something in reserve. Penetrate the level by mutual trust, professional regard and simply friendship, and the last layer is very rewarding.

Bob Mondavi is a great bloke, and a great wine man. He has done more to publicise Californian wine at home and abroad than any man I know. Fit, articulate, engaging, I hope he lives to be a hundred. When I was looking for a vineyard in the Napa in the late 1970s, Bob 'leant' me one of his men, who searched and found the right spot. When I thanked Bob, he grinned and said, 'Glad to have you along.'

A couple of years later, I suggested they try a Napa Valley barrel auction for local charities. Bob said it wouldn't work, but after we lost our vineyard there, I saw the idea promulgated, and it is now very successful. Michael Broadbent runs the auction. I have never received any acknowledgement, but when I chipped Bob about it, he just grinned.

Jim Nassikas's British counterpart, (a Scotsman) is David Levin, who runs the Capital Hotel in Basil Street, London, just a hundred metres from Harrod's. He started as an apprentice cook on Scottish Railways. After working hard in various positions, he married a delightful lady called Margaret, and they renovated a small hotel in the country. One thing led to another, and now they have the Capital (in which I've stayed since 1972), L'Hotel next door, the Greenhouse Restaurant in Mayfair and the Metro Wine Bar. The Capital has a Michelin-starred restaurant, and the staff at the hotel are all marvellous and firm friends. For me it is a home from home.

The English contingent of wine people are incredibly industrious, fine writers with good palates, ever enquiring ever enthusiastic. Eddie Penning-Rowsell, who specialises in Bordeaux wines, came to Australia and was intrigued by the ice-cream boat which serves the yachts in the harbour. We joked and told him that when they served the nude beaches the ice-cream men took off their shorts so that they would be inconspicious. To which Eddie replied, 'I wonder which way they lean, politically.'

Hugh Johnson, the famous wine author, loves Australia, and seizes every chance to visit and taste the wines. He is also an eminent tree-man, a dendrologist, and once gave a New South Wales arboretum an award from the international society of dendrologists. I went with him. The Mayor of the town spotted me and said in surprise, 'I didn't know you were interested in trees.' He had no idea Johnson was a wine man.

There are so many top English wine writers and merchants, eager to share their knowledge, hospitable, opinionated, sometimes slightly patronising but always eclectic and willing to broaden their range. Serena Sutcliffe and Janis Robinson represent the emerging force of the female palate; John Avery, David Peppercorn and Patrick Grubb are all Masters of Wine who delight in sharing a good bottle. And then there's Michael Broadbent of Christies, Master of Wine, international auctioneer, writer, lecturer, Grand Prix holder, International President of the Wine and Food Society. Broadbent is a formidable fellow, sometimes stiff, often stern, the epitome of the English gentlemen, including the eccentricity of riding to work on a bicycle.

When we were touring together, and understanding the sense of humour that lay under this slightly pompous façade, I used to tease him. After one prolonged attack he turned and shouted, 'Oh, Evans, you are a shitty arsehole.'

I've been called many things on different occasions, but never a shitty arsehole, or SA for short. I delighted in the unfortunate remark, and the Honourable Society of SAs was born. We still address each other as SA. When I had a company named after me in France, Len Evans SANS ANONYME, or Len Evans SA, I couldn't wait to get official stationery to confirm my official SA status. But Broadbent had the last laugh. When I received an OBE in 1982 he wrote:

As briefly mentioned in my cable, the governors of the order of SA have seen fit to upgrade you to SE, the E being Earhole, higher, naturally than the A, unless you are standing on your H (or live in Australia).

Unfortunately, the Imperial Award takes precedence over ours, therefore you should run the OBE and the SE in that order—hence, OBESE. Which fits I suppose.

In order to attain your knighthood you must slim. Then you will be dubbed Sir Lean Evans.

'In order to attain your knighthood you must slim. Then you will be dubbed Sir Lean Evans.'

In France friendships may not have the same spontaneity, probably based on this shared sense of humour, yet they can be very rewarding. Of the great chefs, I have special affection for Paul Bocuse, Michel Guerard and Roger Vergé, all of whom visited us at Rothbury, plus of course the late Jean Troisgros and his brother Pierre.

The Champagne families are tremendous people. My particular chums are Christian Billy and Christian Pol Roger of Pol Roger, Alain de Vogué of Veuve Clicquot, Christian Bizot of Bollinger and Henri Krug of the company of the same name. These friends are unfailing in their courtesy and kindness, and their genuine warmth after years of doing business and enjoying Champagne together.

In other areas I have more great wine friends. In Bergerac, near

Bordeaux, Nick and Anne Ryman run Château de la Jaubertie, a fantastic old place beautifully restored by them. Their son Hugh has visited twice to learn Australian wine-making ways. In Burgundy, the 'Queen', Madame Lalou Bize-Leroy, half-owner of the Domaine de la Romanee Conti and owner of the house of Leroy, dominates the old wine market and stands resolutely for absolute quality. She is a famed alpinist, skier, mother, palate, businesswoman and Burgundian to her boots. I adore her. (I like also Marcel, her mountaineer husband, whom I once saw belt a Chevolais bull on the nose with his fist because it was getting too 'stroppy'.) A less grand, but equally delightful man is Louis Vallet, owner of the small shipper, Pierre Bouree in Gevrey-Chambertin. A meticulous wine maker, buyer and shipper, I delight in his company, for to me he represents all that is traditional and good about Burgundian hospitality—genuine love for his vines and wines and courtesy in all business dealings.

All of these people are considerate of the sincere lover of fine wine and food. They meet lots of urgers and would-be's, but they can handle all situations and find time to at least discuss the requirements of those who attend them. Kindness should be remembered. Which brings me back to the Hill Smiths of Yalumba.

I first met some of the family in 1956, when I visited my first winery as their guest. I had come from Mount Isa, and had only one introduction in Adelaide. The lady, hearing I was interested in wine, said, 'You must meet the Hill Smiths.'

I shall be ever grateful. Margie and Mark, and his brother, John, gave me lunch that day and showed me their wines and winery. Seven years later I was their guest at the Barossa Festival, and we've been there for every one since. We watched their sons Michael and Matthew, grow up, and we saw one married. We've also grown very fond of Chairman Wyndham ('Wyndy'), his wife Helen, and their son Rob. The Hill Smiths are mighty people and stand for everything that is good in the traditions of fine Australian wine. The quality of their vineyards, oenologists and equipment is as good as money can make it. Their prices are kept reasonable; their wines are totally consistent yet they never rest on their laurels.

And not the least of things is the social side of events. They lead a quiet life, interspersed with their own visits outside the Yalumba compound and visitors to them. Which, I suppose, makes not for a quiet life. Margie seems quite capable of serving two, twenty or two hundred. I have been with her when she expected four for dinner and sat down sixteen. Yet she never seems in the least flustered or anxious. For this reason, and for her store of frozen sauces, casseroles, terrines, pâtés and delights, I nominate Margie Hill Smith as the best 'caught short' cook I know of in Australia.

'Caught short' cook? One who has the ability to whip up something from nothing, to arrive home late to put something on the table in a relatively short time, to stretch a meal to twice the amount when necessary. Which is what the recipes that follow are all about.

With Jackie Collins of *The Stud* fame.

Margie's caught short mousse

This from Margie Hill Smith, my great mate from the Barossa Valley. She and husband Mark, the Managing Director of Yalumba Wines, have been our hosts for nearly 30 years. In fact, Mark introduced me to the Australian wine industry. Margie is a marvellous caught short cook, able to whip up a meal in a moment, as well as handling the more elaborately planned dinners beautifully.

220g can salmon, bones removed	1 large onion, peeled
capers to taste	½ red capsicum, seeds removed
salt and pepper	½ green capsicum, seeds removed
1 carrot, chopped	½ cup low fat yoghurt
1 small cucumber	Serves 4–6

Into the Magimix put salmon, capers, salt, pepper, carrot pieces, peeled cucumber, onion, capsicum and yoghurt. When blended together in a very fine mix it can be eaten raw, or can be set more firmly by adding egg white or gelatine and poaching in a bain-marie in the oven.

Quick prawns

1kg green prawns	Ketjap Bentene Manis (Indonesian
oil	sauce)
garlic, chopped	Hoi Sin sauce
root ginger	Serves 4

Heat a little oil in a frying pan. Add the garlic, some shaved root ginger (preserved ginger will do) and then quickly cook the shelled (but still tail-bearing) green prawns, literally for seconds.

Add Ketjap Bentene Manis sauce, which can be easily bought, then a touch of Hoi Sin sauce, just enough to meld with the other and coat the prawns. Serve and eat instantly.

Quick tailor, sweet and sour

2 tailor, fresh from the sea	sweet and sour sauce (bought)
1 capsicum, or ½ green, ½ red	ginger conserve
10 spring onions	60g butter
200g bean sprouts	Serves 2

Slice the capsicum and cut onions into lengths. Simmer in a little butter until tender and then add the bean sprouts. Drain, and pour over the sweet and sour sauce and some ginger conserve.

Steam the tailor for a few minutes only, using a proper fish steamer if you have one. If not, any double pan will do. Remove, put on a platter, and take the flesh off the bones. Cover the fish fillets with heated vegetables and sauce.

'The tailor must be fresh, in fact this is for those people who catch them and want to use them before the fish dehydrate, as they do fairly quickly. (Which is why they are so often smoked when caught.)'

Hot bubble and squeak with bacon

This is yet another of a seemingly endless series of quick dishes concocted for the kids. Often the ingredients are leftovers. Speed is always essential.

leftover cooked carrots, potatoes,	*3 eggs*
onions and peas	*Tabasco*
parsley	*2 rashers bacon*
basil	*butter*
salt and pepper	*oil*

Add parsley, basil, salt, pepper, eggs and a dash of Tabasco to the cooked carrots, potatoes, onions and peas. Process in a blender to a 'chopped-up mixture', being careful not to make a paste. Cut the bacon into squares and fry until crisp.

In a small frying pan heat a dab of butter and a drop of oil, then add a large spoonful of the mixture. This will make a round patty about 15cm across. Cook on a medium heat until the patty is brown on both sides. Scatter with crisp bacon and serve.

———————— ❦ ————————

Italo-Chinese cuisine

'Another "caught short" recipe for a hungry horde, composed of "things in the fridge". The kids loved it. As I said at the time, in cooking, confidence is everything.'

500g cold boiled potatoes	*2 stalks celery*
2 bacon rashers	*6 spring onions*
6 salami slices	*soy sauce*
2 onions	*oil*
1 capsicum	

Dice potatoes and sauté in a little hot oil. In another pan fry sliced bacon, salami, onions, capsicum, celery and spring onions. Add a dash of soy sauce, then the fried potato pieces.

———————— ❦ ————————

Quick chicken and vegetables

2 medium-sized chickens	*12 button mushrooms*
oil	*6 spring onions*
60g butter	*12 broccoli pieces*
2 diced bacon rashers	*12 cauliflower flowerets*
3 tablespoons brandy	*2 carrots, chopped*
¾ cup red wine	*1 stalk celery, chopped*
1 bay leaf	*cornflour*
2 cloves garlic, crushed	*parsley*
mixed herbs	*noodles or rice*
12 small onions	Serves 8–10

Cut the chickens into about 8 pieces each—legs, wings, breast and so on. Put some oil, butter and diced bacon in a heavy frying pan and heat. When very hot, place in the chicken and brown. When this is done flame with brandy. Then pour in the red wine, add a bay leaf, the crushed garlic and a pinch of mixed herbs. Cover and simmer for 15 minutes. While chicken is cooking prepare vegetables in sizes according to cooking densities. Small onions, button mushrooms and spring onions may be left whole, broccoli and cauliflower cut into flowerets and carrots and celery sliced into small pieces. Add the vegetables to the pot and stir in with the chicken pieces. Simmer until the vegetables are soft.

Remove the chicken pieces and arrange on a platter. Thicken the sauce and vegetables with cornflour, or butter and flour kneaded together. Pour over the chicken. Sprinkle chopped parsley on top. Serve with noodles or rice.

Quick chicken with tomatoes

1 cooked chicken
500g tomatoes
250g mushrooms
250g onions
parsley
30g butter

1 clove garlic, crushed
salt and pepper
slices of ham
basil
Serves 6–8

'A quick snack stemming from the availability of a large cooked chicken, some cold cooked rice, and masses of ripe tomatoes and hungry kids. The whole affair should take 30 minutes from start to wash-up.'

Drop the tomatoes into boiling water for 30 seconds or so, then remove, skin them and dice. Chop up mushrooms, onions and parsley and simmer in the butter. Then add the diced tomatoes, garlic and salt and pepper. Cook for a further 10 minutes or until sauce is ready. Meanwhile take the chicken meat off the bone and cut it into thin slices. Add chicken, ham, additional parsley and basil to the sauce and warm for five minutes. Serve with rice.

Stir-fried chicken with bean sprouts

350g chicken breasts, skinned, boned
*   and cut into strips*
1 teaspoon dry sherry
1 teaspoon salt
2 teaspoons cornflour

1 egg white
6 tablespoons vegetable oil
200g bean sprouts
½ teaspoon sugar
2–3 spring onions finely shredded

Mix together the sherry, ½ teaspoon salt, the cornflour and egg white in a bowl. Add the chicken and toss to coat thoroughly. Heat 4 tablespoons of oil in a frying pan. Add the chicken and stir-fry until it is cooked through. Transfer to a plate. Add the remaining oil to the pan and reheat. Add the bean sprouts and stir-fry for 30 seconds. Return the chicken to the pan with the remaining salt and the sugar and stir-fry for a few seconds. Transfer to a serving plate and garnish with the shredded spring onions.

Corned beef hash

The Stanford Court Hotel in San Francisco, run by Jim Nassikas, serves the best damned corned beef hash in the world. It is served for breakfast in the coffee shop, with two poached eggs on top. It's delicious, and I never have anything else.

500g cooked pastrami or corned beef   *white pepper to taste*
1 boiled medium-sized potato   *vegetable oil*
1 egg
1 medium-sized onion, diced

Using a food processor chop the corned beef coarsely. Then add the potato, onion and the egg. Add white pepper. Chop again all the ingredients for about 20 seconds. Corned beef is ready to be shaped in 6 patties.

Cook in a frying pan over moderate heat using just a touch of vegetable oil.

Ham leftovers

One of my friend Joan Campbell's recipes. Joan, an amateur (i.e. non-trained) cook, became a leading cook and cookery writer by sheer talent.`

1kg thick sliced ham   *8 cups rich cheese sauce thinned with*
1kg potatoes, parboiled, peeled and   *some cream (sauce must be fairly*
*   cut in thick slices*   *thin)*
Serves 6–8

Layer the ham and potatoes in an ovenproof dish with the sauce. Put some grated cheese on top and cook well in the oven, so that the sauce is absorbed into the potatoes and ham, and the top is brown. Cook slowly for 1–1½ hours or more at about 165°C/325°F. Serve with a fresh green salad.

Trish's hamburgers

Quite simply, my wife cooks the best hamburgers I've ever eaten.

1kg lean, tender beef   *2 carrots, grated*
6 bread rolls   *for the garnish:*
1 onion, finely chopped   *tomatoes*
salt and pepper   *cabbage*
mixed herbs   *mustard*
two eggs   Serves 6

Mix together, beef, finely chopped onion, salt, pepper, mixed herbs, eggs and grated carrot. Cook the patties, being careful not to over-cook them—they should be pink in the middle. Place in the bread rolls and garnish with crisp, sliced tomatoes, cabbage and mustard.

Sharing a joke with Sir Mark Oliphant.

Lamb leftovers

A lovely dish that doesn't take very long to do and gets rid of the cold leg of lamb in a most attractive way.

remains of a cooked leg of lamb, cut
    in pieces
cooked potatoes, sliced
onions, finely sliced
greenery, chopped, (whatever is
    available; spring onion tops,
celery, watercress, parsley, basil,
    lettuce)
stock (chicken or beef consommé, or
    stock cubes if nothing else is
    available)

In a casserole dish place a layer of onions, followed by a layer of potatoes, a layer of lamb pieces and a layer of greenery. Continue layering until all ingredients are used. Top up the casserole dish with stock and place in a hot oven until the onions are cooked.

More lamb leftovers

remains of a cooked leg of lamb, cut
    in small pieces
cooked potatoes, sliced
onions, sliced
salt and pepper

In a frying pan sauté masses of onions until transparent, then add the potatoes and lamb until everything is piping hot. Add plenty of salt and pepper.

'One of my favourites from the caught short and leftover ranks. I like drops of Worcestershire sauce on mine.'

Steak and bean sprouts

prime rib fillet (ask your butcher to
    cut into very thin slices and to
    remove any excess fat)
fresh lettuce
bean sprouts
for the marinade:
1 cup red burgundy
1½ tablespoons sweet Chinese-style
    soy sauce
3 cloves garlic, peeled and crushed
pinch nutmeg
sprinkle of Chinese Five Spice
    powder
1 teaspoon ginger powder or fresh
    root of ginger

'A very quick and easy dish to do and an introduction to the subtleties of Asian cooking.'

Slice steak into very thin strips. Make a marinade by combining the burgundy, soy sauce, garlic, nutmeg, Chinese Five Spice and ginger powder. Press the marinade into the beef with fingertips, then let stand for three hours at room temperature or overnight. Retain the marinade juice.

Fry lettuce leaves in light safflower oil, then place on plates. Lightly fry sprouts, then arrange on the bed of lettuce leaves. Frying should be done at high heat for a very short time.

Gently fry the beef in a lightly oiled frying pan until marinade juices start to thicken and form a smooth sauce. Place the beef on sprouts and lettuce bed, then pour the remaining sauce over the beef. Serve hot with plain or fried rice.

CHAPTER ELEVEN

Desserts: the house on the hill

IN 1968, THE ROTHBURY ESTATE in the Hunter Valley was founded by 11 wine enthusiasts, only three of whom could really be termed wine men. Most of the eight others were keen on wine, and wanted to be part of its making, but they had made their money elsewhere, as accountants, orthodontists, radiologists, store keepers, broadcasters, dentists and surgeons. Consequently, they knew a number of other people who wanted to be part of the grape-growing business, and there was a mad scramble for land. The Wills block which became Herlstone, the block next to Mistletoe (Homestead Hill) and the old Glandor farm, (Brokenback) run by Jack Phillips from which Ringold came before the war, were all bought for various syndicates. And just in case, the old Pinchens block was bought, in between the Andy Phillips farm, which became Woolundry, and the Palmers block, from which Palmers Lane gets its name.

A year later, the Rothbury Board decided that enough was enough, we would plant no more. Almost at once I fancied the remaining 40 hectares and thought it would make a magnificent site for a house. Gerry Sissingh, our manager/wine maker thought the same, and had designs on the site. However, I bought it in 1972, paying Rothbury twice as much as they had paid for it, to offset any feelings of nepotism that may have been harboured among the numerous syndicate holders.

The block just sat there for years. I took hundreds of people there, by four-wheel drive or on horseback, to show them the views and the old water tank in the ground, the only indication that a house had been there in the last part of the 19th century.

During my many trips to the Hunter, I would see a huge pile of old timber at Calga, ironbark about 36 centimetres square, in pieces from 2 to 8 metres long. I decided it would be fun to build frames for a house out of this material. A roof or roofs could be pitched on these box frames, and then the non-weight-bearing walls could be filled in with all sorts of different materials. I enquired about this wood and was told that much of it had come from the Benelong Point Wharf, which had been pulled down to make way for the Opera House. Not only did Adrian Russell, the owner, sell it to me, but he carted it up to my hill himself. Later, Dr Bob Smith, an old mate who had built a

The olive tree and pepper trees shroud the entertainment block of the Hunter house, 1984.

winery in the Upper Hunter from the remains of the Benalla Jail, gave me more of the same kind of timber, for which he no longer had any use.

The timber lay around the site for years. Because it had cost so little to get the materials there, I proudly boasted that I would build my weekender, for that it was all it was to be, for less than $50,000. Foolish man; the plumbing finally cost more than that.

In 1980, we drew up some plans, and Keith Cottier, the architect who had designed Rothbury, put them into a more coherent form. We didn't intend to follow any plans closely. I wanted to build what the Americans call a 'salvage home', out of bits and pieces of materials found in demolition sites and yards and antique shops: French doors, windows, stained glass, firebacks and so on. And we wanted the walls to be of mud brick. We went to see the local council.

The pre-landscaping look of the Hunter house in early 1984.

The council building inspector viewed our application with some suspicion, though not much was said until we mentioned the mud brick walls. That wasn't possible. Mud brick was not an approved material in the area. Keith Cottier pointed out that whole colonies of mud brick houses had been built, particularly in Victoria.

The building inspector was insistent; mud brick wasn't a proven material. Keith explained that other houses built of adobe and pisé had been standing for years, some being over 100 years old. The council wasn't backward, the building inspector pointed out. They had approved a mud brick dwelling in the same lane, and they would see how that turned out. It could take 20 years.

Worse was to come. Unless I was prepared to enclose the veranda leading to the guests' rooms to make it a corridor, the house would be classified as a motel. I protested that I didn't want to build a motel, I wasn't going to take in any members of the public, and I didn't intend to charge for the rooms. No matter, it was a motel. I was instructed to send $200 to the State Planning Authority, with plans and site plans, and request permission.

Their letter came back, stating: 'Permission is granted to build (your) motel, provided you can assure us, there is sufficient off-street parking.' We had 40 hectares which had been shown on the site plan. The house was in the middle of it. The nearest tar-sealed road was nearly a kilometre away and inaccessible. The lane that serviced us was unsealed, full of potholes, and used by a donkey every Pancake Tuesday. All this had been shown on the application. I assured the State Planning Authority that I had calculated there was enough parking for 14,000 cars.

After this initial refusal to recommend my application for mud brick, the building inspector and his successors put no further obstacles in our way. The plans were approved by the council, and the inspectors, once they appreciated the care that went into the house, were most cooperative. Concrete slabs were poured in October, 1981 and allowed to cure. Building was to start the following year.

In December, Peter Fox was killed, and it was then that the house became more significant. Until then, it had been merely a large weekender that I was building for my family and our friends to en-joy. 1982 turned out to be the worst year of my life. Although I was very proud to receive an OBE from the Queen, it did not compen-sate me for the events of the rest of the year.

We tried very hard to save the Evans Wine Company from the demise of Adelaide Holdings. I joined the board of the latter com-pany in an honorary effort to help. We negotiated all over the place. Finally, at one meeting I was told, 'We've got you by the balls and you'll do what you're told.' Not enjoying the sensation, I decided not to continue with the people concerned. I resigned, and was able to borrow sufficient money to buy certain assets of the Evans Wine Company. But we were forced to sell our French and Californian concerns.

These negotiations took a great deal of time and energy. Through it all, we were still attempting to keep things going on various fronts; vines keep growing and produce grapes that have to be crushed and made into wine that has to be matured and bottled and sold. I either fell into an exhausted sleep or tossed and turned all night that year.

And so the building of the house became my major release. Think-ing about it, since the method of construction was ad hoc, distracted my mind from things I had no power to solve. Time and time again I escaped to the country, sometimes only in my mind, to plan, to create, to evolve the house that I now believed would mean a great deal to me in the future.

1983 began with less tension. The resolution of the Evans Wine Company's overseas affairs meant that there was no longer any point in moping. We remembered the good times, and tried to get rid of the bitter taste. The killing drought of 1980–82 appeared to be over and prospects for a reasonable vintage in 1983 seemed sound. And the kids came to the rescue with their enthusiasm and support.

The framework for the house, named Stonehenge by the two carpenters who erected it, seemed to grow quickly. By the end of 1982 the roof was on, and the bare walls were going up. All the old doors and windows that had been stored were on site and marked for inclusion. A bricklayer built the rough walls that we intended to clad with mud of some form, and in the summer holidays of early 1983 we started work.

The kids and their friends and Trish and I plastered the outside walls, cladding them in a mixture of mud, white cement, sand, lime and fire clay, built the verandas of the house, all 35 plus squares of them, and made a large mosaic, measuring six metres by over ten, in the middle of the three blocks of the house. There were problems. The first batch of mud mix contained too little cement, so it dried with large cracks in it and then fell away in huge chunks. Our hands wore out; the surfaces were literally worn away by the grain of the mix, regardless of gloves. We dropped large quarry tiles on our feet and lost toenails. The mosaic was set in wet cement, not on a cement base, and irregularities occurred when it dried because we had fid-dled with designs. Much of the work looks amateurish now, but we

With Joe Franks, head of the CIA (Catering Institute of Australia) and Eric Purbrick of Chateau Tahbilk fame.

wouldn't change it for anything. The greatest compliment we had was from a lady who visited just as we finished the basic work. 'It's marvellous to see people taking the trouble to restore these old homes,' she said.

Champagne and tea sorbet (recipe page 267).

The house began to take the shape of a reversed question mark. The entertainment block consisted of one huge room broken by the barricade of a huge fireplace and a Spanish door. Behind it, and in the middle, was the kitchen, and the dining room was at the other end with another fireplace. The home block consisted of three rooms for the kids; a large bathroom with a bath, two lavatories, three wash bowls and a shower; a laundry; and our bed/sitting room-cum-office, with dressing room and bathroom. The third and final block consisted of a flat for the 'minder', and three guest bedrooms.

Furnishing these bedrooms gave us a bit of fun. Since we had already bought the bedroom furniture we needed, we designed each bathroom around it. One particularly ugly suite of inlaid furniture, purported to have been made by Edwardian apprentices for a visit of the Prince of Wales, was designated the French Brothel Suite. Hence, the bathroom was fitted out with blue and white Parisian tiles, gold taps, a claw-footed bath, and a blue and white loo set in a cedar box. In the Colonial Suite, the furniture and prints are mostly 19th century, and the bathroom is lined with old pine boards and contains a copper bath and a genuine two-seat dunny called 'Madonna and Child', which we finally persuaded the Hill Smiths to part with. The Elizabethan Room posed some problems. The furniture was obvious, a four-poster bed with wood canopy, some chests and chairs and iron work, all 17th century, but what were bathrooms like then? We found panels from the choir of an old church, used a barrel as the bath, and put the loo in a bishop's chair. Maggie Tabberer christened it with great enthusiasm. 'My dear,' she said, 'it's like having a pee in a cathedral.'

In January 1984, the floor of the lounge and dining room block was laid with Mexican tiles, complete with dog paw imprints. After they were cleaned and waxed, we moved the furniture in. Outside, the croquet lawn was the first to be laid, and the garden landscaping will go on for at least five years or so.

One feature took almost six months of weekend work throughout 1984: the 'Tree of Life' mosaic on the southern side of the entertainment block, overlooking the Evans Family Chardonnay vineyard. This mosaic was done on a base with 2.5 centimetre tiles, and apart from almost slicing off the ends of fingers on our left hands with the tile cutters, it was enormous fun. Whoever was visiting for the weekend happily joined in, leaving a small part of themselves in the Hunter Valley.

Future plans are for a library-cum-television hut, set away from the house, alongside the old underground water tank, which we will use as a cellar; an office to be built out of some old wine vats; a tennis court and pool; trout pond and stables. The golf driving range is already in place, and the Suffolk sheep keep it neat. Lower down on

the property, we hope to have a dry run for chickens, turkeys and guinea fowl, and a wet run around a dam and swamp for ducks and geese. Eventually I would like to breed Clydesdales, which I used to work when I was in the Forestry Service in New Zealand. My son Toby has plans that include deer, angora goats and yabby ponds.

Whether or not we remain in the Valley is yet to be determined, but it does seem that we shall spend a lot of time there. The plans for the various types of produce are not entirely daydreaming. There are many restaurants in the district looking for fine produce, and I am taken with the idea of serving our guests food from our own land. The kitchen has the capacity to feed about 20 people without fuss. On Election Day, December 1984, Murray Tyrrell and I hosted the Single Bottle Club at the house. The food was prepared by an ex-apprentice from Bulletin Place, Alex Roser. Francois Henry, who runs Remy & Associates in Australia for Remy Martin, France, attended as a member, and said that it was the best food he had ever eaten in Australia.

So the kitchen, which is furnished mostly with old equipment (a 50-year-old Metters' stove, an old chopping block, and a collection of Victorian and Edwardian utensils), will be able to handle all the entertaining we woud like to do at the house.

Already we are preserving various kinds of peaches, plums, nectarines, greengages and other stone fruit from our orchard. The orchard is not big, but it contains two of lots of things: figs, walnuts, apples, pears, oranges, lemons, grapefruit, limes and almonds as well as the stone fruit. I gain tremendous satisfaction from picking my own fruit after seeing a tree through the year. Various herbs have already been planted, and I plan a large vegetable garden.

Many years ago the family established some priorities. My wife, Trish, likes gardening and I do not. But I like gardens. On one occasion she prevailed upon me to work in the garden for a day. I worked hard and there was tangible evidence of my efforts. 'Well done,' she said. So I asked her to total my efforts in relation to those of a part-time gardener. Trish decided I had been about half as effective. In those days a part-time gardener charged $20 a day, therefore my efforts were worth $10.

'That's it,' I said. 'I can get $100 for an article. I'll write an article for garden money every five weeks. You hire and run the gardener, I'll do what I want to do when I've finished the article and we'll all be happy.' We have been. The fruits from our orchard now provide the basis for one of the easiest desserts to prepare: fruit flambé.

Heat some sugar in the flambé pan and allow it to caramelise. This is essential for flavour. Add a pat of butter, a drop or two of orange juice, some lemon juice and more orange juice, working the mixture over the flame and not allowing it to stick. Add brandy (it is not essential to flame this but you can, in front of your guests) plus any liqueur which is available—Cointreau, Grand Marnier, Benedictine and so on. The liquid should now be quite viscous. Add the chopped segments of whatever fruit you're using, cook through and serve.

Menu

Blinis with Caviar

Coulibiac of Salmon Trout

*Confit of Duck
with Green Beans*

Angels on Horseback

Cheese

Apple Galette

Bowen Mangoes

Coffee—Friandises

Wines

Pol Roger	1947
Pol Roger	1921
Le Montrachet	1962
Batard Montrachet	1929
Meursault	1928
Chateau Mouton	1955
Chateau Margaux	1952
Chateau Lafite	1947
Chateau Margaux	1943
Chateau Rouget	1929
La Tache en Magnum	1969
Chambolle Musigny Charmes	1955
Mazis Chambertin	1947
Beaune Clos du Roi	1947
Vosne Romanee Malconsorts	1945
Chateau d'Yquem	1953
Chateau de Rayne-Vigneau	1945
Chateau d'Arche	1936
Chateau Lafaurie-Peyraguey	1918
Tokay Aszu Essence	1968
Tokay Aszu Essence	1967
Tokay Aszu Essence	1957
Tokay Essence	1957

Cognac Remy Martin, Louis XIII

Honey ice cream (recipe page 267).

.05 bananas

A recipe from an *Australian Women's Weekly* reader. My column in that magazine receives a very large mail on all sorts of topics. I tried this dish and found it quite rich and luscious tasting. Incidentally, the magazine's test kitchen also 'does' all my selections, improvisations and innovations. I'm happy to report that they've all worked. That is, except one. It came from one of the most famous chefs in the world.

6 medium-sized bananas
1/4 cup brown sugar
1/4 cup orange juice
grated rind of one orange
1/2 cup sherry
30g butter

4 tablespoons Bundaberg rum
1/4 teaspoon ground cinnamon
1 tablespoon nutmeg
ice cream or cream
Serves 6

Peel the bananas and place in a flat, buttered baking dish. Combine the brown sugar with the orange juice, rind and sherry. Heat and pour over the bananas. Dot with butter. Bake for 10–15 minutes in a moderate oven. Remove from oven. Heat rum, ignite and pour over bananas. Sprinkle over cinnamon and nutmeg. Serve with cream or ice cream.

Bread and butter pudding

'This is a variation of the famous pudding. I use raspberry jam because I like it, which, after all, should be the principal reason for changing any recipe.'

5–6 slices bread
40g butter
raspberry jam
2 tablespoons raisins
1 1/4 cups milk
3/4 cup cream

2/3 cup sugar
vanilla essence
4 eggs
icing sugar
Serves 4–6

Cut crusts off the bread. Butter each slice and then top with raspberry jam. Line and fill a pudding basin with the bread, scattering raisins in between each layer. Make a custard by combining milk, cream, sugar and a dash of vanilla; bring to the boil, and gradually add beaten eggs slowly. Pour custard around and over the bread. Allow to steep. Bake in an oven in a bain-marie for 45 minutes. Sprinkle with icing sugar and serve.

Fresh mangoes in Champagne

'A great standard. Easy to do and absolutely delicious.'

2 mangoes
1/4 cup Cointreau

1 bottle Champagne (chilled)
Serves 4

Slice the mangoes and marinate them in the Cointreau for 2 hours. Place in the refrigerator. Fill a champagne glass with the sliced marinaded mangoes. Place a little of the juice over them and then top with champagne. Serve immediately.

Fresh poached pear with passionfruit syrup

fresh pears
for the poaching syrup:
2 cups sugar
2½ cups white wine

lemon rind
for the passionfruit syrup:
1 cup sugar
2 cups passionfruit pulp

Make a poaching syrup of 2 cups sugar to 2½ cups of white wine, adding some lemon rind. Boil. Peel the pears and with a Parisienne baller, scoop out the cores. (The pears can be poached either half or whole.) Poach very gently for about 7 minutes, depending on the size and ripeness. Allow to stand until cold.

For the passionfruit syrup, combine 1 cup of sugar to 2 cups of passionfruit pulp which has been passed through a very fine sieve. Simmer for about 10 minutes, skimming off the scum that rises to the surface until the syrup is clear. Chill and serve cold.

Belle orange

2 naval oranges
½ cup sugar
1 cup water
½ cup cream

vanilla to flavour
⅓ cup Grand Marnier
½ cup slivered almonds
Serves 2

Peel the rind thinly from 1 orange and then remove the skin and pith from both oranges. Make a syrup by boiling the sugar and water for 3 minutes. Cool. Whip the cream and flavour with vanilla. Divide the oranges into segments and pour over ¼ cup each of Grand Marnier and sugar syrup. Marinate in the refrigerator for 2 hours. Cut the orange rind into very thin slivers about 2.5cm long. Place them in the remaining syrup, return to the heat and boil rapidly for 5 minutes. Remove the rind, drain and cool.

Place orange segments into 2 Champagne glasses. Divide the peel, sprinkling it on top of the oranges. Spoon over each serving 2 teaspoons Grand Marnier. Place a spoon of whipped cream on each and decorate with almond slivers.

Pineapple poached in maple syrup

1 large pineapple
2½ cups pure maple syrup

2 cups plain yoghurt
Serves 6–8

Peel and core the pineapple. Cut the pineapple down the centre in half. Slice each half in 1.5cm slices. In a heavy saucepan bring the maple syrup to the boil. Add the sliced pineapple and remove from heat. Allow the pineapple and maple syrup to cool in the saucepan. Serve the pineapple with maple syrup at room temperature. Serve the plain yoghurt on the side.

'From Berida Manor, the temple of good health in Bowral, New South Wales. You go there to lose weight, or put it on, or rest, or play golf and tennis, or do anything except work. I don't think this was one of their diet recipes, however.'

Mount Tamborine mango

1½ cups puréed mango
2 tablespoons crème de cacao liqueur
300mls cream, whipped

3 teaspoons gelatine
2 tablespoons water
Serves 6

Dissolve the gelatine in water very slowly over a low heat. Cool and stir into the mango purée. Place the purée into the refrigerator or over ice until it begins to thicken. When the purée has begun to thicken add the liqueur and fold in the whipped cream. Fill a mould which has been previously rinsed out with iced water and place in the refrigerator for at least 2 hours. Dip the mould quickly into hot water and unmould dessert.

Melon merveille

2 medium rock melons
1 punnet strawberries
3 pears
2 egg whites

2 tablespoons sugar
½ cup Cointreau
Serves 4–6

Cut the melons in half and scoop out the seeds, then scoop out the flesh. Wash and hull the strawberries. Peel and cut pears in small pieces. Beat egg whites stiffly and add sugar carefully. Preheat oven to 200°C/400°F. Put a mixture of the fruit in each melon half. Pour over the liqueur and chill for 1 hour. Cover each chilled melon half with meringue and place in the oven for 5 minutes or until golden. Serve hot or cold.

Fresh strawberries in Marsala

'A rather sweet mix. Rudy Komon, one of my mentors and a great friend, used to pour red wine over strawberries. But the latter had to be ripe. Try it.'

1 punnet strawberries
¼ cup white sugar
juice of ½ a lime

⅔ cup Marsala
Serves 4

Hull the strawberries and marinate in sugar and lime juice. Keep in the refrigerator. Pour over the Marsala just before serving, and mix.

Summer pudding

1.5kg raspberries (or blackberries, drained stewed apple, drained stewed strawberries etc.)

1¼ cups caster sugar
plenty of slices of slightly stale bread
whipped cream

In a large bowl mix all the fruits. Make sure there are no stalks and nasty bits. Add caster sugar and mix gently. Do not make it too mushy. Remove the bread crusts, then shape the pieces to fit the bottom and sides of a pudding basin, bowl or soufflé dish. Put the mixture into the bowl, lie more shaped pieces of bread on top. Place a plate on top of this, with a heavy weight. Stand in the fridge overnight. When ready to serve, invert the basin gently over a chilled plate or stand. The bread will have absorbed all the colours of the fruit and be set. Serve with whipped cream.

——————— ✦ ———————

Round fruit salad

200g black grapes
200g white grapes
200g strawberries
150g lychees
250g gooseberries
150g watermelon balls
150g rock melon balls

150g honeydew melon balls
150g pawpaw balls
3 nips Grand Marnier
juice of 2 lemons
1 tablespoon caster sugar
300ml cream
Serves 6

Mix all ingredients in a large bowl and pour Grand Marnier, lemon juice and sugar over. Stir occasionally, marinading for a total of two hours. Whip the cream, mixing it with some of the marinade, and serve the liquid separately.

'Most blessed of all puddings, so easy to do and so easy to adapt. The English use raspberries as a base, as well as redcurrants, blackberries and so on; whatever berries are in season. But I've done it with blackberries and apple and it's possible with other fruits if they are stewed for a little while and then the liquid is removed.'

——————— ✦ ———————

Champagne and tea sorbet

2 cups Champagne
½ cup strong tea
⅓ cup lemon juice
1 teaspoon lemon rind

½ cup orange juice and sugar syrup
  (2 cups of sugar plus ½ cup
  water)
¼ cup Grand Marnier
1 egg white

On a medium heat melt together the lemon juice, lemon rind, orange juice and sugar syrup. If you want to heat the alcohol out, add the Champagne, otherwise leave the mixture to cool before adding. Add the tea, Grand Marnier and egg white. Mix well and freeze.

'This delightful interlude course was served by Anna Landragin of Yellow Glen Wines near Smythesdale, Ballarat, at a luncheon given for the Hugh Johnsons and myself.'

——————— ✦ ———————

Honey ice cream

½ cup honey
4 eggs
pinch salt

2 cups cream
Serves 6–8

Bring the honey to the boil and let it boil for 2–3 minutes. Beat the eggs, adding a pinch of salt. Pour the honey into the eggs, stirring all the time. Allow this mixture to get thoroughly cold, stirring from time to time. Whip the cream and add to the mixture. Pour this into a mould and freeze.

Serve with one or a mixture of the following: raspberries, boysenberries, redcurrants or small strawberries.

Blackberry sorbet

For all the gadgets, sometimes the old ways are best, though I do use a blender to make this sorbet.

250g blackberries
250g apples, peeled and sliced
caster sugar to taste

1 egg white
lemon juice to taste

Place the blackberries, apple pieces, caster sugar, egg white and lemon juice in a blender and purée. Transfer to a shallow tray, and put in the freezer. Take out every hour or so, and mash the edges (which get colder first) into the middle, until completely done.

'It's like having a pee in a cathedral . . .'

Pernod chocolate royal

From a competition promoting Pernod. I judged the final which was won by Claudette Xuerb of North Sydney Technical College.

3 canned pear halves
½ cup Pernod
1 cup ice cream
100g chocolate
¼ cup almonds, chopped and toasted

2 tablespoons whipped cream
1 cup Dairy Farmers custard
300ml cream
Serves 4–6

Soak the pears in 3 tablespoons of Pernod, allowing long enough for the flavour to penetrate. Blend 2 tablespoons of Pernod into the ice cream, place into a cooled mould and put in the freezer. Melt half the chocolate, and grate the rest. Fold the chocolate and almonds into the whipped cream. Place this mixture over the ice cream and refreeze. Blend together the custard, cream and 1 tablespoon of Pernod. Slice the pears and arrange on top of the frozen cream layer. On top of this pour the custard mixture. Freeze until set.

Pot de crème au chocolat

50g dark chocolate, unsweetened
4 egg yolks
1 cup cream

pinch salt
Serves 3–4

Beat egg yolks together. Bring the cream to boiling point and add the chocolate. Cook this mixture until the chocolate is melted, but don't allow it to come to the boil. Take the pan from the heat. Add a little of the hot cream mixture to the beaten egg yolks and then pour these into the cream and stir until the mixture has cooled a little. Add the salt and strain into small custard cups. Chill the custard overnight in the refrigerator.

Crêpes suzette

for the crêpes:
1 cup plain flour
pinch salt
2 large eggs
1 cup cold milk
30g butter, melted
vegetable oil for frying
for the sauce:

125g butter
1 tablespoon caster sugar
4 tablespoons Grand Marnier,
    Cointreau or Curaçao
1 level teaspoon grated orange peel
1 level teaspoon grated lemon peel
2 tablespoons brandy
Serves 8

To make the crêpes, place flour, salt, eggs and milk into a bowl and whisk until well blended. Add the melted butter and combine. Heat the oil and cook the crêpes like pancakes. Fold the crêpes in half and then in half again. To make the sauce, melt the butter in a large pan over a low heat. Add sugar and Grand Marnier, Cointreau or Curaçao. Heat until the sugar melts. Place the crêpes back into the pan, adding the orange and lemon peel to them as they are heating. Swish about in the pan juices. Meanwhile, heat the brandy to lukewarm in a small saucepan. Ignite. Pour over the pancakes. Serve when the flames have subsided.

I made sweet crepes for years using any liqueur to hand for the sauce. Wondrous indeed were the results. Then I came across an excellent book, *Spirited Cooking*, by Sonia Allison, which listed all the various names for crêpes using different spirits and liqueurs:

Crêpes Annette: substitute Grand Marnier, Cointreau or Curaçao with Kahlua or Tia Maria. Omit the orange and lemon peel. Use brandy to flame.

Crêpes Babette: use Parfait Amour and flame with French Mirabelle Eau-de-Vie or any plum liqueur.

Crêpes Claudette: use crème de cacao with navy rum for flaming.

Crêpes Ginette: cherry brandy with gin for flaming.

Crêpes Georgette: green or yellow chartreuse and flame with vodka.

Crêpes Ninette: Crème des Bananes with whisky for flaming.

Crêpes Paulette: use mandarin liqueur and add 1 level teaspoon of finely grated lemon peel to the pancakes as they are heating. Use Armagnac for flaming.

The Colonial Bedroom at the Hunter house.

Emperor's pancake

We used to visit Fritz Feiersinger, the owner of the Morritz Lodge at Perisher. He's now expanded to Austria and Fall's Creek. Fritz is a wonderful character, truly a man of spirit, the traditional life and soul of every party. This rich dish was served at one of his dinners for us, and is a speciality of Chef Sepp Schenkenreiter.

2 tablespoons sultanas
3 tablespoons dark rum
4 egg yolks
3 tablespoons sugar
½ teaspoon salt
½ cup milk

½ teaspoon vanilla essence
1 cup sifted flour
5 egg whites
60g unsalted butter
icing sugar
Serves 4–6

Place the sultanas in rum and soak for 30 minutes, drain and dry. Beat together egg yolks, sugar and salt until a thick, pale yellow mixture forms. Stir in milk and vanilla essence then beat in flour gradually. When the mixture is smooth, stir in the sultanas. In another bowl, beat egg whites to a stiff consistency and then fold into the batter until completely mixed together. Over a low heat melt a quarter of the butter in a heavy pan. Pour in enough batter to cover the bottom of the pan to a depth of half a centimetre. Cook until the pancake has puffed up and browned slightly (approximately 4 minutes).

Turn the pancake onto a plate, add another quarter of the butter to the pan, reheat and return pancake to the pan, uncooked side down. When cooked, pull the pancake into 6 or 8 pieces and remove to a warm plate. Repeat with the remaining mixture to make another pancake and divide into similar pieces. Return the first lot to the pan and cook both lots together over a medium heat for about two minutes, turning all the time. Place on a plate, sprinkle with icing sugar and serve with fruit or fruit compote.

Crêpes Fitzgerald

'Served by Brennan's of New Orleans. The Brennan clan entertained Graham Kerr and I on a trip we made in 1967. This dessert has remained one of my favourites, and is always rapturously received.'

for the crêpes:
2 eggs
¾ cup sifted flour
1 teaspoon sugar
pinch of salt
milk
vegetable oil
for the filling:
8 heaping teaspoons Philadelphia
   Cream Cheese

8 tablespoons sour cream
for the sauce:
2 cups strawberries
sugar
butter
strawberry liqueur
Kirsch
Serves 4

To make the crêpes, mix the eggs with flour, sugar and salt. Add milk until the batter is the consistency of condensed milk. Beat until smooth. Heat a 15cm skillet oiled with a pastry brush dipped in vegetable oil. Pour 2 tablespoons of batter into the pan, tilting quickly to distribute batter evenly. Cook 1 minute or so until brown, then turn and brown the other side. Oil the pan with a brush and repeat. Keep cooked cakes warm in a towel. To make the filling, roll the cream cheese and sour cream in the crêpes and put on a plate. To make the sauce, in a chafing dish, cook the strawberries in sugar and butter. Flame in strawberry liqueur and Kirsch and pour over crêpes.

Iced lemon soufflé

If there is one thing cooler than a cucumber it is an iced lemon soufflé. Cold soufflés are not baked, and they rise above the rim of the soufflé dish and stay there, unlike cooked ones. It is the gelatine, egg whites and whipped cream that enable them to hold their shape. When you chill cold soufflés in a bowl with a waxed paper cuff, the gelatine sits so that the cuff can be removed, leaving a good collar of fluffy soufflé standing firmly above the bowl.

1 envelope gelatine
2 tablespoons water
grated rind of 4 lemons
½ cup strained lemon juice
1 cup caster sugar
7–8 egg whites

1 cup cream
whipped cream, extra
slices of lemon
fresh mint leaves
Serves 6

'If there is one thing cooler than a cucumber it is an iced lemon soufflé.'

In a small saucepan soften the gelatine and water. Add lemon rind, lemon juice and sugar. Stir over low heat until the gelatine is thoroughly dissolved, then chill to syrup consistency. Beat the egg whites until very stiff. Beat into the lemon gelatine mixture. Whip cream and fold into the lemon meringue until thoroughly mixed. Tie a double band of waxed paper around the top and on the outside of a 3 cup soufflé dish. Pour in the lemon soufflé and chill.

Remove the waxed paper collar before serving. Decorate top of the soufflé with additional whipped cream, paper-thin slices of lemon, and fresh mint leaves.

———————❧———————

Cold raspberry soufflé

From an excellent book, *The French Kitchen*, by the accomplished Melbourne cook and lecturer, Di Holuigue. Di set out to adapt French cooking to Australia and did a great job.

1 punnet raspberries, puréed
6 tablespoons caster sugar
4 egg yolks
3 teaspoons gelatine

water
1¼ cups cream, whipped
5 egg whites, whipped to firm snow
Serves 8

Cream sugar and egg yolks over hot water until mousse-like. Soften the gelatine in a little cold water, melt and add, then immediately add puréed raspberries. Continue beating until the bowl is cool. Set bowl over ice, stirring frequently as the mixture starts to set. When texture is the same as the whipped cream, fold in the cream and then the beaten egg whites. Pour into a 3-cup soufflé bowl with an oiled grease-proof paper collar. Refrigerate until set. Decorate with rosettes of cream, topped by a raspberry.

As a substitute for the raspberries, you can use pureed mango, strawberries, kiwi fruit or ½ cup passionfruit pulp with the juice of 1 lemon and an extra tablespoon of sugar.

Soufflé glace aux fraises

1 cup puréed strawberries
5 egg whites
1¾ cups sugar

2 cups water
1 cup cream, whipped
Serves 4

Beat egg whites stiffly. Boil the sugar with water to 120°C/240°F. Tie a band of paper about 2.5cm wide around the rim of a deep straight-sided soufflé mould. Fold the sugar syrup carefully into the stiffly beaten egg whites. Place in a freezer tray and chill until it is mushy. Remove from the refrigerator and carefully stir in the strawberry purée and stiffly beaten cream. Pour the mixture into the soufflé mould and place in the freezer for 2 hours. Remove the paper band before serving.

The mosaic at the Hunter house.

Tamarillo bavarois

4 tamarillos puréed
4 egg yolks
⅓ cup sugar
⅔ cup milk
¼ vanilla bean, split

3 leaves gelatine or 20g powdered
    gelatine, dissolved in ⅓ cup hot
    water
300ml cream, semi-whipped
Serves 4–6

Lightly butter and coat with icing sugar a 3 cup mould (or equivalent in small moulds). Beat the egg yolks and sugar until the mixture forms a ribbon and changes colour. Heat the milk with the vanilla bean to boiling point. Add the tamarillo purée to the egg yolk mixture and while beating add the boiling milk. Return to the heat and cook over a gentle flame, stirring constantly until it coats the back of a wooden spoon. Add the gelatine and beat well with a whisk until dissolved. Remove the vanilla bean. Pour the mixture into a bowl, set over ice and stir until it begins to thicken to a thread consistency. Be sure to run the spoon over all surfaces of the bowl so than no lumps are present in the custard.

Beat the cream until it is of slightly stiffer consistency than the cooled, thickened custard. Fold the two mixtures together carefully but thoroughly. Put into a mould or moulds. Leave for 6 hours at least before unmoulding. Serve with a fruit purée sauce such as strawberries or kiwi fruit.

Salzburger nockerl

5 egg whites
60g butter
⅓ cup cream
3 egg yolks

6 teaspoons flour
⅓ cup sugar
icing sugar to dust
Serves 3

Preheat the oven to 180°C/350°F. Beat the egg whites stiffly. Place the butter and cream into an ovenproof dish, place in the oven and let them melt. Beat the egg yolks with the flour and sugar and then fold them very gently into the beaten egg whites. Place 3 large 'blobs' into the foaming butter and cream. When the bottom of the mixture is just set (about 1 minute) place the dish very quickly into a heated oven and leave until the *nockerl* are browned (about 10–15 minutes).

Remove and dust with icing sugar, and serve immediately.

———— ❧ ————

Grandma's favourite

This is a tasty dessert topping for whatever. You can serve it with cream and/or ice cream. Easy to do and a favourite with a horde of kids.

1 cup caster sugar	1½ cups milk
1 tablespoon butter	2 eggs
2½ tablespoons self-raising flour	Serves 4–6
1 lemon	

Cream together the caster sugar and butter. Add the flour and the juice and grated rind of the lemon. Add milk and beaten egg yolks. Lastly fold in the egg whites, which have been beaten until stiff. Place in a casserole dish (without the top) and stand in a baking dish of cold water in the oven. Bake slowly for ¾ hour at 180°C/350°F.

———— ❧ ————

Apple, pear and blackberry tart

Quick and easy to make. you can do this with individual tartlets rather than one big tart and work on the presentation a bit.

3 medium, crisp eating apples	pinch of flour
3 medium pears	75g butter
80g frozen blackberries	1 tablespoon caster sugar
220g puff pastry	brandy

Roll out the pastry to a 2mm thickness on a lightly floured surface. Place on a baking tray brushed with cold water and cut out a circle 22cm diameter. Using a fork or small knife prick the pastry. Keep in a cool place. Peel, halve and core the apples and pears, cutting each half into 8–10 evenly sized segments. Place in a frying pan with a little butter and quickly sauté for 2 minutes over high heat. Add the sugar. Pour in 2 tablespoons of brandy and ignite. Leave to cool.

To assemble the tart, arrange alternate cold apple and pear segments in an attractive rosette pattern on the pastry. Preheat the oven to 240°C/475°F. Bake the tart in a very hot oven for 12 minutes. Thoroughly drain the thawed blackberries. Remove the tart from the oven and arrange the berries in a heap in the centre of the tart. Return to the oven for a further 3 minutes cooking. Serve with cream.

'An astounding dish I enjoyed years ago with Hans Sternik when he was boss of the Vienna Intercontinental. He has since become President of the chain. We had had a marvellous dinner, though it was of Viennese proportions. When the huge plate of nockerl *arrived we thought we were done for, but it was so light and airy it was no trouble at all.'*

Chartreuse and banana tart

1 tablespoon green chartreuse
6 bananas
2 tablespoons icing sugar
1 tablespoon water
few drops of vanilla essence

for the short pastry:
1½ cups plain flour
90g butter or margarine
⅓ cup milk
salt
Serves 12

'*This is from one of those promotional cookbooks trade people love to put out. However, it does work, and I've included it because green chartreuse is my favourite liqueur.*'

Prepare the pastry and line the tart tray. On a plate mix the icing sugar and vanilla essence. Peel the bananas and cut them lengthwise. Roll them in the sugar and place them on the tart. Cook in a medium oven for 20–30 minutes. Meanwhile mix the green chartreuse, water and vanilla essence. Pour over the tart as soon as it is cooked. Leave to cool before serving.

Melon tart

From Hermann Schneider's Two Faces Restaurant in South Yarra, Melbourne.

2 medium-sized fully ripened
    rock melons
¼ cup sugar
1 glass Sauternes
2 tablespoons Kirsch
3 teaspoons gelatine
for the pastry:
1¼ cups sifted flour

80g ground macadamia nuts
    (substitute ground almonds if not
    available)
100g butter
1 egg
1 tablespoon sugar
2–3 tablespoons water

To make the pastry, mix flour, ground nuts, sugar and salt together in bowl, add softened butter and gently rub with fingers until the mixture becomes a sandy texture, then add egg and enough water until you have a smooth pastry, but work gently and do not over work the pastry. Let rest for 1–2 hours before use. Roll pastry between two plastic sheets and then line an 20cm pastry ring, prick pastry well before baking and use a blind baking filling such as beans or rice during initial baking. Bake approximately 20 minutes in a moderate oven. Let cool.

Make approximately 24 melon balls with a melon baller, soak these in half glass of the sweet wine, cook the remainder of 1 melon together with sugar for approximately 5 minutes and while still warm add remaining sweet wine and half of the gelatine. Pass through a fine sieve, do same with flesh of melon and blend together. Add Kirsch, and just before setting fill the cooked pastry shell and decorate with melon balls. Dissolve remaining gelatine with sweet wine retained from melon balls, and give whole tart a generous coating. Chill well before serving.

Pecan pie

3 large eggs
½ cup sugar
½ teaspoon salt
3 tablespoons melted butter
1 cup dark or light corn syrup
    (Karo)
1 cup chopped pecans
whipped cream and extra pecan
    halves to decorate

for the pie shell:
1 cup plain flour
¼ teaspoon salt
3 tablespoons butter
2 tablespoons water
Serves 8–12

To make the filling, beat eggs lightly, add the sugar, salt, butter, corn syrup and pecans and stir well to combine. Pour into a pie shell and bake in moderate oven 180°C/350°F for about 1 hour or until the filling is well browned and just set. Decorate with whipped cream and pecan halves.

To make an unbaked shortcrust pie shell, mix ingredients together in a food processor or rub in butter and flour as in traditional method. Roll very thinly to fit a 23cm pie plate.

'This great, stodgy, jaw-stopping dish came from a visit to the Stahmann's property in Moree. They are now Australian citizens, but came from Houston, Texas, to find the right property for pecan production. They now have almost 80,000 trees, plus a nut-shelling plant in Toowoomba. This tremendous enterprise is a most valuable export earner, only about 10 per cent being retained for the home market. I like this version of Pecan Pie, which is less sweet than most.'

Macadamia nut pie

100g macadamia nuts
1½ tablespoons gelatine
2 tablespoons cold water
½ cut milk
½ cup maple syrup
pinch salt
2 egg yolks
¼ cup cream
1 tablespoon rum

for the pastry:
1 cup plain flour
½ teaspoon salt
2 tablespoons desiccated coconut
⅓ cup cooking oil
1½ tablespoons cold milk
egg white
Serves 8

To make the pastry, preheat the oven to 220°C/425°F. Sift the flour and salt into a bowl with the coconut. Combine cooking oil and milk and beat until milky. Tip this over the flour and stir with a fork until blended. Press the dough into an ungreased 23cm pie plate with fingers. Glaze with the egg white and bake for about 15 minutes. Cool.

To make the filling, dissolve the gelatine in cold water. In a double boiler, stir milk, maple syrup and salt. When hot, pour part of this over the beaten egg yolks and then add the warmed egg yolks to the double boiler. Stir for a while then add the gelatine, and stir this until all the gelatine is properly dissolved and it becomes a custard. Chill.

Whip the cream till really thick and fold into it the finely chopped macadamia nuts and rum. Whip egg whites till stiff, and fold into the cream, nuts and chilled custard. Pour this into the pie shell and refrigerate.

New York brandy truffles

2–3 cups evaporated milk
185g cooking chocolate, roughly
   chopped
2½ cups crushed plain sweet biscuits
¾ cup icing sugar

250g chopped walnuts
⅓ cup Australian brandy
chocolate nonpareils
Makes 6 dozen

Heat the milk and chocolate pieces until chocolate melts and mixture thickens, stirring constantly. Remove from the heat. Add crushed biscuits, sugar, walnuts and brandy. Mix well. Stand at room temperature for 30 minutes. Shape into 2.5cm diameter balls and roll in chocolate nonpareils. Refrigerate. Nice with a good Spatlese.

———————— ❧ ————————

Orange brioche with two curds

20g fresh yeast
¼ cup of warm water
¾ cup of tepid milk
¼ cup sugar
1 heaped teaspoon salt
3 eggs
6 egg yolks
3 cups plain flour
170g unsalted softened butter
grated rind of 2 oranges

1 cup chopped candied orange peel
1 egg yolk
¼ cup cream
for the lemon curd:
6 eggs
rind and juice of 3 lemons
240g caster sugar
120g unsalted butter
Makes 18

'I first met Gay Bilson when she and Tony opened the Bon Gout in dilapidated downtown Elizabeth Street. They arrived in Sydney with little except a broken down Porsche, which "expired as we drew up outside our future restaurant". Their success was almost immediate, and many of us remember those days with great affection. I don't think either of them had quite the same attitude they have today. Each knew less, and there were times of gorgeous experimentation and improvisation.'

To make brioche, dissolve yeast in warm water. Add ½ cup flour and work into a soft dough. Form dough into a ball and cut a cross on top. Place ball in a bowl of warm water where it will very quickly double in size and form a sponge on top of the water. Put the remaining flour into a bowl, add the sugar and salt and make a well in the centre and beat in the eggs, egg yolks, warm milk and drained yeast sponge. When everything seems well mixed, beat in the softened butter. Place dough in a greased bowl, cover with a damp cloth and put in a warm place to rise for 1 hour. Then knock the dough down and beat in the grated orange rind and candied orange peel. Place in a greased bowl, cover with plastic wrap and leave in the refrigerator overnight. In the morning the dough must be treated gently to keep the brioches as light as possible. Make 18 small balls and place in buttered individual brioche moulds. Allow to rise for 20 minutes. Brush with beaten egg yolk and cream. Bake in a hot oven 220°C/ 425°F about 15 minutes or until golden brown.

To make the lemon curd, place all ingredients in a saucepan and whisk over gentle heat until first bubbles appear and it has thickened. Immediately strain into a bowl and cover. To make the passionfruit curd, substitute 200ml of strained passionfruit pulp for the lemon and proceed as for lemon curd. Warm the brioches and place on a plate with a small bowl of each curd.

Roxi's strudel

6 apples
2 cups fresh breadcrumbs
90g unsalted butter
4 sheets filo pastry
sugar to taste

⅔ cup sultanas
lemon rind
powdered cloves
cinnamon
icing sugar

Peel, core and dice the apples. Fry breadcrumbs in unsalted butter until golden brown. Butter, individually, four layers of bought filo pastry, placing on top of each other. Spread golden buttered crumbs down one side leaving spaces at the side, top and bottom for tucking. On top of the crumbs heap plenty of raw diced apple. Sprinkle with sugar to taste. Sprinkle with sultanas. Add a generous pinch of a mixture of lemon rind, powdered cloves and cinnamon. Roll up, tucking ends in so that mixture cannot escape. Bake at 165°C/325°F until pastry is a crisp golden colour. Take out, sprinkle with icing sugar and serve.

'This is a recipe from the snow country. I ski at both Thredbo and Perisher Valley, having a style once described as that of "an aged, drunken wombat". One evening, I had dinner at which this great strudel was cooked by a delightful girl. I can't remember the ski lodge but I do know her name was Roxi.'

Almond blocks

125g unsalted butter, at room
    temperature, cut into 8 pieces
½ cup firmly packed dark brown
    sugar
¼ cup granulated sugar
2 large eggs
¼ teaspoon pure almond extract

1¾ cups flour
2 teaspoons unsweetened cocoa
½ teaspoon bicarbonate of soda
2 cups sliced almonds, preferably
    blanched

Makes 6 dozen

Use the metal blade of a food processor to process the butter, brown sugar and granulated sugar until smooth, about 20 seconds, stopping once to scrape the bowl. Add 1 of the eggs and the almond extract and pulse 3 or 4 times to mix. Add the flour, cocoa and baking powder and process until thoroughly blended, about 20 seconds. Transfer the dough to a mixing bowl and, with a wooden spoon, work in 1¼ cups of the sliced almonds. Reserve the remainder. Remove the dough to a sheet of wax paper and shape it into a 23cm x 7.5cm x 2.5cm brick. Smooth the sides with a knife or metal spatula dipped in water. Wrap in plastic wrap and refrigerate for 2–3 hours, until firm enough to slice.

Preheat the oven to 180°C/350°F. Line 2 baking trays with cooking paper. With a sharp knife cut the brick of dough in half lengthwise. Then cut each bar crosswise into 5mm slices. Place the biscuits 1.2cm apart on the baking trays. In a small bowl beat the remaining egg with 1 tablespoon of water; brush the tops of the biscuits with the egg mixture. Place a slice of the reserved almonds on the centre of each biscuit. Bake in the lower third of the preheated oven for 8–10 minutes or until firm. Remove from the oven and let the biscuits cool completely before removing from the paper.

Chocolate mounds

*125g unsalted butter, at room
    temperature, cut into 9 pieces*
½ cup icing sugar
½ cup flour
pinch of salt

60g chocolate, melted
150g cooking chocolate
teaspoon vegetable oil
Makes 4 dozen

Use the metal blade of a food processor to process the butter and sugar until smooth, about 20 seconds, stopping once to scrape the bowl. Add the flour and salt and process for about 30 seconds or until the mixture resembles coarse meal. Add the melted chocolate and process until well blended, about 15 seconds, scraping the bowl twice. Divide the dough in half and roll each portion into a cylinder about 45cm long and 2cm across. Refrigerate the cylinders on wax paper until firm enough to cut, about 1 hour.

Preheat the oven to 180°C/350°F. Line a baking tray with parchment or cooking paper. With a sharp knife cut the cylinders crosswise at 2cm intervals, taking care to cut the slices straight. Place the biscuits cut side down on the tray about 2.5cm apart and bake in the lower third of the preheated oven for 15–18 minutes or until firm. Remove from the oven and slide the parchment onto a counter. Let the biscuits cool completely on the parchment.

Melt the cooking chocolate with the oil in the top of a double boiler over barely simmering water. Remove from the heat. Dip each cookie into the melted chocolate so that one side is coated. Place on cake racks until the chocolate has hardened.

Cold raspberry soufflé (recipe page 271).

White chocolate timbale with boysenberry coulis

Another Kables special from the Regent Hotel, Sydney.

280g white chocolate
½ cup milk
2 tablespoons brandy
2 tablespoons water
3 teaspoons gelatine
1½ cups fresh cream

4 egg whites
for the coulis:
200g boysenberries
⅓ cup sugar
2 teaspoons cassis liqueur
Serves 8

Melt the chocolate in a double boiler. Add the milk. Combine the brandy, water and gelatine and melt together. Add the gelatine mix to the chocolate. Add the cream. Fold the beaten egg whites into the chocolate mixture and pour into a round mould.

To prepare the coulis, heat the berries with the sugar and liqueur. Cool.

Set the unmoulded timbale on the cold coulis and decorate appropriately.

Macaroons

200g packet almond paste
2/3 cup icing sugar
1/4 cup granulated sugar

2 large egg whites
6 red glacé cherries, cut into eighths

Makes 4 dozen

Preheat the oven to 160°C/325°F. Line a 38 x 30cm baking tray with cooking paper. Use the metal blade of a food processor to process the almond paste, icing sugar and granulated sugar until well blended, pulsing 6 to 8 times and then processing for about 30 seconds. With the machine running add the egg whites through the feed tube and process until incorporated, about 20 seconds, stopping twice to scrape the bowl. Transfer the mixture to a large pastry bag fitted with a 1cm star tip. Pipe rosettes of the mixture onto the baking tray about 2.5cm apart. (If you do not have a pastry bag, place rounded teaspoonfuls of the mixture onto the baking trays.) Put a piece of cherry on the centre of each biscuit. Bake in the lower third of the preheated oven for 15–20 minutes or until golden and firm. Remove from the oven and slide the paper onto a counter. Let cool for 10 minutes and then remove the biscuits from the paper.

Apple, pear and blackberry tart (recipe page 273).

Hussar's love

1/2 cup hazelnuts
1/2 cup flour
90g unsalted butter, at room
    temperature, cut into 6 pieces
3 tablespoons granulated sugar

1/2 cup flour
1/2 cup seedless raspberry jam
icing sugar

Makes 6 dozen

Use the metal blade of a food processor to process the hazelnuts and flour until the nuts are finely ground, about 1 minute. Set aside. Use the metal blade to process the butter and sugar until smooth, about 15 seconds. Add the flour and the reserved hazelnut and flour mixture and process until well blended, 15–20 seconds, stopping once or twice to scrape the bowl. Divide the dough in half and roll each portion into a cylinder 25cm long and 2.5cm across. Place the cylinders on wax paper and refrigerate until firm enough to slice, 1 hour.

Preheat the oven to 180°C/350°F. Line 2 baking trays with buttered cooking paper. With a sharp knife slice each cylinder crosswise at 5mm intervals. Place the biscuits on the trays about 2.5cm apart and bake in the lower third of the preheated oven for 12 to 15 minutes or until firm. They should not brown around the edges. Remove from the oven and slide the paper onto a counter. Let the biscuits cool completely on the cooking paper. In a small saucepan melt the jam over low heat. Remove the pan from the heat and let cool for a few minutes, until the jam has thickened enough to barely hold its shape. Sift icing sugar generously over the tops of the biscuits. Put the thickened jam in a parchment cone and cut a 5cm opening. Squeeze a dot of jam onto the centre of each biscuit.

CHAPTER TWELVE

Wine: Rothbury, Petaluma and the Evans Family Company

Light-heartedness is an essential part of wine enjoyment. Too many people take wine too seriously. It is not a cult, it is a drink. The banter which should be at all wine tables is one of the great joys, and has been part of the lives of civilised people for centuries. Yet recently, a young wine maker, after spending a day with me, said how suprised he was that I was so 'flippant' about wine. 'You don't seem to take it very seriously,' he said.

I thought about this for some time. Finally, I agreed with him, but only in part. 'I take wine extremely seriously,' I said, 'from the vineyard to the wine making to the maturation to the blending and bottling. Once it's in the bottle I'm quite light-hearted about it.'

Even that is not completely true. My wine-judging career, which began in the early sixties and once covered every major show in Australia, still continues, with chairmanship of the National Wine Show at Canberra, the Royal Easter Show in Sydney and the International Judging View in Melbourne in 1985, which brought together the greatest range of judges I've ever seen. Wine judging is a serious business, though there are refreshingly amusing moments in between the serious.

From early days I had a 'cellar', first under the marital bed, then in a disused fireplace in our Paddington flat, then in a proper cellar at Greenwich. The establishment of the cellar I took seriously, though the result was pure enjoyment. Having a cellar of mature wine to call upon has always been an important part of my life, and laying one down need not be an expensive practice. We've been broke nearly all our lives, simply because we've always enjoyed life.

A cellar should contain a selection of different grape varieties, styles, regions and even countries. A selection from Australia should contain a mix of the best varieties from the best areas, a selection of what each area does best. A top Rhine Riesling from the Clare or Eden valleys of South Australia, Cabernet Sauvignon from Coonawarra, Pinot Noir from southwest Western Australia, the Yarra Valley, or the Hunter, Chardonnay from many areas in all wine states, Shiraz from the Hunter, Coonawarra, Barossa or McLaren Vale, and Semillon from the Hunter alone.

Over the years, I have been accused of being a fanatical supporter

With David Lowe, wine maker, and Denis Power, General Manager, at Rothbury in 1984.

of the Hunter Valley, no doubt because I have chosen to live there and because the Evans Family Company has its biggest investment there. I am tired of people from other wine areas accusing me of bias, though they themselves are full of it. The Hunter produces great soft wines of certain styles: Shiraz or Hermitage, which is out of fashion; Pinot Noir, which is becoming more important; Chardonnay, which has the capacity to produce good wines in many regions; and the classic Semillon, which is the greatest white grape of the Hunter and makes possibly the best style of its kind in the world.

Many other areas make great wines, each of their own style. For too long Australia has produced too many different varieties in each wine-producing region, and it will soon be time for those areas to produce only what they do best.

Of all the wine areas, I think that Coonawarra is superior in pro-duction/quality terms. The Adelaide Hills and the Yarra Valley are Australia's prettiest wine districts, and they each have tremendous potential. Tasmania may become an important wine State, and I revere the attitude, balance, common sense and community spirit to be found in the Barossa Valley. The great things about the Hunter Valley are its lovely soft wines, the sweep and light of the district, and its proximity to Sydney. Max Lake once said, 'The tragedy of Coonawarra is that it's not a hundred miles from Sydney.'

One has to start somewhere, and in 1968 we started wine produc-tion, on a small scale, in the Rothbury parish of the lower Hunter Valley. This was by no particular design and was not part of a pro-found, ambitious scheme.

One day, Murray Tyrrell, talking of the various people who almost everyday spoke to either him or me about 'getting into grow-ing vines and making wine', said, 'I'm going to sell my home block, move across the road from the winery and build a house. The old block we'll cut up into ten-acre vineyards which we'll grow for all these people.'

'Why don't you form a syndicate instead?' I asked. On such casual statements are empires founded, or foundered.

Rothbury has had some quite severe problems since conception. At the time of the red wine boom we planted too much shiraz (her-mitage), not foreseeing the end to the demand for it; we planted too many vines on soils that could not sustain an appropriate yield; we had faith in the true Estate concept of 'from own vineyards to bottle', and too many other 'Estates', buying material and wine from any-where, ruined the name; we were the wrong size, being too big for a boutique and too small to compete with the major wineries; we suf-fered badly from the drought of 1980–83, the vineyards sometimes yielding less than a tonne per hectare, and we were affected by the wage explosion of the mid-seventies, making it necessary to plan loss years and to re-finance the Company.

Yet Rothbury has been a forerunner in many ways. The Rothbury Estate Society gave members a unique deal: quality wines at lesser prices, since we were selling directly from the winery; wine educa-

At Rothbury with the great André Tchelistcheff, the dean of Californian wine makers, and Murray Tyrrell.

tional dinners with schools and seminars; jazz festivals, operas, operettas, renaissance music concerts, showjumping, Edwardian cricket weekends. We organised extensive interstate tastings, invited top overseas chefs to host the Great Chefs dinners that supported the work being done by Australian restaurateurs, and made educational tapes on wine tasting and appreciation. In short, we stirred up such an interest in the valley that the availability of accommodation blossomed, and tourism flourished. Nick Whitlam, the head of the State Bank told me, 'Rothbury has been the pivot of development in the valley over the last 15 years. You should be very proud of that.'

We made some damned good wines, too. James Halliday, the noted wine scribe, stated that the best Semillons consistently came from us, and that we had taken the responsibility of making them from Lindemans. Praise indeed, when one considers their great whites of the 1950s and 1960s. We made great red, particularly in the 1979 and 1983 vintages, and I'm devoted to our development of the Chardonnay and Pinot Noir styles. The last is particularly fascinating, and David Lowe, our wine maker, is developing the carbonique maceration method of fermentation into an art. Rothbury has made some marvellous wines, yet I feel the best is still to come. It's ironic I suppose, to be proud of a company that is yet to recover its losses, yet I could not be more so. Rothbury will still be a shining light when others have failed.

At Petaluma we started on the right foot, and apart from a minor falter or two, progress has been swift. We didn't actually start Petaluma, we joined in.

Brian Croser, a brilliant wine maker who had trained initially in South Australia before studying at Davis University in California, left Thomas Hardy and Sons in 1975 after a period as head oenologist. He had become too desk bound and production system orientated, and wanted to make his own wine. Establishing the oenology course at the Wagga Wagga School of Advanced Education allowed him time to make his own batches of wine, and this he started in 1976 with riesling fruit from Mitchelton. In 1977 he used Cowra fruit to make his first Chardonnay (there was also a Traminer), and in 1978 he made another Chardonnay.

During this year, we had discussed the Evans Wine Company's requirements after its purchase of vineyards in Coonawarra and Clare. Brian, who was thinking about moving to Echuca in Victoria, suggested that he build a winery under contract for the Evans Wine Company in the Adelaide Hills, which he would use while making our wine. We agreed, and when the results of the 1979 vintage were successful, we decided to put our South Australian interests together under the Petaluma name. The 1979 Riesling, from Clare, was a great success, establishing a new style of full-flavoured wine of the dry Spatlese style (grapes picked late but fermented out quite dry). The 1979 Coonawarra Red was also successful, and these wines resulted in Petaluma becoming established at the forefront of quality wine.

With Joseph Levin, son of David Levin who owns the Capital Hotel in London, and Sally and Toby, two of my three kids, at Rothbury at the 1984 vintage.

Opening the Bollinger at the Also Rans Racing Club annual picnic at Thredbo with my other daughter Jodie.

Brian is managing director of the company, and runs it capably. My role as chairman includes being his alter ego, adviser, policy framer and taster. The last occupation is probably my favourite, greater even than spotting a young wine, before anybody else, which becomes a great wine. To me it's a thrill to discard early each part of the make that you think is unsuitable, to mature and cherish the rest, to taste again and again during development, and to finally line up all the components on the bench prior to the final selection. Brian and I enjoy arguing, discussing, changing percentages without disclosing information, testing, probing, discovering.

Expansion of pinot noir and chardonnay vineyards in the Adelaide Hills led to another exciting development: the restoration of the old Bridgewater Mill in the heart of the Adelaide Hills, and its establishment as the centre of Pelatuma's new sparkling wine venture. Bollinger, the famous Champagne house, will guide us in this, having become shareholders in Petaluma.

The quest for wines of the highest quality supports my *Theory of Capacity*. Published originally in my 'Indulgence' column in the *Weekend Australian*, the theory was printed and sold for charity.

With Peter Fox and Brian Croser at Petaluma.

The Len Evans Theory of Capacity

1. *There is an awful lot of wine in the world, but there is also a lot of awful wine.*

2. *No sensible person drinks to excess. Therefore any one person can drink only a certain predictable amount.*

3. *There are countless flavours, nuances, shades of wine; endless varieties, regions, styles. You have neither the time nor the capacity to try them all.*

4. *To make the most of the time left to you, you must start by calculating your total future capacity. One bottle of wine a day is 365 bottles a year. If your life expectancy is another 30 years, there are only 10,000 odd bottles ahead of you.*

5. *People who say, 'You can't drink the good stuff all the time' are talking rubbish. You must drink good stuff all the time. Every time you drink a bottle of inferior wine it's like smashing a superior bottle against the wall. The pleasure is lost forever. You can't get that bottle back.*

6. *There are people who build up huge cellars, most of which they have no hope of drinking. They are foolish in overestimating their capacity, but they err on the right side and their friends love them.*

7. *There are also people who don't want to drink wine and are happy with the cheapies. I forgive them. There are others who are content with beer and spirits. I can't worry about everybody.*

8. *Wine is not meant to be enjoyed merely for its own sake; it is the key to love and laughter with friends, to the enjoyment of food and beauty and humour and art and music. It rewards us far beyond its cost.*

9. *What part is wine of your life? Ten per centum? Then ten per centum of your income should be spent on wine.*

10. *The principles of this theory should be applied to other parts of life.*

The theory attracted many disciples, including a man who beat me at golf after he had told me I had changed his life, and others who went a bit beyond my thesis. Bruce Petty, the famous film maker and cartoonist, told me he would have to seriously examine how many famous books he would be able to read. Another disciple told me he would attend major sporting features all over the world, and that this would curtail the expansion of his company.

But back to the development of quality. Chardonnay has remained a popular wine since its inception in Australia, though I'm not sure how much damage will be done by the people who blend from other areas and other varieties and still pass off their wines as top regional Chardonnays.

I even worry about the quality wine industry. Approximately 80 per cent of wine, in 1984, was sold in bag-in-box, flagon or in bulk. Of the 20 per cent remaining, I would estimate a total of five per cent would sell as premium wine, and of that less than half is what I'd call very good Australian wine. About two per cent of all wine made in this country is therefore representative of what Australia, at best, can do in the wine making world. This isn't very much, when one considers the almost endless areas suitable for wine, the climate, and the enthusiasm for the top wines, which rank among the best in the world. It's all very well to talk about how good our wines can be, when the vast majority of wine is made to be very ordinary indeed.

It's never been my game. I'd rather write or breed horses or build antique collages (a hobby!) than make ordinary wine. The Evans Family Chardonnay is a wine for which we have high hopes. The vineyard below the house in the Hunter Valley was planted in 1976, 1977 and 1978. It bore well for the first time in 1984, when over 20,000 bottles were made. We try very hard with this wine, buying new wood every year, cold maturing, blending and discarding. It's a totally authentic wine, entirely from Chardonnay, entirely from our own vineyard. Apart from the hot vintage of 1981, no wine has developed to its full extent, so we don't yet know its potential. It will be a joy to find out.

Early stages at Petaluma in the Adelaide Hills, 1979.

These chapter introductions are more autobiographical than I had intended. I was asked to write my memoirs, but I refused, saying that I was still living them.

As for the future, there is still so much to do, so many projects and ideas. I hope we shall be able to achieve some of them. You should live each day as if it were your last, but you should plan your future as if you will live forever. Twenty years ago I had dinner with Keith Dunstan, the celebrated Australian journalist and author. The first red he served was one he had saved for years for just such an occasion; it was a 55 Penfold's Grange. I slurped and sipped in total appreciation. 'That's great,' I declared, finally. 'What's next?' That became the epitath he gave me. He says it exemplifies my life:

WHAT'S NEXT?